JOURNEY OF AN INTROVERT

HOW AN EXTREME INTROVERT'S 52-WEEK BATTLE WITH FEAR OPENED HIDDEN DOORS TO UNDERSTANDING

Dan N Cass

Dan Cass/52 at 52 Productions
San Rafael, CA
www.52at52.com

Author's Note: I have tried to recreate events, locales and conversations from my memories of them. In order to maintain their anonymity in some instances I have changed the names of individuals and places. I may have changed some identifying characteristics and details such as physical properties, occupations and places of residence. In some cases, I have compressed events; in others I have made two people into one.

Editors: Travis Wood, Robin Gound
Cover Design: Damonza, Tracy O'Neill

Journey of an Introvert/ Dan N Cass. -- 1st ed.
ISBN: 978-0-9992757-0-2

Dedication

This book is dedicated to my sister Natalie Kae, who preferred to go by her middle name, Kae. She lived her short life with a ravenous appetite for happiness. Complete opposites—a boy and a girl, type A and type B personalities, an introvert and extrovert—we began as competitive siblings, moved into separate social circles during school before eventually becoming close friends as adults. Quickly arriving at the heart of any matter, each of us discussing thoughts and ideas from our unique perspectives, I always knew where I stood with her. Her gentle candor rarely hid expectations of what a brother "should" do or left unsaid assumptions on the table.

Kae, I know you're watching what I'm doing with this beautiful dream called life. Thank you for the gentle puffs of wind during light-wind water-starts while I windsurf. I dedicate this book to how you lived life on your own terms. I know you've left this life, but I prefer to think of you on an extended adventure in a remote part of the world. I expect to see your smiling face when I meet you at the next dimension's arrival gate. I miss you.

Everything you want

is on the other side of fear

—George Addair

Contents

Introduction

"Moderation?" He leaped up on the desk, like an evangelist. "Moderation? It's mediocrity, fear, and confusion in disguise. It's the devil's reasonable deception. It's the wobbling compromise that makes no one happy. Moderation is for the bland, the apologetic, for the fence sitters of the world afraid to take a stand. It's for those afraid to laugh or cry, for those afraid to live or die. Moderation"—he took a deep breath, getting ready for his final condemnation—"is lukewarm tea, the devil's own brew."

—Socrates

Way of the Peaceful Warrior

by Dan Millman

"Why are you always so serious? Why don't you smile more?" From parents to girlfriends. From wives to a few close friends and many workplace acquaintances, it's been a constant refrain. From every possible perspective I've heard some variation of, "Why can't you relax, be silly, and have a little fun?" It's been gently pointed out with maternal concern by classroom teachers. It's been shared by objective observers whose opinions I respected. I'm sure my mother, a bubbly social extrovert, always excited to meet new people, has often wondered if I was mistakenly switched at birth in the hospital nursery.

Echoing in the back of my mind for years, I've been on the receiving end of a girlfriend's wrath, laced with frustration, sarcasm and ridicule: I was embarrassing her. I couldn't relate to her verbose girlfriends and certainly hadn't developed the extroverted social skills necessary to fake a shallow hug and an empty air kiss on the cheek. I've tried being silly, conforming to fit in, but instead of feeling like part of the crowd, I usually felt awkward and distant. I'm sure the group around me felt the same.

Why isn't it enough to enjoy the simple pleasures of a mindless day without trying to compete, sometimes with others, but mostly against the face reflected in the mirror? Why does the unrelenting desire to learn and grow turn everything into a mission? A number of times I've tried letting go pretending to be a leaf on a stream. Existing without purpose, passively accepting life as it came, I hated every complacent minute. Instead of relaxing into the moment, I was fighting an internal battle. Without a significant load, an impossible goal, or at least a set of challenging problems, the relentless engine of my mind implodes from boredom.

I'm fifty-two now so why can't I surrender to age, safely sliding through the rest of this life before slipping into a soft hospital bed and a quiet, peaceful death? It's because I've never been able to let go. I don't know any other way of living. I relish the adventure of life and the interesting problems it presents. Swimming in deep pools of curiosity, I continue to savor the intensity of new challenges as I examine the unfolding mysteries of the world.

I stepped into my first martial arts dojo at twenty-eight. I started water-skiing on a slalom course at thirty-two. I ventured into the Canadian Rockies at thirty-eight to learn how to snow ski. This year at fifty-two I entered the dynamic worlds of motorsports, heli-skiing, and skydiving. The more difficult the obstacles, the more unexpected twists and turns, the greater the satisfaction during the journey. I have an unyielding need to explore, expanding my knowledge, not only of the natural world, but what I'm capable of as a man.

When I reached five decades of life, I frequently heard new questions. "Dan, when are you going to stop doing these crazy things? When are you going to quit playing and join the adults?"

My response? "Never. And I'm not playing."

The questions surprised me. Why would I knowingly walk away from pleasure? What possible reason could I find to deliberately close a door on curiosity? When do I become too old to set new goals? I don't want to retire from work *or* play, sublimating my thirst for new challenges. The interest and intensity pursuing new goals have never diminished. I continue to discover and sometimes rediscover, untapped physical and mental abilities. Most interesting is when I experience deeper levels of emotion, particularly the distinctive resonance of satisfaction. I want to savor all of it until the moment I depart this life.

I hope I meet my end on a steep mountain-side skiing at the limit of my ability, on a golf course admiring a long slow draw falling towards the green, or slumped over a chess board, my mind intensely contemplating the variations of moves six steps ahead. Better yet, my heart pumping its last ounce of oxygen-filled blood, I'd prefer to die in the arms of a woman I trusted enough to set aside the thick armor of my emotional protection.

At fifty-two I've spent most of my life immersed in the hyper-competitive worlds of banking, technology, and sports. I've devoted years to introspection, carefully observing my thoughts and reactions to structured process and long, drawn-out strategies. With a little maturity and perhaps a tiny bit of wisdom, all built on a mountain of mistakes, I've made inroads into the moments when I perform well. These rare moments of inspired performance have always followed a process of setting a large, almost impossible goal before developing an incremental, step-by-step plan to achieve that objective.

This book began as a daily journal charting my attempt to challenge an internal monster: my lifelong fear of heights. Once the journey began, I noticed my entries becoming an evolving mystery. Each day revealing new insights, I wondered how fifty-two years of life had prepared me to challenge my most dreaded foe. Would I finally overcome it once and for all, another satisfying checkmark of achievement or slip into the dangerous shadows of my many weaknesses? My journal, unfolding into a day-by-day mystery, eventually became a memoir, a mirror into an intimate relationship with fear.

This is that story.

CHAPTER ONE

Trapped, with nowhere to run

I must not fear.
Fear is the mind-killer.
Fear is the little-death that brings total obliteration.
I will face my fear. I will permit it to pass over me and through me.
And when it has gone past, I will turn the inner eye to see its path.
Where the fear has gone, there will be nothing.
Only I will remain.
—Frank Herbert
Dune

I'm buried alive. After fifty-two years of avoidance and a well-rehearsed chorus of irrational lies, it all fell apart. I'd finally reached the bottom. Helpless and isolated, I was suffocating in an emotional coffin six feet below ground. I've been acutely aware of my fear since childhood, but with nowhere left to run, tonight was the first time I began pounding my fists against the coffin's silk fabric inches from my face. Furiously screaming to escape, my battle with the fear of heights began on a dark mountain road.

Since 1998, every weekend from early December through the end of March, I've skied in the Sierra Mountains of Northern California at a resort called Kirkwood. I make the three-and-a-half-hour drive to South Lake Tahoe from San Francisco every Friday evening, skiing Saturday and Sunday. I prefer Kirkwood because of its steep terrain, challenging runs, and narrow chutes hiding secret stashes of deep powder. More important for an introvert, with the exception of holiday weekends, rarely are there throngs of people impatiently crowding into chaotic lift lines.

When I first began skiing Kirkwood, I took the quickest route like every rational person from the congested Bay Area trying to save a few precious minutes of time. That weekend ski trip follows a path east to Sacramento on I-80 before veering south on Highway 50. During the twisty, winding climb into the Sierra mountain range, Highway 50 gradually builds to an altitude of seven thousand feet. Five minutes before the trip ends with a steep descent into the South Lake Tahoe valley, drivers are forced to traverse a small stretch of road I've jokingly christened, "*The Cliff.*"

Cut into the side of the mountain, the narrow, quarter-mile section of road creates a sheer, almost vertical drop-off. It's wide enough for two lanes of passenger vehicles, but when semi-trucks or buses approach from opposite directions, side-view mirrors are in danger of colliding. To prevent vehicles from sliding off the snow-covered winter road into oblivion, the California Department of Roads built a low rock curb masquerading as a barrier wall.

To my vertigo-affected vision the cliff seems to extend straight down. The reality is the incline is probably only forty-five degrees: perfect if I had a pair of snow skis attached to my feet. But on an unlit, icy winter road, even in the relative safety of my four-wheel-drive truck, it became my weekly nightmare. During the first year in California, I simply forced my way past the terrifying section of road, but I eventually surrendered to my fear. For the last eight years I've been using Highways 16, 49, and 88 which took an hour longer.

For the last six weekends I've somehow been able to force my way past my excruciating decision point, the junction of Highways 50 and 16. I always flirted with the decision, mentally dancing around its frightening edges until the last possible moment before turning south to emotional safety. Tonight would be different. The bed of my truck stuffed with ski bags full of boots, goggles, and gear, I left a grinding week in the office escaping San Francisco's crowded Financial District.

I always look forward to the solitude of the three-hour drive. Unburdened with nonstop e-mails, meetings, or conference calls, I thrive on the moments of privacy allowing me to decompress. I don't even turn on the radio. Similar to the peacefulness of early mornings, the critical time alone provides the clarity to step back and contemplate the patterns, metaphors, and symbolism swirling around my life. Still in objective work mode, the logical, problem-solving part of my brain completely engaged, I headed east, reflecting on an impromptu meeting that ended when I asked a key staff member to calculate her return on investment of the significant amount of time she spent worrying, both in and out of the office.

She'd come into my office with the open-ended question, "Can we talk?", implying, "Can I tell you my problem and then you'll handle it so I won't have to confront a difficult co-worker?"

Calmly but purposefully checking my office wall clock before slowly looking back to her, I told her she had exactly fifteen minutes before my next meeting. As she happily closed the office door eager to indirectly add to my already long list of priorities, the meeting began when I told her she had an important choice to make: "If you want to vent, burning off some emotions, I can sit here, empathizing with your problem. If you want me to *'do'* something, you'll have to explicitly ask me the question. As you know, I'll need a concise sentence of nouns and verbs followed by a deadline, but no adjectives."

I've been in this situation too many times and am slowly learning from my mistakes. Too often trying to be helpful, I've offered observations and suggestions to friends, co-workers, girlfriends, and even wives, but most of the time they didn't need or want solutions. They simply needed someone to listen.

It took years of painful missteps before I understood that my desire to help not only wasn't helpful—it was often a curse. With someone I loved or deeply respected it was torture watching them drown in six inches of water when all they needed to do was stand up. In the office with peers or staff, my approach was often different. I could empathize, but learned it was better to detach and avoid being pulled into the shifting tides of emotional drama.

Clearly understanding the distinct choices of assigning her boss a new task or venting her frustrations, she chose the latter. The conversation quickly shifted from her concerns with a co-worker's poor attitude to the real, underlying problem: how much time she spent worrying, from minor issues all the way to full-blown disaster scenarios, both of which would likely never come to fruition. She then shared she often worried she was worrying too much. Uneasily glancing down to the desk before looking up to meet my eyes, she finally confessed that in the rare moments she wasn't worrying, she felt guilty about it. With habits fully developed from years of unconsciously misusing her imagination, she'd become a fully functioning expert in worry and guilt.

After listening to the incredible amount of time she spent on useless emotions, an idea to help appeared. I often see people as patterns of actions, not words or emotions, so instead of patronizingly telling her to quit worrying—or worse, telling her to "Work the problem, not worry the problem"—I gave her a practically impossible assignment.

On my desk at 8:00 am Monday morning I expected a professionally prepared Return On Investment analysis of her worry. As she waited for the punch line of my obvious joke I continued. Without blinking I told her the analysis must then provide another quantitative breakout using worrying about worry as the compounding exponent. When her shocked eyes acknowledged I was completely serious, I gave her the last and perhaps most difficult part of the assignment. The analysis should also include a measurable breakout of the time she wasted, her emotional opportunity costs, feeling guilty when she wasn't worrying. I knew she'd agonize about the assignment and purposefully didn't give her a definition how to quantify worry or guilt, (I didn't know either). I also didn't tell her that at our Monday morning review, her next assignment would be to put thirty minutes of focused worrying into her daily schedule. She could still worry, but not outside of that small window of time. At least not in the office.

The unusual assignment wasn't a punishment. I considered her a close friend; otherwise I'd never have bothered. I was showing her a door, but not to a solution. Behind the door was an elaborate room of mirrors, a carnival funhouse of her mind. It was necessary for her to examine each distorted image she was creating. After that she could choose denial, obsessively keeping each distortion clean with rags and a bottle of Windex, or she could choose the solution I preferred: bring a hammer, leaving ugly shards of guilt and worry littered on the floor. I had no illusions her problems would be solved by Monday morning but at least it would provide her with a new, possibly painful, perspective to start from.

As the asphalt highway sang a duet with my noisy off-road truck tires, I wondered how my highly skilled staff member might calculate her moment-by-moment, compounding investments in worry and guilt. I also thought, *what did she get from it all*? Ultimately, no matter how much compassion I had, regardless of any type of elaborate motivational plan I could create to guide the way, this was her problem to solve. Ironically, I also wondered how much time and energy I'd wasted over a lifetime avoiding my own tension, discomfort, and fears.

Regardless of my calm, reflective state, it all began the moment I arrived at the rolling Sierra foothills east of Sacramento. An internal voice I knew all too well started whispering about the Cliff. As each mile on the steepening roads passed, the voice became insistent, each syllable growing louder. Taunting and torturing me, my mind always starts the revolving list of worries, but it's my body that spontaneously responds with familiar feelings of dread. Merging together with perfect, circular precision matching the twisting turns of the winding road, my mind and body oscillate between an unrelenting mental dialogue and painful physical reactions.

Closer and closer to the cliff, each left and right turn through the narrow mountain passes brought more negative thoughts increasing in velocity and volume. *Will it be icy? Will some self-absorbed idiot follow too closely behind me on this snow-packed stretch of road? What's my plan of action if an oncoming car veers into my lane?* Escaping from a cocoon of a thousand irrational thoughts, a beautiful butterfly finally appeared. Floating on delicately painted wings, hovering a few inches out of my grasp, fear was now mocking me, continuing the endless game of "What if? What if? What if?"

Mile upon agonizing mile through the winding roads up into the Sierra Mountains, I obsessed about the Cliff. The faster I drove, the faster my butterfly chased me. Around curve after curve, up into blind cutbacks, back down into the next sweeping turn on the snow-packed road, my butterfly wouldn't relent. As I strangled the steering wheel, the physical tension escalated until my vision became a blurry, grayish tunnel myopically focused on the asphalt road directly in front of my bumper. A few miles before arriving at the Cliff my emotional and physical exhaustion reached a climax. In one moment, other than my labored breathing, the only sound in my truck was the noise of the road. In the next, the cab of my truck was filled with a screaming voice, "stop it! Stop It! *STOP IT*!"

Without knowing how I had stopped in a narrow mountainside pullout just before Echo Summit, the highest point on Highway 50. I was desperate, trying to relax, silently waiting for rational thoughts and feelings to emerge before returning to the road. Trying to control my emotions with deep abdominal breathing, when tears of rage and frustration began welling up in the corners of my eyes, I knew it was pointless. I rarely cry, but if I do, it's usually to release built-up anger or frustration. It's rarely about sadness. Tonight's tears were confusing. I didn't know if they were from the stress of this evening's drive or the purging of tension from a lifetime of fear. With no immediate answer, I waited until I was completely drained from the release of emotion.

I'm fully aware millions of years of evolutionary DNA have been passed down to help me avoid danger. I've inherited the necessary survival genes to avoid falling from a cliff, being burned alive in a fire, drowning in a raging river, or being savagely ripped apart, eaten alive by wild animals. I have well-honed tools of logic and reason helping me steer clear of dangerous men with clubs, spears, and guns—or, worse, men with pens and microphones wanting to dictate everything I do or think. My heavily relied-upon tool of rationality can be comforting, but it doesn't mean anything when I'm shaking in frustration, isolated, and alone in the mountains. My co-worker had become an expert in negative emotions. I've done the same thing, slogging through an exhausting cycle of fear and avoidance for years.

As a small boy, I hid my terror from my parents each time our family crossed the Nebraska City Bridge on monthly visits to my grandparents. Every trip was the same. As soon as our tires began whining across the grated metal bridge I became the boy hiding beneath the covers, the murky waters of the Missouri River, silently waited for me hundreds of feet below. I'm also wary of precarious ski lifts and swaying skyscrapers. I even have recurring nightmares driving over steep, unknown bridges with minimalist guardrails. My fear is so deep-seated that although I've lived in San Francisco since 1998, I've purposely never walked across the Golden Gate Bridge.

Alone on a dark mountain road, exhausted and not knowing what to do, I took an action I've rarely, if ever used: purposeful inaction. Practically impossible for a control freak used to directing or at least influencing external events, I remained on the side of the road for over twenty minutes. Little more than an empty vessel, I sat in silence, desperate to be filled with the peaceful stillness of the moonlit, snow-covered mountains.

Rolling down the drivers-side window, the cold air chilling my skin where the tears had fallen, I was beginning to understand. Somewhere, at some point in my life, without understanding how or why, I accepted and internalized the thought, "I AM afraid of heights." No one forced that unwelcome gift on me. I don't recall attending an elaborate ceremony where I received a beautiful wooden plaque, hand engraved with a collection of thoughts and emotions destined to haunt me. I certainly don't remember finding a present from Santa, wrapped in ornate paper tied off with a shiny bow under the tree on a chilly Nebraska morning. I have no memories of birthday parties as a young boy unwrapping my horrible secret under the flickering candles of a frosted cake.

Physically and emotionally exhausted from the cathartic release of tears, for the first time in my life I was having a coherent conversation about heights. It was obvious: I'd been avoiding fear at every opportunity, running a race I'd never win. Instead of continuing my avoidance it became imperative to begin a new path, explicitly confronting the ugly, whispering voice. To do that, I needed specifics, not the generalized evasion and distraction techniques of the world. Most importantly, I had to *do* something.

So instead of helplessly whining, "I hate this," or passively accepting the rationalization "I've always been afraid of heights," I began asking a series of exacting questions requiring unemotional responses. "Why am I still so afraid of heights and in particular, of roads like this? What is my fear and where is it? How does the contagious momentum of fear, little more than a thought, build into painful feelings of dread? When have I ever been in real danger? What would it take to not be afraid of heights? How would it feel to live my life controlling or at least managing these feelings?"

Question after question began emerging from a new perspective. Able to remain separate from the painful physical reactions, I returned to where I'm the most comfortable—my logical thinking mode. An outside observer objectively viewing the problem through a new prism, I specifically didn't ask the plaintive question, *"Why is this happening to me?"* For the first time, I clearly understood. I wasn't the victim: I was the cause—my mind was the playground bully and victimizer.

I wondered how many times I'd chosen the greyish, colorless road to avoid my fears. A thousand? Ten thousand? More? It's likely the times I decided not to confront fear, either my massive fear of heights or the little fears and challenges of daily life that slip by unnoticed, couldn't be counted. I certainly wasn't going to take the easy way out, deflecting my personal responsibility, trying to shift the blame onto someone or something else. I also needed to replace emotional adjectives with verbs—verbs of action. Enveloped in the mountain's stillness, the lid of the coffin had opened a crack. To begin my escape to freedom, an important question waited for my answer:

What would the man I'm striving to become do in this situation?

Although I'd prefer to say he shared a moment of profound mysticism, a personal epiphany, or even a spiritual revelation, it was the opposite. His response was simple and obvious. "You've been running from fear since your earliest memories as a child."

He was right. It's time to bring out the beautifully wrapped gift of fear carefully hidden in a shadowy closet of my mind.

For me.

CHAPTER TWO

I've always been afraid

Courage is not the absence of fear,
but rather the judgment that
something else is more important than fear.
—Ambrose Redmoon

In fifty-two years of living, I can't recall a single moment when I was comfortable with heights. My first memory confronting that specific fear was as a young boy climbing trees with neighborhood buddies. As feelings of anxiety and dread surged through me, I'd watch from the ground as they confidently scaled the tree into a haphazard club-house or casually sat on swaying limbs, their skinny legs dangling in the breeze.

Only after memorizing their intricate foot placements and handholds would I begin my self-doubting, nerve-wracking climb. As my friends expectantly looked down from their safe perches, I'd clumsily start my ascent. At a certain juncture, usually about ten feet up where the trunk of the tree separated into smaller branches, any false confidence I'd tentatively built on the ground instantly evaporated. Preventing any coordinated movements, my chest cavity had constricted into a rigid ball leaving no room to inhale the calming effects of oxygen.

Physically and emotionally defeated, clinging to the rough bark of the tree, I couldn't move up or down. I was stuck, staring blankly at a small section of roughly textured tree bark, six inches from my face. Overwhelmed with fear, I ached worse than suffering through a feverish bout with the flu. I'm sure if one had been available my pulse would have challenged the upper limits of any heart-rate monitor Polar could build. With an unusual but insightful compassion a couple of my buddies recognized what was happening, exhorting me to keep climbing, shouting down that they had had the same fears. Regardless of their youthful enthusiasm and support I awkwardly shimmied down to the safety of the ground. I wanted to be part of the group but when my feet hit the ground, feelings of helplessness and isolation I would learn to know all too well enveloped me.

I grew up in the small Mid-western town of Lincoln, Nebraska. In 1964, the city government built an Olympic-level swimming pool called Woods Municipal equipped with standard one-meter and three-meter diving springboards. The pool also had a five-meter, a seven-and-a-half-meter, and—the tallest—a ten-meter concrete diving platform. On a warm summer day filled with shouting kids, I decided flinging my skinny body off the ten-meter platform would eliminate my fear. My reasoning was simple: if I could jump off the tallest diving platform, I'd vanquish my terror once and for all—the vertical descent to the water serving as the magical silver bullet of instant success.

The idea seemed reasonable, but the innocence of my approach had a significant problem. Too young and inexperienced, I didn't have any type of plan other than stubbornly climbing to the highest platform and jumping. Ten years old and ninety pounds dripping wet, I was trying to slice through the thick scales of my terrifying dragon with nothing more than willpower. I had zero understanding of how to jump or dive off safely. My sword was dull. Without building a step-by-step progression first, slowly becoming comfortable and proficient on the lower platforms, in youthful ignorance I was ultimately reinforcing my fear of heights.

Even climbing the steel ladder was a challenge. Dripping wet, uncomfortably waiting in a line of screaming, pushing kids, any type of breeze created instant goosebumps magnifying my anxiety. Consumed by internal doubt, it got worse when it was my turn to climb the ladder. With every tentative handhold, my fingers trying to grasp the cold steel, I worried I'd slip, falling helplessly to the concrete deck. To avoid looking down I focused on the horizontal rungs of the ladder with piercing, absolute tunnel vision. Just like climbing in neighborhood backyards or trying to scale the intimidating thick climbing rope in gym class, my field of vision was focused and frozen, inches in front of my face.

Every torturous climb to the concrete summit ended where the only possibility was to descend—either off the platform into the blue, chlorine abyss or back down the slippery ladder. I often stood paralyzed on the platform, scanning Lincoln's horizon for over fifteen minutes of self-induced misery, struggling to convince myself I really wanted to be up there. Ignoring suntanned lifeguards impatiently shouting at me to jump, I retreated down the ladder a few times until I learned that slow descent was even more terrifying than jumping.

When I finally made the decision to jump, I couldn't confidently stride up to the edge of the platform, looking straight down before stepping off, merging with the forces of gravity. I always had to take a couple of running steps in order to build momentum before leaping. Plummeting feet first toward the water, my arms cycling backward to keep my balance, I prayed I wouldn't tumble out of control, landing on my back or side.

After absorbing the physical shock of the impact, the explosion of bubbles muffling all sound, I'd make the short swim to the edge of the pool where I could tentatively inspect myself for injury. Instead of confidence-building feelings of satisfaction and accomplishment, I felt nothing but the relief of survival, confirming to my reptilian brain the obvious: *See? I told you. All people have fears, and yours is heights. Accept and submit to your fear just like everyone else. Use common sense, fall back on our extensive social conditioning, quit these crazy challenges, and go back to being a good boy. It's a much easier way to slide through life.*

I tried challenging my fear almost every time at the pool, but I learned little from the experience. With no context or process for learning, my approach was little more than a simplistic bungee jump. I didn't have access to coaches skilled in platform diving or seasoned in helping people overcome fear. I certainly hadn't developed the self-awareness to ask for help. In the late 1960s, there wasn't a self-help section at the local library or a Barnes and Noble. The Internet didn't exist, giving me access to others willing to share their acrophobic fear. At the time, any type of external support system probably wouldn't have mattered anyway. I wanted to defeat fear alone, on my terms.

I couldn't comprehend its lifelong ramifications, but a deep competitive streak masquerading as juvenile stubbornness was emerging. Stubbornness was an important tool I'd learn to depend on, but to successfully challenge my fear, I was missing two critical ingredients. First was a credible long-term plan with an incremental, structured process. Secondly, I needed a different type of motivation: an emotional catalyst built on a lifetime of pent-up fear and frustration bursting at the seams, waiting to be released.

CHAPTER THREE

Rage overwhelms my fear

It is in your moments of decision that your destiny is shaped.

—Tony Robbins

Chronologically I'm fifty-two years old today. My abused body, full of scarred muscle tissue connected to aching joints and broken bones healed with smooth lumps of calcium, constantly screams for deep massage—or at least a few days of total rest. Instead of resting, forty-two years after my misguided escapades on a swimming-pool platform, I was looking over the edge of another vertical drop-off. The difference is this platform, called the Wave, has an impact zone of soft, white snow instead of blue, chlorinated water. The Wave is a ski run on the backside of the Kirkwood ski resort in Northern California where strong winter winds create a huge wave-shaped cornice of snow.

I've skied the sides and edges of the Wave for years, staying safely on the periphery of my fear but have never dropped in from the top because of a variety of readily available excuses: "The person I'm skiing with can't do it", "I'm feeling tired today" or "It's too icy (or rocky) for the landing." On the days when the internal voice of fear whispered, "I *could* get injured" or "I *should* be careful" I retreated into the rationalization that maybe I needed more conditioning in the gym or more training miles on the bike. The problem was determining where to draw the line. How much more training was needed and when would it be enough? The worst thoughts were when the voice warned, "I *should* act my age" or asked, "What would people think?"

I've been at this spot many times before, warmed up ready to ski off the edge, so why is today the day to challenge gravity, ice, and rock, deliberately endangering my safety? Why not ski more realistic runs before returning to the warmth a ski-lodge bar, drowning my fears in a torrent of alcohol. It's because I'm already intoxicated. Surging through me was the volatile cocktail of rage mixed with anger. Last night's rage on the Cliff and today's anger on the Wave were directed at the unceasing cycle of negative thoughts pouring in and out of my mind.

I'm tired of living with the feelings of a ten-year-old boy trying in vain to climb a tree or leap from a diving platform. I can't take one more day of the negativity of fear, an ugly virus painfully eating away at my soul. I want to know what it's like to live without fear. Today is the perfect day to begin challenging heights. If I don't start now, I'll die, trapped in my mental coffin.

My skis sliding back and forth, the tips peaking over the cornice edge, I was perfectly balanced, my ski boots snuggly wrapped around my feet and ankles. My leather encased hands confidently gripped the handles of my lightweight carbon ski poles. I was physically prepared from countless years in the gym. I had the right equipment and had spent years methodically developing my skills for this moment. The distance from the top of the Wave to my landing point was only about fifteen or twenty feet, but it was into deep powder: ideal conditions for what I wanted to accomplish. Purging my mind of 'could, should, might or what-if,' a deep breath of cold mountain air filled my lungs.

When a comforting slice of wind brushed my face sending a frisson of pleasure through each muscle and tendon of my body, I harnessed fifty-two years of pent-up frustration aggressively pushing off with my poles, driving my hands ahead of my knees. Empty of thought I fell through gravity to a perfect landing in an explosion of snow. As powerful currents of satisfaction surged through me I skied forward a few yards before a roll of my knees stopped me in the waist-deep powder. With a primordial exaltation, my arms reaching up to a perfect cloudless sky, I roared out to the universe, my guttural scream announcing rage and anger could conquer my fear.

Slowly turning my head to defiantly gaze up at the newly conquered cliff of snow my ecstatic explosion of emotion quickly turned into a disturbing sense of ironic déjà vu. I've been here before. Fifteen years ago I was in exactly the same position looking back up at another shear 15' drop-off with the same internal smile of delicious satisfaction flowing through my body.

For a three-year period starting in 1994 I worked as a banking-technology consultant in Vancouver, British Columbia. Able to drive to Whistler-Blackcomb, a world-class mountain in less than two hours, I took full advantage of the opportunity. When I first went to Blackcomb I didn't know how to ski. Growing up in Nebraska meant that unless I wanted to ski on an icy bluff with a fifty-yard ski run and a sun-bleached rope tow I'd have to make a ten-hour road trip to Colorado. I made a few trips during college to Breckenridge, Steamboat, and A-Basin but was too poor and stubborn to spend any money on lessons. Doing little more than using brute strength to force my way down the mountains, I didn't learn, or appreciate, anything about skiing's subtle beauty.

My first year on Blackcomb was simply skiing the beginner and intermediate runs putting miles under my skis. I'd ski the steeper blue runs early in the morning when my legs were fresh before moving back and forth between green and blue for the rest of the day. My ski days, filled with crashes, tumbles and a steep learning curve, always ended with an exhausted but contented smile.

During the first year I was also introduced to a famous run called the Sudan Couloir. I first saw it from a distant chairlift and couldn't believe people actually skied something so steep and treacherous. It's so incredibly dangerous the resort created a bumper sticker with an emblem of a fighter pilot's helmet complete with oxygen mask, signifying big altitude, big attitude and death-defying risk.

Intrigued by the almost impossible challenge I decided to become skilled enough to ski the Sudan within three years. The key difference with my goal was quality. I didn't want to cautiously sideslip my skis down the run so I could sit in a crowded après-ski bar, loudly boasting to others in a vague half lie, "Yeah, I skied it without falling." I was selfish. I wanted to ski it for me, with power and grace, fully in control of my turns, body position, and vision. To achieve my goal, I skied Blackcomb every weekend from Thanksgiving to the end of May and sometimes into June for three years.

I spent the second year challenging steeper runs, moguls, and tiny bits of air, but my problem wasn't desire. I had too much desire, far too much testosterone, and power from the gym. What I needed was technique which would only come from expert instruction. Instead of choosing a twenty-three-year-old male instructor filled to the brim with youthful bravado I chose the oldest instructor on the mountain: Lorne McFadgen. Lorne was in his mid-sixties but could ski any run on the mountain flowing through mogul fields like water through a boulder-filled stream never breaking a sweat. Lorne was a perfect instructor for me, his skills on the mountain surpassed only by his patient ability to teach.

Outside of weekly lessons with Lorne I spent long hours on a favorite ski run called "the Wall." I skied the Wall hundreds of times, sometimes falling, many times crashing, but day by day my skiing was improving even if just a tiny bit at a time. As long as I was learning, however slowly, I enjoyed the work. Each improvement in technique or understanding became progress, evidence I was advancing toward skiing the Sudan with power and grace.

One of the great advantages of the Wall run was its relative position on the mountain. Access to it was easiest by taking chair seven, the Jersey Cream Express quad. Traversing directly over the Wall was ideal, because I could visualize new lines on my next run. The chair rides also provided a good view and constant reminder of my eventual goal, the Sudan. It was a perfect setup, where my favorite training field and ultimate goal were within sight of each other.

Toward the end of the second season one of my most important daily drills was to ski up to the fifteen-foot drop-in point of the Sudan, inch my skis out over the almost vertical entry point, before visualizing a perfect ski run. Intellectually I knew it was possible; I saw dozens of people ski it every day watching from the Sudan's entry point. I saw them ski it during my rides up chair seven. I'd even ski in from an easier run to watch others from below. My conscious mind was wary, but my subconscious saw it was possible. I only needed time, instruction, and the repetitions necessary to build my physical and mental confidence.

After three years and hundreds of days of preparation I rolled out of bed at 5:00 a.m. to an exciting mid-February forecast: three feet of fresh, dry snow was patiently waiting for me on Blackcomb's steep terrain. I rushed out of my apartment beginning another early morning drive north on the winding Sea-to-Sky highway. A few miles past the tiny logging town of Squamish and the imposing two-thousand-foot granite slab of the Stawamus Chief, an energizing chill raced through me.

For three winters I'd fallen into a predictable pattern of behavior. I used the same parking lot, the same lifts, and the same mountainside restaurants, but that day's arrival was filled with a new tension: my first attempt to ski the Sudan. A Friday with minimal crowds, the cold, clear weather provided the perfect ski conditions. Everything had fallen into place. I was nervous but excited, deliberately falling back on my mental and physical preparation. After patiently following my normal warmup routine of stretching and a few ski runs, I arrived at the edge of my oblivion: The Sudan's vertical entrance.

My ski tips were positioned over the edge, fifteen feet off the ground, but just before making the final push-off with my poles, I noticed a few people standing above me to the right on a small granite overlook. As they looked back and forth at the treacherous drop-off into the Sudan and then back at me, I recognized the bewildered look on their faces, the disbelief someone could, or would want to, ski that run. I had had the same thoughts three years earlier. As my skis smoothly slid back and forth creating a perfect two-inch channel of melted snow I began my final visualization effort. After hundreds of sessions I had a perfect image of success playing out frame by frame: exactly what would happen on each turn, how I would feel, and even how the grunts of exertion would explode from my throat.

Using gravity and the extreme angle of the mountain to propel me forward, before I knew it, it was over. I barely remembered falling through the air. After landing in a blinding eruption of snow, I made a few powerful, grunt-filled turns before stopping. Consuming liters of chilly mountain air with each breath I savored the sweet exhilaration of "I did it!" until bone-shivering waves of irony began washing over me. Looking back up at the narrow entry point, anticlimactic thoughts began assaulting my short-lived victory. *That was it? I trained three solid years for that? That was one of the easiest things I've ever done. What happened to my fear?*

Today's emotions under the Wave are exactly the same as fifteen years ago under the Sudan. I've been here too many times with the identical feelings of sublime pleasure, the unique blend of chemicals and enzymes coursing through my veins. After watching NBA stars Jerry West and John Havlicek competing against each other on TV, I spent an entire fall semester in sixth-grade recess learning how to execute a basketball jump shot. Without a coach or an instructional book, I had no idea what I was doing. I was jumping but not shooting. I was shooting but not jumping. Eventually, it began to fall into place. With a rhythmic motion allowing me to extend into the air before my wrist softly released the shot, it was both bliss and validation: I could do anything I wanted. I simply had to decide before putting in the work.

I drank the same beautiful cocktail of emotion at the end of my seventh-grade summer. I was mesmerized watching Olympian Bob Beamon explode off the ground, bicycling his legs through the air in a ballet of power and grace as he broke the long-jump record during the 1968 Mexico City Olympics by an incredible two feet. After weeks wondering what he'd felt like collapsing to his knees in a moment of cataplectic ecstasy, I spent the rest of the summer alone at the track teaching myself the same hitch-kick long-jump technique.

The harmonic feelings of satisfaction from achievement are well-known. I'm very familiar with the late-night pleasure, alone in my bedroom staring at a darkened ceiling, when a private smile warms my face. Once the delicious taste of setting and then working toward a difficult personal goal passed my lips, it became an addiction. Since then I've lived a life of goal setting, internal discipline, and the gratification from accomplishment. I thrive on the challenges, the goal setting, the intricate planning, and especially the grind of the work. I relish the struggle and the search. It's when I feel the most alive.

Of course, there is a downside. My problems have always begun when the physical pleasures and the addictive rush of excitement fade away. When the warm feelings of accomplishment begin to wear off, when the excitement dies down and the sports equipment is put away, familiar feelings of tension and discomfort slowly reemerge. Sometimes it takes hours or even days, but today's problem began only seconds after looking back up at the Wave. The irony is that every achievement has always ended with the same melancholy realization; "Now what?"

"Now what?" If the feelings of accomplishment have always been *exactly* the same, why seek them out again? Why spend three exhausting years working on a goal to ski the Sudan? Why let rage propel me off of a fifteen-foot, land-locked ocean-wave of snow? Why not settle for contentment, leaving personal challenge to the past, accepting an easier life? It's because I don't know what else to do. I don't know any other way of living. Contentment has always been the enemy.

I've always felt a dull ache; a strange off-balance sensation I'm awakening from a dream within a dream. Searching for something important, a memory long ago forgotten, I feel homesick but can't remember where or even what home means. The memory teases me, always on the tip of my tongue. Then it tortures me. A millimeter beyond my fingertips, the answer to my life hides in an early morning fog of amnesia. My quest to remember compels me, helping me grow by setting challenging goals, relentlessly moving forward, regardless of my age.

I skied the rest of the day under Northern California's crystalline skies basking in the chemicals of satisfaction rhythmically flowing through my body. The release of tension last night on the Cliff created room for anger on the Wave to nourish me, propelling me to the addictive feelings of power and confidence. When I ski, typically the time on the chairlift is used to catch my breath, analyze mistakes on the previous run and adjust a piece of equipment before preparing to improve my technique on the next run. At rare times, if the person sitting beside me has a calm energy, I'll even engage in casual conversation about the weather or snow conditions.

Today? I was in my comfort zone, alone with my thoughts, trying to comprehend and appreciate the ironic twists and turns in the magical dream of life, in particular, my own.

CHAPTER FOUR

I won the birth lottery

Invincible. Just like you feel. The world is their oyster. They believe they're destined for great things, just like many of you. Their eyes are full of hope, just like you. Did they wait till it was too late to make from their lives even one iota of what they were capable? Because you see, gentlemen, these boys are fertilizing daffodils. But if you listen real close, you can hear them whisper their legacy to you. Go on. Lean in. Listen. Do you hear it? Carpe…carpe…carpe diem. Seize the day, boys. Make your lives extraordinary.

—Mr. Keating
Dead Poets Society

I've always been an athlete. Born from an athletic gene pool, my exposure to the beauty of sports and the dignity of competition began early. In a noisy, crowded gym in the tiny town of Hamburg, Iowa, I slept cradled in my mother's arms as my father played point guard for his high-school basketball team. Attending in person meant I arrived early in their lives. My father was seventeen and my mother sixteen when I was born on February 4, 1957, in Nebraska City, Nebraska. I was the oldest of course but was joined eighteen months later by my sister Kae. Our youngest sister, Julie, joined the family five years later.

We lived a typical middle-class American life: my mother stayed at home raising the three of us, while my father worked as an Architect Representative to support the family. My grandparents lived in Hamburg, Iowa, a short, twenty-minute drive away, so in addition to frequent weekend trips, we spent Thanksgiving, Christmas, and other major holidays with a large, supportive family. Although I'd won the birth lottery, being born to two loving parents, I certainly didn't begin life with a silver spoon in my mouth. My parents started their young life together with absolutely nothing except love for each other, high-school degrees, and an incredible work ethic.

Mom and Dad
Gilson's Café Hamburg, Iowa, 1956

1960 Three-years old

I enjoyed Abraham Maslow's ladder of the basic necessities of life—its hierarchy's first two rungs comprising food, clothing, shelter, and safety. Maslow's third rung, belonging and love, were easily filled. My childhood was filled with structure, tough love, and consistent discipline. My parents have always shown they loved me, their actions matching their words, and I felt it—deeply. I never had to suffer a daily personal hell, a parental version of original sin, where whatever I did, no matter how hard I worked, wasn't good enough.

I was never given the tiresome, ugly burden that their expectations for me superseded my dreams. I never silently cried myself to sleep worrying if I didn't become a doctor, attorney, or a "success" I'd be letting them down, the pressures of filial obligation an impossible weight I could never carry. I was spared the soul-crushing words, "You'll never amount to anything." I never heard them whisper, "If you do *that*, what will the neighbors think?" Not having to live up to external expectations, I've never taken an explicit action where the ultimate goal was to please or prove something to my parents. It wasn't necessary. I already felt their deep love and acceptance.

Even at such a young age, my parents were wise enough to let me struggle. I had to learn how to solve problems on my own, slowly building the survival and coping skills necessary to live an autonomous life. When I was old enough they assigned me responsibilities without discussion or my consent, but I wasn't being punished; I was being prepared. My favorite responsibility was taking care of the family dog, Sam—a beast of a basset hound who had an appetite for food and mischief as large as his floppy ears. My job was to keep him fed, walked, and to pick up after him in the backyard.

My least favorite job was to keep our huge yard mowed in the spring, summer, and fall. A twice-a-week, two-hour, sweat-and-grass-stained event doubled to a four-hour ordeal of misery if I procrastinated from the weekly schedule. It was also my responsibility to keep our driveway and sidewalks clear of snow, regardless of the brutal Nebraska winters. I didn't look forward to taking two or three hours mowing the yard or scooping heavy winter snow, but afterward I felt good seeing the results, knowing I was responsible. At only ten years old I was already developing a sense of Maslow's self-esteem needs: the fourth rung.

Although young, they were parents first, doing what was necessary to prepare me for the world. I was protected but never coddled. When it was necessary to learn about the symbiotic relationship of actions and consequences they didn't take the easy way out. I received serious adult-to-child discussions, verbal scolding, time-outs, and groundings. Technically I'm still "grounded" for almost burning down our home in an explosive Fourth of July fireworks campaign. Before an evening out with friends my parents had given pointed instructions to a babysitter: I wasn't allowed outside to play with my buddies during the summer holiday. It, or I, was too dangerous. Frustrated and unamused, ignoring the babysitter lounging in our living room, I began firing bottle rockets from the windowsill of my bedroom. It was going great until the bedroom curtains burst into flames, instantly catching the ceiling on fire. Although I put out the fire quickly, when my furious and frustrated father saw the charred curtains, windowsill, and ceiling, not knowing what else to do, he grounded me for life.

One of my most lasting punishments was self-inflicted. Instead of earning money mowing more yards, I planned an elaborate $6 shoplifting heist to equip my platoon of twelve-inch soldiers with more gear. Scheming for days, trying to figure out how to make a clean getaway, I decided to buy a $.29 notepad the same size as the shrink-wrapped equipment so I could walk back to the toy section and insert the unpaid-for item into my sack. Escaping from the store, my heart pumping out of my chest with terror and satisfaction, I didn't know I'd set myself up for real punishment. Every single time I played with the stolen equipment I felt ashamed. After watching my parents earn everything in their lives, I was too mortified to admit to them what I'd done. I also didn't want to suffer the embarrassment of facing the store owner when I returned the gear to the store.

My worst punishment was being on the receiving end of corporal punishment. Hearing my mother say "Wait till your father gets home" was awful, but receiving the spanking from him wasn't the worst. The worst was after the physical consequences. Sliding off his lap as huge tears fell down my face, I was more embarrassed than hurt. But it wasn't until I saw *his* crying face that I instantly understood the full weight of my actions. I was absolutely crushed when I realized I had forced him to act. It was devastating knowing I was the person responsible for deeply hurting my father, making him cry.

Eventually, my parents moved our family to Lincoln, NE. Moving to a new city meant attending a new school. It also meant leaving my neighborhood friends. Already shy and reserved, moving to a new school introduced me to a new problem I'd face for the rest of my life: acute social awkwardness. When the second grade at Bethany Grade School began, I was dropped into an environment completely unprepared for new kids and social expectations.

Miserable and lonely, too young to understand I would meet new friends and adapt to the environment, I wasn't adjusting well to my new classmates or surroundings. After the first two weeks of school, I finally decided to assert my independence.

Every morning and afternoon our class would head to the playground for a twenty-minute recess to burn off boisterous enthusiasm. One fateful morning after our teacher called us back in I went to the washroom with everyone else, but instead of returning to the classroom, I waited. As the washroom emptied and the shiny hallway floors echoed in silence I snuck out of the building to walk home, over a mile away. Enjoying the autumn sun warm my face, I was extremely pleased with my strategy to escape the new kids and teacher. What I didn't know was my mother had received a phone call from a frantic teacher and principal: the seven-year-old boy they were responsible for was missing.

Upon my victorious entrance home, my mother's emotions quickly cycled from relief, her young son wasn't missing, to anger when I lied that school had been let out early for the day. After a quick call to the principal confirming my safety, my mother drove me back to school. Confused and overwhelmed, I reluctantly returned to my small wooden desk. Compounding my embarrassment and social awkwardness, in front of staring, bewildered classmates I was choking back tears. When my teacher asked in front of the class why I'd run away from school, I could only mumble through puffy lips and salty tears, "They always call me the the new kid in the green shirt." I had no way to explain I was an introvert, suffocating in a room of noisy people. I thought I just different and weird.

Although the tension was different from school I especially didn't (and still don't) like the unwanted attention of birthday parties—especially being on the receiving end of "Happy Birthday to You." I'd awkwardly stand in front of the candlelit cake hoping the song would be over as soon as possible before blowing out candles to the cheers and clapping of neighborhood friends. The annual ritual always seemed odd. I didn't understand what we were celebrating. I had survived another arbitrary period of time—a year? It wouldn't be until decades later the reasons for my escape from the chaos of grade school and my reluctance to attend birthday parties would be discovered.

Outside of the trauma of second grade and unwanted birthday parties I enjoyed a full, if not idyllic, childhood. My days were filled with a small number of neighborhood friends, Cub Scout camping weekends, Sunday school, and a Midwestern social ethic that allowed us to leave the doors to our home unlocked for weeks, if not months, at a time. It was so safe that all the local neighborhood children, sometimes up to twenty of us, played without adult supervision far past sunset and into the darkness of the evening or until the parents stood on porches, yelling their children's names to get them to come home for dinner.

Many neighborhood events were instigated and coordinated by my sister Kae. She was as outgoing and social as I was shy and detached. After only a short time in the new neighborhood, she had amassed a small army of friends, acquaintances, and allies. She wasn't overbearing in her methods of coordinating the local group of kids, but when necessary she could be persistent, persuasive, and sweetly cajoling. I often marveled at how she could simply walk up to a complete stranger, gregariously introduce herself, and within five minutes have a new friend for life. Her golden-blond hair, stretching down to the middle of her back wasn't her defining characteristic. It was her dimpled smile, a well-used instrument projecting joy and wonder to all around her. With a gracious ease and delight, she could disarm the hard shell of even the most distant person she might encounter in the many adventures in her life. Except me.

Like most siblings, we had our differences and competitive rivalries, but the most striking difference was in the ways we each responded to fear. We were just wired differently. If I was afraid my actions typically revealed my fear, which at this stage of life usually manifested in some form of crushing shyness. In the rare times Kae was afraid she seemed to have an innate ability to mask her fear and at the same time engage in the challenge of the moment. Our differences were never more evident than at 14,264 feet above sea level on a remote peak in Colorado named Mount Evans.

Our family typically took annual two-week fishing trips to Minnesota in the summer, but one year we decided to drive to Colorado to enjoy the magnificence of the Rocky Mountains for the first time. One morning over breakfast in the mountains my father enthusiastically suggested the day's activity: driving up the highest paved road in the world—Mount Evans. This was to be a new adventure and bonding experience for our family. Although not as famous, Mount Evans has inclines steeper than Pikes Peak and is paved all the way to the top.

Most of the journey up the mountain was without guardrails with only a foot of pavement separating safety from oblivion. Worse was that asphalt at the edges of the pothole-filled road had broken away in chunks as large as a county-fair-winning pumpkin. On top of no guardrails and loose pavement, the last five miles of road to the peak didn't have a painted centerline and was barely wide enough to accommodate two lanes of traffic. Further complicating an already treacherous drive were the cold, gusting winds sufficient to rock a full-size vehicle startling even the most self-assured drivers. Terror-inducing roads and the lack of guardrails aside, the real and ever-present danger on the trip was my mother.

My description of that infamous Sunday-afternoon drive is purely anecdotal. I was slumped down in the back seat so I wasn't forced to look out the car windows. Further avoiding my fear, my head was buried in the pages of a book I was desperately trying to read. In the rare and unpleasant moments when I'm forced to dig up old memories of the trip my eyelids begin an unconscious quiver and my ears echo with my mother's terror-filled screams demanding my father stop the car on the narrow road and turn around. While I'm afraid of heights, my mother has a fear of heights that can't be measured which begs the obvious question, 'what was my father thinking when he suggested we drive to the summit of Mount Evans?'

As we ascended the winding road my mother's fear began to build at a rate easily surpassing the increase in altitude. As each narrow mile of crumbling pavement passed beneath our car's tires the smothering tension of her fear escalated. Ignoring my father's impassioned voice forcefully telling her to shut up, her suggestions to stop and turn the car around soon became pleading cries of agony. Eventually, when she couldn't take it any longer, her pleas transformed into panic-induced horrifying moans begging my father to go back. Fortunately, my father had the good sense to ignore my mother: turning around on that narrow road is probably one of the most dangerous maneuvers a driver could perform. Even Kae, the only calm person in the car, was begging my mother to be quiet. I have no idea what Julie was doing.

Kae sat in the back seat next to me seemingly without an ounce of fear or at least she had it cleverly hidden. Unconcerned with the obvious danger she strained to look over the edge of the vertical drop-offs. With certain death only inches away she seemed to revel not only in my fear but also that she and I were different in this way as well. Sometimes teasing but mostly supporting me, she'd suggest, "It's not that bad, Danny. Look out the window." But each time I looked out, I was moments from becoming sick. Like my first horror movie, I watched most, if not all of the movie called *A Family Road Trip* through sweating fingers. Of course we made it up and down the mountain safely and we've laughed about it for years at family gatherings.

The day after the horrific trip up Mount Evans my father coordinated an afternoon trip to Golden Colorado to watch the summer training camp of the Baltimore Colts. After watching them on TV it was exciting to see the elite players in person. I savored every moment until my father handed me a piece of paper and a pen before suggesting I join the unruly horde of frantic boys pushing each other out of the way to get autographs. Instead of jumping into the chaotic melee I was frozen in place, almost indifferent, before I watched Kae roll her eyes at me in disbelief. Impatiently snatching the paper and pen from my hand she physically asserted her way through the mob of screaming boys. Standing triumphantly in front of NFL stars Johnny Unitas and Tom Matte, she waited patiently, but expectantly, for their autographs.

It was the first time I'd had an opportunity to ask for an autograph but my reluctance to fight for their signatures on a flimsy piece of paper wasn't because of shyness. Although I read about them daily and watched them on TV every Sunday I'd never put either player on a lofty, unreachable pedestal worshiping them as omnipotent heroes of the gridiron. I wanted much more than a simple bit of ink scratched on paper to show my friends. I wanted one of them to pull me to the side, wrap his huge, callused hand around mine, look me straight in the eye, and tell me I could achieve anything if I worked hard enough. Instead of an autograph, I wanted something of value: their words encouragement. I wanted one of them to say, "Danny, look at me. If I can do it, you can do it too." I could see it was possible, but I wanted to hear it as well.

I'd already received that type of attention and inspiration. In addition to the love and support of my birth parents, my lottery ticket was stamped with great athletic genetics. My father and maternal grandfather had been fantastic athletes, excelling in football, baseball, and track. When my father had the time away from a busy work schedule, he spent evenings and weekends patiently teaching me how to throw a football correctly or demonstrating the nuances of swinging a baseball bat the most efficient and powerful way. When not practicing in the backyard with my father, I spent my free time playing baseball with much older neighborhood boys, competing and reveling under the hot summer sun.

My friendships in grade school were the opposite of Kae's, and not surprisingly would mirror my social needs as an adult. I had many arms-length acquaintances but spent most of my time with two neighborhood boys, one whose personality was dramatically different. Like Kae, my friend Kevin was outgoing, but our relationship centered on playing sports or roaming the neighborhoods together on our bikes. My other friend Brad was as quiet as I was. We played sports together but most of our time was spent on the battlefields of chess, electric football, or backyard G. I. Joe missions. I was comfortable with both of them and had little interest in having a large group of friends. At the time I wasn't self-aware enough to pay attention to the dynamics but when the three of us got together, I was more comfortable moving to the background letting Kevin drive and dominate the conversations.

I survived the social trauma running away from my second-grade class but have rarely worn a green shirt since. It took years but I somehow buried the painful screams of my mother on Mount Evans. I healed quickly from high-speed bicycle and skateboard crashes. Although I survived mischievous Fourth of July fireworks expeditions, all extremities intact—ten fingers and toes—I almost lost my right eye. After a firework exploded too close to my face I was bandaged for a couple of weeks not knowing if I'd be able to see after that. Fortunately, the frightening time under the gauze patch ended and I had healed.

I received good grades, began playing the trumpet, and met new friends, but the social expectations of school were challenging. It wasn't until I could escape the classroom chaos of screaming kids into the structure of sports that my life began to change. Sports would become a vehicle of expression without being forced to talk. Although never the center of attention at a party, loudly monopolizing every conversation, I could dominate the playing fields. Of course I didn't recognize or appreciate it at the time, but competition, especially in the world of sports, would eventually provide the structure and foundation to challenge my fear of heights.

CHAPTER FIVE

Creating an intimate game, with fear

Our truest life is when we are in our dreams awake
—Henry David Thoreau

Last night's purge of emotion on the Cliff and today's anger-induced fifteen-foot drop in from the Wave fueled a day of confident, powerful skiing. Heart pumping, thigh-burning mogul runs contrasted with calm, introspective chairlift rides. Eventually, muscular fatigue signaled an end to my climactic weekend. The physical power from the adrenaline rush burned away, I made the awkward ski-boot walk back to the parking lot and an ice-cold beer.

Bootless feet resting on the gate of my truck, the February sun softly warmed my face in the wind-protected Kirkwood valley. Unwinding in the comfort of a sun-faded lounge chair, today's "après' ski beer" was sweeter than usual. As each icy swallow mixed with the crisp mountain air, blissfully burned the back of my throat, I reflected on the tumultuous weekend and the ebbs and flows of my adult life. After years of avoidance the Cliff had broken me down, rupturing my false sense of safety and control. Then my frustration-fueled anger on the Wave spurred me to action, all thoughts of physical safety or self-preservation rendered unimportant. I often have random thoughts crystallizing into deep insights, but it's been years since I've felt the intoxicating satisfaction coming from the last twenty-four hours. The question was, "why?"

I'm fully aware that compared to millions of others on the planet, my life is great. I've always felt the deep, unconditional love of my parents and family. I've never been hungry, abused, or abandoned. I've never been in real danger or in any type of serious trouble. In a moment of timeless perfection, I've looked across a restaurant table into the eyes of a woman I'd fallen in love with thinking I was looking into a reflection of my soul. Professionally, my work in technology and banking allows me to make a very comfortable living and working in some of the great cities of the world: San Francisco, Vancouver, British Columbia, and Bermuda.

Competitively, I've been a member of successful sports teams from the sixth grade through college. Because of my athletic abilities I also had the opportunity to graduate from college, the first in my family's history. I've never been trapped by the economic legacy of my blue-collar, Midwestern birth. The truth is I have a better standard of living than all the kings and queens in the history of the world: better health care, a longer projected life-span, abundant healthy food, and safer, convenient transportation. If I'm brutally honest, my life in the West, and particularly the United States, has been filled with opportunity. What more could I want?

Balancing out my good fortune, I've also been penniless, precariously living check to check, every month a delicate balancing act between eating, paying the rent, or repairing my rusting car held together with duct tape. I've been fired and laid off from jobs. In my early thirties, already firmly seated on the merry-go-round of material success, I stretched my arm out grasping for the golden ring of happiness only to discover it was a trap.

I've failed in almost every possible way. I've somehow survived multiple divorces and dozens of painful relationship endings. Witnessing the deep pain and suffering of others, I've been exposed to life's fragility. From less than fifty feet away, I watched a football teammate sentenced to quadriplegic life in a wheelchair, his neck broken in a fraction of a second during a tackle. I've witnessed friends and families devastated by alcoholism, infidelity, drugs, and personal dysfunction too awful to comprehend and too difficult to fix. I've helplessly watched close friends sent to prison after each made a long series of bad personal decisions. The most devastating pain came from watching my sister succumb to pancreatic cancer within six months. I've even committed 'premeditated' murder and got away with the crime.

Why can't I accept the balance of good and bad, settling for '*My life right now is good enough?'* Why can't I be content my family is healthy, I have a few close friends, and my life in general—at least from an outside perspective—is great? Why isn't it enough to get—and *stay*—married? Isn't a career filled with peers I respect acceptable over the long-term? I've been here before. I'd reached another point in my life where acceptance, settling, and contentment had turned into disgust. The trajectory of my personal universe is out of geometric alignment. Again.

Hidden far beneath an external layer of material success and physical comfort is a heavy burden, an unconscious feeling something was wrong. I have a monster inside of me. Cycling through the seasons watching life unfold, I've always been haunted by deep feelings "I'm capable of more." Material social comforts, my avoidance of fear, and the lack of impossible challenges are incongruent to how I want to live as a man.

I've always spent most of my time in my head observing and analyzing the world, but I'd forgotten the most satisfying parts of my life were spent competing. I competed against other athletes, a low score in golf or a technology project delivered on time. The business world is satisfying not because I can make a good living, but because of the complex problems to solve. The work is interesting. I savor the mental challenge competing over a chess board watching my opponent create devious attack plans. Primarily, I competed against myself, constantly striving to grow and expand.

While I laugh about it now, I wonder how I've missed this for so long. I was only one decision away from changing the direction of my life. Again. I just needed a reason. The best decisions in my life, like today's on the Wave, have always been internal. The Wave became the catalyst, not only to action but to remembering the addictive feelings from my past. I've always been the happiest when I've gone inside, trusting my heart, paying attention to the feelings flowing through me. I've always been the most successful when I lived in a world of '*I am'* instead of '*I should.'* My authentic spark of insanity bursting into a beautiful flame of purpose, setting audacious—if not impossible—goals, has always been the key. Even if I could find an accurate definition for the words, I didn't want to settle for "realistic or normal." A barometer if I was on the right path was when 90 percent of people around me thought I was crazy.

In junior high, at a skinny one hundred thirty pounds, I brashly told unconvinced teammates I'd be an all-city and all-state running back in high school. During high school, I did the same thing, self-assuredly telling the same disbelieving friends I'd play Division I college football. It wasn't boasting, but a method of creating tension: I'd be forced to deliver or face their ridicule. From the sixth grade until I graduated from college, the single, practically impossible goal I worked toward was to play football in the NFL. Although I had no idea how to ascend the massive NFL mountain I'd decided to climb, I was one-hundred percent committed to drive my personal flag into that snow-capped peak. Not even out of junior high school, I was already exploring what I was capable of as a man—reaching for Maslow's fifth and final step: self-actualization.

Motivated again, reengaging with the purifying energy of competition, I began forcefully pushing back against an imposing, intimidating opponent: my overwhelming fear of heights. It's been a complex chess match I've expertly avoided, the black and white pieces patiently waiting for me to finally make a move. Finishing the last swallow of today's celebratory beer, I made a promise not to get sidetracked by the mundane, obfuscating clutter of day-to-day

Western life. A challenging new door of opportunity had opened. It was time to let the inspiration from the last twenty-four hours fuel a return to the eternal wisdom of a ten-year-old boy embarking on new, almost impossible journeys.

Obstinately standing before fear, I moved pawn to e4 attacking the center, beginning the most difficult challenge of my life: skydive by my fifty-third birthday. My new game with deadly consequences had its genesis last night on the terrifying drive along the Cliff. Today a cornice of snow yanked me out of comfort and complacency, illuminating the way to proceed: compete. Deciding to jump from a plane wasn't because of an existential mid-life crisis where I don't know how to be happy or what to do with my life. It was the opposite: I've always known; I just had to remember.

Could I do it? Could I jump from an airplane in fifty-two weeks? My answer is "*Yes*." Fear is comfortable chasing its prey, but it's not used to its prey stopping for a fight. I'm looking forward to the stubborn contest of wills against my new competitor. Accustomed to winning since I began competing athletically as a boy, I expect to win the game.

Again.

CHAPTER SIX

Initiation into the world of men

We have not even to risk the adventure alone, for the heroes of all time have gone before us—the labyrinth is thoroughly known. We have only to follow the thread of the hero path, and where we had thought to find an abomination, we shall find a god; where we had thought to slay another, we shall slay ourselves; where we had thought to travel outward, we shall come to the center of our own existence. And where we had thought to be alone, we shall be with all the world.

—Joseph Campbell
The Hero with a Thousand Faces

Up until the sixth grade, outside of my father, most authority figures in my life had been women. Warm, sincere, and caring, my Sunday-school and grade-school teachers taught and nurtured me, but I never felt I could fully express myself. I was trapped in a structure of school subjects I didn't care about, expected politeness to people I didn't respect, and a schedule geared solely to the group. Whenever possible I had always avoided any type of social confrontation, at home, at school or with friends. It was exhausting.

I was also the classic underachiever. My teachers and parents struggled, frustrated because they knew I had the ability to excel scholastically if only I'd apply myself. The problem was I was busy with more important things. After hearing or reading it once, I could recall every sports statistic for any player at will. I could sit motionless over a chessboard for hours, analyzing potential moves and strategy. I was also a voracious reader, devouring two or three books at a time—only they weren't the books assigned at school. It wasn't that I didn't care or was too stubborn to give in; I simply wasn't interested in the rote memorization required by schoolwork. The difference in my interest and focus between school and my personal reading assignments was vast.

1966 Unimpressed with the group.

Everything changed after my introduction to the intensity of organized, full-contact football. Lurking inside, unseen and misunderstood, the need to fully express myself finally had a stage. The violence of football provided an outlet to express myself without restraint. In school, church, or social settings, I was often tongue-tied. It was extremely frustrating coercing the concepts and ideas trapped in my brain along the long, circuitous journey to my tongue. In contrast, in motion on an athletic field, especially football, my muscles, thoughts and emotions flowed, almost without effort.

Football, the ultimate team game, also became my initiation into the world of men. I quickly learned that while I appreciated the nurturing support from women, I needed respect and inspiration from men. With the exception of military confidence-building obstacle courses, I'm not aware of any remaining tribal rites of passage into Western manhood and certainly can't recall any challenges for building my character step by step. The closest I got to any type of initiation into a group was participating in the Oklahoma drill, famous in fall camps across the country. Inside the blocking dummies laid on the ground, with my teammates screaming their support, I could hit someone as hard as I wanted. I loved it.

1968 The intensity begins.

When I joined the Elks Club sponsored “C” team in Lincoln, two local firemen, Bob King and Hop Cook, spent their off-days coaching impressionable young men in the basics of football: correct tackling and blocking skills. More importantly, they reinforced my parents’ lessons of accountability, teamwork, and discipline. I thrived on the intoxicating, addictive feelings competing in organized sports. Sports had referees, rules, and structure, making it easy to immediately see the results of my efforts. It was simple: at the end of a play, we had made yards or had scored. At the end of the game, we had won or lost. We weren’t awarded a meaningless gold star or participation trophy, empty of satisfaction or lasting memories.

I was lucky to have such a strong support system around me. I was surrounded by disciplined male authority figures as coaches and my parents provided an extremely nurturing and predictable home environment. But if I wanted something, I had to earn it. No one was going to give me anything. If I wanted a starting position on the team, I'd have to earn it during practice. If I wanted something more tangible, such as a new baseball glove, I had to mow yards, scoop snow from sidewalks, or clean our garage. I did earn a starting position on the team and the other material things I coveted: the first leather basketball in the neighborhood, a Wilson Jet, and an authentic NFL "Duke" football. At the end of my first year of contact football, I also received the first of many athletic awards. I was selected to the Elks All-Star team as an imposing eighty-two-pound middle guard.

The late sixties saw the rise of the sports dynasties of the Red Auerbach driven Boston Celtics, the John Wooden led UCLA Bruins, and the Vince Lombardi coached Green Bay Packers. Each coach focused on teamwork, character, and discipline. It was also the inspiring period of the Apollo moon landings, where nothing in life was impossible. The timing and confluence of events surrounding me were perfect. My competitive inner personality was beginning to blossom, expressing itself to the outer world.

While I was adapting to the cascade of male hormones fueling my growing body, I was being exposed to a new form of motivation: watching the NFL on Sunday afternoons. Sitting on our living-room floor, captivated and spellbound, I watched Steve Sabol's NFL films blend a dynamic soundtrack with a dramatic narrative read by a deeply masculine voice extolling the virtues of teamwork, discipline, and sacrifice. In awe and wonder, my desire to play in the NFL only intensified when the films were set to slow motion and football became a ballet, the grace and beauty of a moving human body highlighted by the explosions of raw emotion and the violence of the game. At the innocent age of twelve on a crisp fall morning, I set a goal to become a running back in the National Football League. I didn't know where the thought came from; nor did I care. I never asked for permission or thought it necessary to receive any validation before I made that decision. It was mine.

A critical factor was not having anyone constantly telling me what I should or shouldn't do. In particular, my young parents, wise beyond their years, were loving enough not to steal this or any other dream. Other than telling me to study hard in school, they never told me I should be more realistic how I lived my life. They left me to my heart, not living their lives through me with a manipulative barrage of "You should," or, "You must," or, "It's safer to…." If anyone knew my NFL goal was far more than a naïve, whimsical thought, I would have been labeled completely naïve, delusional, or mentally unstable. It wouldn't have mattered: I'd already learned how to remove the 'you should' guilt bullets from everyone's guns.

At the same time, I received an influential Christmas gift, a book about Vince Lombardi called *Lombardi*. Every night for months, I fell asleep wearing my Packer helmet while reading through the face mask. Tossing a football in the air with one hand while flipping pages of the book with the other, I consumed and memorized every motivational sentence. Thinking they'd created a robotic, goal-driven machine, my parents, and particularly my mother, probably regretted giving me the book, but it didn't increase my focus or discipline; I was already that way. It just made me feel like I wasn't alone.

Outside of our family doctor, who strongly suggested to my parents that I stop playing all sports and spend more time indoors to avoid a childhood bout of allergies, I wasn't burdened with a self-anointed, well-intentioned *expert* in life or an organization, church, or school guiding me down a well-worn path of Nordic *Janteloven*. I was fortunate to be sheltered from people wanting to help by "fixing" me or keeping me safe from wasted effort and the likely, if almost certain, heartbreak of failure. If my parents had obeyed our doctor, ignoring the joy they could see I received from sports, my life would have been irrevocably different.

My life would also have been different if I hadn't been sensitive to an inner voice. Being popular or friends with a large group of people usually fell into the same general categories of disinterest, boredom, or both. I had many arms-length acquaintances, but only a few close friends. The first Christmas break in my seventh-grade year a classmate invited me to his house one Saturday night to hang out with his friends. When I arrived I thought it peculiar that no adults were present and as the evening progressed things got worse. With a rebellious gleam in their eyes they began pouring drinks from their parents' liquor cabinet and lighting cigarettes.

To be part of the group I took a tiny sip of whiskey, but the taste was as awful as most of the evening. Trying to look cool I held a cigarette to my mouth but I couldn't bring myself to inhale. As the evening continued a distinct sense of foreboding gripped me like a vise. I didn't belong there. I was in some type of real, but unknown, danger. My first reactions have never been to submit to the peer pressure of a group. If I'd been a 'people pleaser' I could have gone down a dangerous road filled with tragic consequences. Later that evening when I returned home I felt a deep sense of relief and vowed never to hang out with these boys—and their strange desires—again. When the winter break ended I returned to my comfort zone: the structure of sports and teammates. Sports and my self-preservation instincts protected me from the rebellious boys who would eventually move from alcohol and cigarettes to heavy drug use. That was an important lesson, but I would also learn that in addition to people who were a positive influence on my life, I would soon be meeting others who would coldly introduce me to the cruelty of the world.

My junior-high athletic career was wildly successful. I played basketball and ran track under an influential coach: Dean Cell. Following the blue-collar, middle-class work ethic of the Northeast Lincoln community, coach Cell was a fiery, no-nonsense coach who demanded peak conditioning and fundamentals. Accustomed to and expecting success, individually and as a member of a team, I was the starting guard for the basketball team for three straight years, only losing one game and earning three city championships. A co-captain in track and field, I competed in the sprints, long jump, shot put, and discus on another city-championship team. Under coach King, I was the quarterback of the eighth-grade Elks team with a record of 8-1-1 taking third place in the state championships. I also led the league in scoring, passing, and rushing.

1970 Elks A Team City Champions

It was a great time but forces in life I couldn't control were well underway. Sports and my buddies in the locker room had always been a priority, but school was changing—and it seemed to have happened overnight. The hallways were now filled with strange new creatures: young women. I walked the hallways in a constant state of inebriation, the effects of new hormones flooding my adolescent, little different than alcohol. The skinny girls had developed curves, wore makeup, and the smell of perfume permeated my senses as they strolled by. Although I had no idea how to talk to them, I was certainly paying attention.

CHAPTER SEVEN

Setting the game in motion

A rock pile ceases to be a rock pile
the moment a single man contemplates it,
bearing within him the image of a cathedral.
—Antoine de Saint-Exupéry

Leaving Kirkwood's muddy parking lot beginning the long drive back to San Francisco I wasn't burdened with the usual physical exhaustion at the end of a weekend ski trip. Instead, feeling light and free, embarking on a new, unknown journey of adventure and mystery, the clarity of my thinking was as bright and clear as the blue skies above the snow-capped mountains. As mile after mile slowly turned through the odometer, ideas, structure, metaphors, and patterns of my life's successes and failures fell into place.

I've gone through life's institutional processes: school, church and work. Grade school, junior high, high school and college consisted of annual and monthly milestones broken down into weekly subdivisions and sub-processes. The broad topics of Math, Science, History and English were separated into smaller, more manageable pieces. The learning structure of mathematics was divided into arithmetic, algebra, trigonometry and calculus. Those sub-categories were further broken into the weekly syllabus. It's a practical implementation of divide and conquer.

The levels of advancement in my professional career are similar. Junior Programmer, Programmer, Programmer-Analyst, Senior Business Analyst and Project Manager, all leading up to my current position of Chief Information Officer. After thirty years of solving challenging finance and technology problems my professional toolbox is much more refined but I still fall back on fundamentals: breaking large problems into smaller, more manageable pieces, prioritizing with careful deliberation before putting a plan in place.

I know how to work and maneuver within a process. I was part of the obvious structures, frameworks and progressions in school and work, but I've been doing naturally with athletics in some form or other since the sixth grade. Unleashing a cascading river of motivation, my early attempts at process, although raw and unrefined, usually began with a football game on TV, an intriguing book, or interesting movie. I used the energy, writing down exactly what I wanted to do and achieve. I followed my goals with a detailed plan always including dates, milestones and contingencies. Reviewing and refining my plans on a daily basis, I was rarely distracted by the noise of the world. Staying disciplined has always been easy for me: it's just a simple function of never forgetting exactly what I want. Outside of intimate relationships, I've been relatively successful using this process—in sports and my career.

I followed a structured process snow-skiing when I learned the basics of turning and stopping on the bunny hill. Once I had those fundamentals learned, I developed new skills, practicing on the green and blue hills. After developing sufficient technique, confidence, and conditioning, I moved to the black and double black-diamond expert runs. The martial art Tae Kwon Do has similar step-by-step advancement. Starting with a white belt, I methodically developed my skills, moving up in rank from white to yellow, green, blue, red, and finally black belt.

In the past, my fear was usually the unwelcome result of some activity. Now, the emotion of fear *is* the activity. I'm curious to see if the habits I've developed over a lifetime are enough of a foundation to develop a new skill: the ability to become comfortable feeling uncomfortable. I'll apply my skills, both professional and personal, to challenge my ghostly phantom, but with a new twist. Instead of coldly setting aside the emotional distraction of fear, I'm explicitly inserting it into the plan.

I need to do more than buy an affectless, two-dollar *No Fear* bumper sticker, my public statement to the world. I want to '*Know My Fear'*, journeying into its labyrinth, creating a deep understanding. I want to seek it out, deliberately challenging it at every opportunity. Step-by-step, similar to snow skiing, education in school or the martial arts, I'll challenge fear with a structured process. Instead of a series of impotent reactive emotions, moment by moment, one mental brick after another, I'll build a pillar of emotional defiance.

I have no idea how I made the the three-and-a-half-hour drive home. The driving was an unconscious blur of traffic. My mind was elsewhere, consumed with ideas. I arrived home with an exciting plan for the year swirling around in my head. I had created a bunny, green, blue, black, and double-black skiing progression to explicitly confront my fear. I'll execute the plan in small, manageable steps over the next fifty-two weeks making minor adjustments as I learn and evolve. A base camp of structured ideas for the assault on the summit of my personal Mount Everest was in place.

The year long, week-by-week, immersion process will allow my mind to adapt to increasing levels of discomfort in general and more specifically, heights. I need an extended period of time to slowly push my internal boundaries. I don't want to fail like I did at the swimming pool, flinging my young, skinny body off of a concrete diving platform hoping the universe would reward my impatience with a quick solution. I'll still work my normal sixty-hour week in the office, continue the physical grind in the gym, but I'll use the evenings, weekends, and vacation time to play my new game.

Week		Sunday	Monday	Tuesday	Wednesday	Thursday	Friday	Saturday	Participant Plan	Spectator Plan
	Feb-09									
1	1				52		ski	ski	Powder ski Kirkwood	
2	8	yoga/massage		ski/film			Teatro Zinzanni			Teatro Zizanni
3	15		Gym			UB 100s	Phoenix (?)	[illegible]	[illegible]	
4	22							ski	Backcountry Awareness/Transceiver Clinic 2/28	
	Mar-09									
5	1	ski	yoga	yoga	lift	yoga	ski/film	ski kirkwood	ski	
6	8	Fly South Dakota					Fly SFO/ golf		Kirkwood mogul photo shoot	
7	15	golf/yoga				New boots/Reno	[illegible]	alare	alare Fri 3/20 thru Sun 3/22	Ballet
8	22	alare/40" powder		LIFT		Strength TKD		ski kirkwood	ski	
9	29	ski kirkwood	yoga	lift	yoga	Strength TKD				
	Apr-09									
10	5	boot fitting/ski kirkwood	ski Mt Rose/lesson	keigwin thunderhill				**ski kirkwood**		
11	12	ski kirkwood						ski kirkwood		
12	19	ski kirkwood					ski kirkwood	ski kirkwood		Opera
13	26	Fly South Dakota	SD Rest	SD Rest	SD Rest	SD Rest	Fly stokes! (?)	Golf demo/lift UB (?)		
	May-09									
14	3	Fly Las Vegas		Gartner speak/Fly SFO		sick	sick	sick	Speak at Gartner conference Las Vegas	Shark Reef Mandala Bay
15	10	sick	sick	sick	sick	sick	Fly Maui	maui	**Maui**	Museum
16	17	Maui	Maui	Maui	Maui	Maui (Scuba Dive)	Maui	Maui (Scuba Lanai)	Scuba Dive/Surf Maui	AMA Superbike (Infineon) (May 17)
17	24	Maui	fly sfo					Sail the Delta	Delta Photo Shoot	
	31		run/yoga		core strength/yoga		run yoga	Golf/yoga		
	Jun-09									
18	7	The Hill/Yoga!		run/yoga		Lift UB		2009 CBR	blackbelt exam	
19	14	Walk 3 miles	Met Christopher Sorrenti	Strength TKD		lift ub		CBR riding		
20	21							Walk/run	horseback riding	
21	28	Fly South Dakota	Lift UB		FLY SFO	Strength TKD	CBR Training	Walk/run	Waddell photo shoot	
	Jul-09									
22	5		Lift UB		Strength TKD		Walk/run		Golden Gate Bridge Photo shoot	Laguna Seca (Moto GP)
23	12	Lift UB	fly SD	Strength TKD		walk/run	FLY SFO	Bike Training		
24	19	samurai exhibit	lift ub		core strength/yoga		walk/run	Bike Training	SFO Dainese track day tuning	samurai exhibit
25	26		Core Abs		Walk/run 3.5		Lift UB	Bike Training		
	Aug-08	Muir woods 10 mile hike		Core		Yoga/TKD				
26	2							L.A. Dinner	Track days	
27	9						Fly Portillo		Portillo Ski/Heli Trip	
28	16	Portillo	Portillo	Portillo	Portillo	Portillo	Portillo	Portillo		Museum, Pablo Neruda's home
29	23	Portillo	Fly SFO		La Follie			**Bike Training**	The Gorge photo shoot	
30	30	Walk 1 hour/Windsurf Delta			Jardiniere		Mikael Crissy 6.2 (?)		Go karting refresher course	
	Sep-09									
31	6	Minden Glider	Water Ski	Yoga	Yoga			**Diablo Shores**	Whistler	Skin Two Rubber Ball (London)
32	13	Diablo Shores/Sail Delta						**Air Combat**	blackbelt exam	
33	20		Jim Russell	Jim Russell	Jim Russell				Air Combat Fighter lead in (2k) 9/19 - 20	
34	27							Sail Crissy	Water Ski photo shoot	
	Oct-09									
36	4									
37	11	iSky	TKD			Lift	FLY San Diego	FLY PSC	Punta San Carlos	
38	18	PSC	PSC	PSC	PSC	PSC	PSC	FLY San Diego	Punta San Carlos	
39	25	FLY SFO			Massage	Swim lesson 1			Float Plane over Golden Gate	Paris
	Nov-09									
40	1		TKD			TKD			Shark Dive Farralons	
41	8		Infineon	Infineon		TKD			Moto gp	Mr.Ms. Olympia
42	15		TKD			TKD		Warren Miller Marin Center		
43	22		Kendo		Laguna Seca		Laguna Seca		Motogp	
44	29		TKD			TKD		Zoom Zoom track day		
	Dec-09									
45	6	Zoom Zoom Track day								
46	13									
47	20	Skydive Perris								
48	27							Top Gun Jets		
49	Jan-10									
50	17									
51	24									
52	31					53				
	7-Feb						heli ski	heli ski	**heli ski**	
	14-Feb	heli ski	heli ski	heli ski	heli ski	heli ski	heli ski	heli ski	**Heli ski**	
	21-Feb									

The original 52-week plan

The foundational building block, the bunny hill of my process, will accomplish three specific goals. The principal goal during the months of February, March and April will be spent learning the technical aspects of the sport of skydiving. I'll study the terminology and physics building a base of knowledge, becoming familiar with the equipment and safety techniques. Because it's the winter ski season, I'll also seek out more fear inducing, challenging locations on the ski-mountains. I'll find more uncomfortable, unfamiliar situations with real physical consequences: steeper pitches and a few feet more air under my skis during jumps.

The second goal is to begin studying the physiology of fear. What does the human body do when it's in danger? How does the breathing function affect how the brain views possible harm? How does the nervous system affect the intricate web of fascia holding our bodies together? How do people with little or no fear of heights deal with other fears—for example, the fear of water or claustrophobia?

The final goal, a key building block in all of my personal successes, is visualization. I need to begin visualizing the critical moment jumping from the plane before freefalling towards the surface of the earth. This visualization piece isn't just mental. I need to project from my mind, into my body, the smell, sound and feelings being in an aircraft at twelve thousand feet. Although my ultimate goal is twelve months away, I also need to begin vividly imagining a perfect picture of success from the time I drive up to the jump site until the time I'm taking off the parachute with a huge smile of accomplishment deepening the creases of my face.

The foundation [illegible] accomplishment [illegible] months of [illegible] March and [illegible] agent [illegible] technical aspects of the sport [illegible] and [illegible] building [illegible] equipment and safety techniques [illegible] I had to seek out [illegible] [illegible] and [illegible] physical consequences [illegible] [illegible] jumps.

[illegible] to be [illegible] [illegible] [illegible] [illegible] affect how [illegible] does the nervous system affect [illegible] [illegible] 25 percent [illegible] [illegible]

The [illegible] a key [illegible] success, is visualization [illegible] moment, jumping from [illegible] surface of the earth [illegible] to project from my mind into [illegible] being [illegible] altitude of twelve thousand [illegible] goal is six months away [illegible] perfect picture of success [illegible] until the time [illegible] accomplishment [illegible]

CHAPTER EIGHT

Feeding on the cruelty of the world

Pay no attention to what the critics say;
no statue has ever been erected to a critic.
—Jean Sibelius

I've made thousands of decisions in my life but this weekend's decision to challenge heights felt eerily similar to setting the goal of playing in the NFL. Regardless of how audacious it seems in hindsight, I couldn't have understood the life-changing importance of my football dream. Setting such an impossible goal and never giving up taught me to focus and prioritize—avoiding the constant irritations and distractions life would set before me. Although I was never sat down at a dinner table and explicitly taught how to make a personal choice, I was constantly learning from the examples of other people's actions.

I can't remember of course, but probably one of the first things I learned as an infant was how to avoid the inherent danger of various household objects. As I grew older interacting with other small children, I was taught to be nice, share my toys, and learn the social niceties providing the glue for a society to function. Watching my parents, siblings, close family members, and friends, I mimicked their behavior, positive or negative, looking to them for guidance and a sense of belonging.

I probably watched and listened a little too closely, in particular to my father. Around the age of four, I attended an extended-family Christmas dinner at my grandparent's home. Extremely proud of what Santa had left under the tree, I paraded around wearing my new cowboy hat and gun belt with matching cowboy boots. When a distant relative loudly entered the crowded living room shaking hands with everyone I decided to assert my personality, repeating what I'd heard. Hands on hips, swaggering up to him in the middle of the festive gathering, I kicked him in the shins before meeting his eye, defiantly stating for all to hear, "I don't like you and my dad doesn't either." After that, I'm sure my parents were much more careful what they said in front of their unusually observant son.

At five years old the shift to the structure of school began. Grade school was laid out with the basic classes of reading and writing, arithmetic, history, science and the arts. I also began to receive societal lessons in how to take direction, conform and submit. "Get in line. Be quiet! No pushing or shoving. Get good grades, study hard, and don't bring attention to yourself."

Junior high school was a critical period of assimilation. It was assumed I knew how to be happy and what to do with my life. Unfortunately, although I was taught history, math, and science, I wasn't explicitly taught how to carefully create and set the dreams and goals of my life. When given aptitude tests designed to show me what I might be good at, unfortunately, I believed the results. I'd never held a drumstick but when the results of the musical-ability tests came back, I was dead last in percussion. I thought being a drummer would be fun, but I let a test, a teacher, and her "system" tell me what to do.

High school and college didn't actively teach me how to live a unique life. There certainly were no courses called Planning and Achieving Your Personal Goals, Making Life Changes, or Facing your Fears Using Process. Instead, I was unconsciously taught a way to conform and slowly die day by day: "Just be a good boy and do what you're told." I was given a coloring book but was told it was safer to stay inside the lines. Most social institutions—school, work, the media, churches, and the government—spoke in vague generalities, consistently teaching me to ignore and sublimate my feelings and desires. I was bombarded with thousands of messages full of feel-good pluralism telling me what to do, what to think, and what to feel, but the messages weren't designed to inspire me. Most often the message was laced with hidden layers of fear, self-doubt, and, worst of all, a staggering helping of guilt imploring me to conform to the trap of safety and security—a perfect recipe for unhappiness.

Ironically, at the same time I was being implicitly trained and conditioned to conform, I heard the lofty but hollow platitudes I could do or be anything I wanted. The problem was when I asked how, I was usually met with a pair of eyes as empty and glassy as a Hindu cow's. Society's institutions left me to fate, falling into life situations helped along by a series of seemingly random events little more than accidents in time. I was taught it was dangerous to be an individual in a world where non-conformity met stifling resistance. Society's collective taught me how to be a good boy, hypnotizing me into believing that after graduating from school, I'd be happy if I had a job, a wife, children, and debt.

From a competitive standpoint, society taught me winning is all that matters, but after winning or achieving a goal I wasn't taught how to deal with success and the uncertain transition into what to do next? In competition or in general day-to-day life, society certainly didn't teach me how to fail with dignity. More accurately, society consistently taught me it was imperative not to fail, embarrassing myself in front of others, the ultimate shame.

But I was exceedingly fortunate. On a daily basis, my parents modeled how to be an autonomous, self-directed adult. They were active in our local church, participating in and volunteering for many activities and events. For as long as I could remember every Sunday morning meant getting up, putting on a suit with a clip-on tie before attending Sunday school and church services. One bright spring Sunday morning I came into the living room appropriately dressed only to find my parents in the living room wearing bathrobes over their pajamas, lazily sipping coffee as they read the morning paper. Surprised when told we wouldn't be going to church "for a while," I happily scrambled back into my jeans and sneakers heading off to the sandlot baseball field. Although too young to understand, years later I was told a family with the wrong color of skin had attempted to join the church. When the church leaders emphatically said "no", my parents despondently but resolutely walked away from organized religion.

A few years after setting the goal to play in the NFL, a second life-changing event presented itself as I prepared for my ninth-grade season. As long as snow wasn't on the ground, I'd suit up in my Packer uniform complete with a shiny, forest-green #15 Bart Starr jersey and head to our backyard to practice. Starting in a three-point stance, I'd bark out an imaginary play before sprinting at full speed up and down the backyard. Carrying the football, I evaded trees and dodged bushes I imagined as opposing tacklers. For hours. I'd even turn on our backyard lights at sunset when I had the energy to continue. When my father had time after work he'd spend hours throwing pass after pass until his arm was so tired he'd announce we'd better practice handoffs for the rest of the evening. I practiced from the bitter cold of January into the scorching heat and humidity of July and August. I was never under pressure to be in the backyard, and as a matter of fact my, father constantly told me I was training too much.

In the middle of August, a couple of weeks before the freshman season was set to begin, Northeast High School started official practices. Wanting to learn more about football, if only by attendance and proximity, I'd ride my bike in full football gear one and a half miles to the practice field to watch. In addition to soaking in the structure of practice, the school's blocking sleds and green canvas tackling dummies were available. For hours before practice I'd set up the tackling dummies in different formations, running imaginary plays, dodging a new set of tacklers rather than backyard trees. On a seemingly insignificant but life-changing day, one of the hottest of the summer, I had been practicing alone for about an hour before players on the sophomore team began gathering at the other end of the practice field.

As the blocking dummies were being dragged into formation, from far across the practice field I heard one of the sophomore players yelling, "Hey Bart, throw me a pass." At over seventy-five yards, I knew it was too far to throw a pass to them, but then I realized it was a cruel attempt at ridicule.

Stunned and shocked not by their exact words, but of their intent, I couldn't understand why one of the last boys in the line was making fun of me wearing my Packer uniform. I was practicing so I could eventually wear the same black and white Northeast uniform they were wearing. At such an early, impressionable age, I'd just begun to recognize that the sharp pinpricks of ridicule, often disguised as good-natured jokes between friends, were really meant to hurt. I also began noticing the inaudible, inner voices of doubt and uncertainty, but this was the first time the outside voices of the world had shown up in such an ugly way. At first I was embarrassed and for the briefest of moments thought '*maybe it is weird to be here practicing by myself in my Packer uniform.*'

I was fourteen, too young to have developed a thick protective shield of emotional scars or calluses. I hadn't yet learned the world would consistently deliver the harsh lessons I hadn't been exposed to at home. I was completely alone without coaches, parents, or authority figures to protect the innocence of my feelings. This new problem was mine and I would have to face it on my own.

Feeling a seed of self-consciousness trying to sprout into embarrassment I knew I couldn't slink away in submission. If I walked to my bicycle, my head down in shame and started to pedal home, I'd be enraged—not at the taunting young men hiding in the back of the line, but at myself because I gave in, letting them distract me from my goals. Because I didn't have any experience or skills confronting people trying to get me to quit I simply had to bear down, enduring their sarcasm and ridicule. Alone. As the sweat poured down my face inside my helmet I kept practicing, stubbornly and angrily dragging the imaginary players into position for the next play.

On that day, alone on a practice field, I learned how important it was not to care what other people said or thought, especially about the dreams I wanted to live. Although I hadn't been taught how to confront cruelty, I was completely motivated, striving for something I wanted with a long-term goal. When I rode home, unbelievable feelings of freedom and satisfaction washed over me. I was beginning to understand the moments of struggle were often more satisfying than the achievements. I enjoyed the goal setting and the planning followed by the small, day-to-day sacrifices leading to constant but tiny improvements. The droplets, no more than one-percent improvements at a time, would eventually cascade into a flood of opportunity.

The boy's destructive cruelty opened a hidden, internal door. Behind the door I discovered a private room fortified with a defensive shield of unyielding competitiveness. I learned to harden my mind, protecting my goals from people who wanted to control me, dragging me down into their ugly world of complacency and stagnation. A single, private moment taught me to bear down, ignoring the soulless voices of the world trying to make me feel small. In a bizarre if not ironic way I should thank the undisciplined, unmotivated boys shuffling around in the back of the line, their jerseys not tucked in, their socks bunched sloppily around their ankles. Later in life when my career was in full swing, I'd meet up with them again in a much more dangerous form—the belittling office narcissists, dream stealers trying to crush the goals of everyone around them.

I was fortunate to be exposed to the harshness of this lesson early in life. The boys in the back of the line gave me an important tool, a new form of personal motivation to develop and transform into something useful. I didn't know the term at the time, but I'd become something of an alchemist. Instead of letting their energy slip through my fingers unused, I learned to feast on it, turning it into something useful. I turned the initial shock and embarrassment to internal disbelief. My disbelief grew into anger, before ending in steely determination. Once my determination was strong enough it became physical action fueled by a white-hot laser beam of focus. Their ridicule also made my life easier because I didn't have to worry about being nice to them. I could ignore them with the pleasure of indifference.

I was back on the practice field in my green jersey the next day, the day after, and all the days up until official practices began. A single, impressionable moment on a humid day in August could have been the start of learning how to accept defeat, shrinking away from life. I was unaware of the moment when I accepted my fear of heights, but I was acutely aware of the lifelong implications on the dusty practice field. Accepting their gift of ridicule could have initiated a lifelong sequence of decisions, where a fraction of a second at a time I'd give in to outside, soul-sucking influences destroying my goals, dreams and my life. If I'd have left my dreams, littered on the ground like the green dummies never to be pursued again, my life would have been irretrievably different.

Because I had the protection of a long-term goal, I kept moving forward on a practice field in Lincoln. Without my impossible dream, I could have easily succumbed to, accepted, and internalized their ridicule and cruelty. Instead, I did the opposite: I didn't forget what I wanted and stubbornly pushed back against them and their ugly world. Pushing back against the world became the key that would open hidden doors to a magical period of success in high school.

CHAPTER NINE

I've signed a binding contract

Remembering that I'll be dead soon is the most important tool I've ever encountered to help me make the big choices in life. Because almost everything—all external expectations, all pride, all fear of embarrassment or failure—these things just fall away in the face of death, leaving only what is truly important. Remembering that you are going to die is the best way I know to avoid the trap of thinking you have something to lose. You are already naked. There is no reason not to follow your heart.

—Steve Jobs

I've been overconfident, ignorant, arrogant and naïve—an exceptionally dangerous combination in any environment—but off-piste, deep in the backcountry, that combination can be fatal. Skiing about twenty-five days a year for the last fifteen years, I've always believed I was safe on a mountain but I've been in danger, perhaps not to others, but certainly to myself. I like to ski deep powder and some of the best areas on a mountain where powder accumulates are between huge granite boulders called chutes. Often barely wide enough to make a ski turn, the danger is if the snow breaks free into an avalanche, a skier can be trapped unable to escape.

I've been that ignorant skier. Little more than a red-and-white pin in a bowling alley of stone, it would only take a few pounds of pressure to trigger a ten-ton bowling ball of snow to crush me. If I were lucky, I'd be killed instantly from head trauma after hitting silent, immobile trees or rocks patiently waiting at the bottom of the slope. If I were as unlucky as I was unprepared, I'd be encased in a concrete tomb of snow slowly asphyxiating. I often ski alone, so in any type of avalanche the probabilities of my survival would be remote.

The strategy this year is to get into situations where I'm uncomfortable, providing escalating levels of tension, uncertainty, and challenge. I've never traveled to South America or flown in a helicopter. I'm confident on a pair of skis, but I've never been heli-skiing. Deciding to take on the opportunities constrained by the word *never*, I booked several ten-day ski excursions. The first, a February trip to Portillo Chile in August with one day scheduled for heli-skiing. I also scheduled a ten-day heli-ski trip to the Cariboo and Monashee mountain ranges of British Columbia for next February.

To prepare for heli-skiing in the backcountry where I'd be landing on tiny, precarious mountain peaks I signed up for an American Institute Avalanche Research and Education (AIARE) course at Kirkwood. AIARE provides avalanche awareness instruction to skiers, snowboarders, and the snowmobiling community who traverse the backcountry. In the United States alone there are on average twenty-eight avalanche-related deaths per year. The course began with a basic introduction to avalanche weather patterns, cornices, vertical-slope angles, and run-out zones. Next, the safety equipment—the shovels, probes, and transceivers—were exhaustively explained and demonstrated. After the classroom exercises, we turned our attention to "on-mountain" training exercises. Here, we would dig avalanche pits and determine the quality of the snowpack as we looked for buried transceivers pretending to be snow-covered victims.

During the course, the instructors, expert backcountry ski mountaineers, shared story after story of unprepared skiers, snowboarders, and snowmobilers rescued by search-and-rescue teams after long, cold nights alone in the mountains. For the unfortunate few, rescue missions turned into body-recovery missions. Each story was a variation of unprepared, dismissive skier wearing a thin parka, carrying no food or water, and certainly no backcountry-safety equipment. As each story unfolded, I hypocritically rolled my eyes, smugly thinking I'd never be in a situation where I'd have to be rescued.

I couldn't imagine facing the tired eyes of a seasoned rescuer who risked his life to help me until I realized: I've been one of those people. Windsurfing in dying winds in Bermuda, I've been rescued two miles offshore by the Coast Guard. I've also been towed over a mile back to shore by a fellow windsurfer in the shark-infested waters of Tomales Bay in Northern California after my mast snapped in two during a jibe. In both instances, I'd been naïve, unprepared, and entirely overconfident in my ability and had caused someone else to take a significant risk for me.

While I received my avalanche-training certificate, it came with a huge dose of humility. Thinking I was prepared for skiing steep powder runs in the backcountry, the course opened my eyes. Without respect for the power of nature in the mountains, I had no fear. In hindsight, I've been extremely lucky during my snow-skiing adventures. I've relied on my physical abilities to get me out of trouble on steep, isolated mountainsides. Although I've acquired the necessary survival equipment: transceivers, probes, shovels and packs, what's missing from my backcountry toolbox is a foundational layer of knowledge refined with years of experience.

As much as I might want to, I can't buy or borrow the tool of experience. I'll have to earn it brick by brick with carefully placed layers of sticky mortar. I need constant practice using the equipment, preparing and honing my skills so I can get out of a jam without endangering myself or others. During my research into fear, I read about Hollywood stunt men and other adventurers. The common theme among the most successful was discipline and constant preparation followed with a massive dose of math and physics. They survived with their brains, not their bravado.

Being forced to swallow such a bitter pill, admitting my backcountry skiing skills to stay relatively safe were lacking, initiated an internal conversation about my plan to skydive. I can't make the same naïve, avoidable mistakes. A few months from now, I'll jump from a plane, freefalling to the earth before flying a nylon canopy back to the ground. If I make a mistake, a 911 call to search-and-rescue teams waiting to retrieve me from an avalanche won't be possible. If I can't develop and hone the necessary skydiving tools, I'll die.

Perhaps it's uncommon but I don't find it difficult thinking about what's on the other side of the translucent veil called death. Around the world 150,000 people die every day: almost two human beings per second. I'll eventually be one of those statistics, but I use that upcoming reality as a motivator. I could be dead in six months from pancreatic cancer—I saw it happen with a healthy family member I dearly loved. I could be killed in an avalanche like too many of the world-class skiers I've watched on DVD. I could be dead in six minutes from a heart attack or a brain embolism—untimely events that have happened to people close to me as well. I could die in my sleep, like my close friend Bill.

Intense rivals playing for opposing schools in junior high and high school, Bill and I quickly became friends on the Nebraska football team. Because we both played on defense, we spent hours together in meeting rooms, lifting weights, and running. We often ended our weeks with Friday-evening marathon racquetball games that finished only when the janitors turned off the facility lights, forcing us to go home. Beginning in August of 1975, it only took a few months for him to go from a competitor I wanted to dominate to a respected friend I wanted to protect and support. A year later, after a great training week together in August of 1976, I was stunned to read the early-morning newspaper headline that my good friend had died in his sleep from an enlarged heart. I had no idea what to do or even what to feel. I was numb. When I went to Bill's funeral, my first, I began to understand that life is constantly changing. Nothing ever stays the same. Nothing.

I could be killed by a drunk driver while on the way to work—I read about it daily and saw it first-hand driving to a summer construction job during college. Sharing an early-morning ride to the job site with co-workers we arrived at a chaotic accident scene only minutes after a violent, head-on collision. With vehicle debris littering the road we slowly drove by the carnage until we recognized one of the cars in the accident, the mangled metal of our co-worker's Datsun 280Z. We quickly pulled over but were shocked when we got a closer look. For the first time in my short life I saw the world with spiritual eyes and instantly knew that souls existed. A broken, lifeless body was slumped over the steering wheel. His body, no longer supported by his soul, was a carcass of flesh, no different than a slab of beef hanging in a meat locker. Our friend was gone.

Before I saw my co-worker's lifeless form, I often wondered why as a young boy I wept for weeks when our family dog died but barely had a sniffle at my grandmother's funeral, even when passing by the open casket. Her funeral, my second, was fifteen years after Bill's. Feeling confused and guilty, I couldn't believe I could be so callous. I carried that guilt with me for years until I saw my co-workers body. I knew then that I hadn't cried at her funeral because the cold, inanimate shell of flesh wasn't my grandmother. The body in the casket was the same lifeless, crude physical matter occupying the driver's seat of my co-worker's car. The truth of who they really were had left their physical bodies.

All these scenarios are sudden deaths out of nowhere. Do I want to die asphyxiated in an avalanche? Of course not, but when I die I want to be doing something I love in a place I enjoy. I don't have a death wish. I have a life wish, but I don't believe the purpose of my life is to live as long as possible staying safe in a protective bubble of dullness and complacency. Long ago I signed a binding contract with my eventual death. I don't want to be in denial ignoring my destiny, thinking I have all of the time in the world. When I was twenty I took my health and youth for granted. My thirties were focused on my career, avoiding morbid, distracting concepts such as death. In my forties, I began to understand that time and age were real.

Now? I'm fifty-two. The standard mortality statistics say I'll likely live until about seventy-five, giving me about twenty-three more years to live. That's 8,390 days. I've lived 70 percent of the average statistical life-span. As a reminder of the obvious fact that death is part of the natural cycle I've created a visual cue, my version of a *memento mori*, of the number of days I might have left. I have two large vases on a table just inside the entryway into my home. One vase holds a number of silver ball bearings representing the number of days I've lived. The other vase holds the number I may have left. Each day before walking out the door, I move a ball bearing from one vase to the other. It's my own daily wake-up call to pay attention, fully live my life and never take anything for granted.

CHAPTER TEN

Accepted into my first tribe

Our subconscious minds have no sense of humor, play no jokes, and cannot tell the difference between reality and an imagined thought or image. What we continually think about eventually will manifest in our lives.
—Sidney Madwed

Regardless of my junior-high athletic success and rapidly building confidence, when I tried out for the high-school team I wasn't sure what to expect. Each fall Lincoln Northeast had over 140 players trying out for its teams. With so many participants the school had to have three separate teams—sophomore, junior varsity and varsity. Normally sophomores played only on the sophomore team. In rare cases a sophomore with enough talent would be moved up to the junior-varsity team. Almost never would a sophomore make the varsity team, playing with the seniors.

Tryouts began in the middle of August and continued until classes started in September. Every day was filled with blocking, tackling and conditioning drills, learning new plays, and sprinting up and down the grassy field. I wasn't sure how I was doing compared to other players, but I was prepared. Doing everything possible to develop my skills, I'd already spent hundreds of hours in the backyard dodging bushes and trees or catching passes from my father. Pretending to be Bart Star alone on a practice field, I learned to ignore the cynical voices of the world. After watching every game on TV or devouring the sports pages of the newspaper, I fell asleep every night dreaming of football. After weeks of punishing two-a-day practices, the coaches posted rosters on the locker room bulletin board. Although my work had been rewarded I was surprised to see I was the only sophomore who had made the varsity team.

Being the only sophomore was extremely satisfying, but it wasn't until shaking my father's hand later that evening that I began to understand the simplicity of what I needed as a person. I had performed the simple act of shaking his hand many times before, but it was always as a boy shaking a father's hand. Arriving home from practice, I found him in his bedroom after a long, hard day at the office. After quietly sharing I was the only sophomore who'd made the varsity team he didn't say a single word. He looked me straight in the eyes, silently nodding his respect and acknowledgment of how hard I had worked before holding his hand out in wordless understanding. A gentle, but penetrating look of his eyes. An unpretentious, almost imperceptible nod of his head. A firm handshake between a father and his maturing son. His eyes carried a depth and meaning in a single, timeless moment telling me that our relationship, always to remain a father and his son, had now changed to two men.

As a boy I'd always sat at the children's table at Thanksgiving and Christmas dinners but after that handshake, a chair at the grownup table was now waiting for me. A silent moment of mutual respect over in no more than two or three seconds would set the stage for the rest of my life. Years later, fully distracted by the world, I'd often forget its importance, but the holy trinity of a wordless look of respect in someone's eyes, an accepting nod of understanding and a firm handshake were all I would ever want or need.

The second time I felt I was becoming a man, a part of and responsible for something other than my personal goals, happened in my senior year of high school. From the seventh grade up until then, we had been boys, a group of individuals. Informally preparing without coaches for the upcoming season during Nebraska's summer heat we had become a team. Ten out of eleven of those who had played with me on the championship Elks teams were on this team, and we expected the same type of success. Although my teammates voted me co-captain I wasn't the outgoing cheerleader type vocally exhorting my teammates toward success. I enjoyed being looked to for leadership, but my style was much more subdued: I lead with my presence and intensity.

I didn't fully understand the responsibility of being a leader until the initial Friday-night game of the season. Sitting alone in a corner of a noiseless locker room I was nervous. It got worse as we warmed up, the opposing team preparing just across the field. I was close to throwing up until my anxiousness evaporated into a hypnotic focus when we began the ritualized pregame jumping jacks. Jumping jacks were a part of every practice but the tension-filled game time warmup created a unique sense of urgency and importance.

Lined up in four rows of ten, the stadium lights reflecting off our white uniforms, with each synchronized movement of our hands above our heads forty young men came together in perfect unison, shouting the letters of our school, "N-O-R-T-H-E-A-S-T!" We moved and yelled in a coordinated, increasing crescendo of combined force, and as the last *T* of *Northeast* was shouted, we would end with, "Rockets, Rockets, Rockets!" We only performed a total of twelve jumping jacks but the electricity flowing between us sent chills running up and down my spine. If I sit quietly, recalling these memories from far back in time, it still brings feelings that reverberate today.

It wasn't the letters, the words, or the competition to come that mattered. It was the experience of bonding. The game of football—and it was just a game—wasn't so important either. This was our version of an ancient aboriginal dance, the tribesmen surrounding the flickering nighttime fire as they prepared together for the hunt. We had become one, a group of young men with a common goal: compete fairly against the other team and win. In two hours, we would know—not by integers on the scoreboard but by looking into each other's eyes. A handshake from my father had introduced me to the world of men. I was now the leader of this young tribe. With that responsibility, more than anything, I did not want to let them down.

Other than losing a game there wasn't a single part of football I didn't enjoy. Peering up through my facemask at Nebraska's humid August skies while stretching on the itchy grass practice field, I was ecstatic on the first day of practice—the off-season was over and I was playing football again. I loved the tranquil pregame ritual in the training room getting my ankles taped. I reveled in the simple pleasure of pulling stretchy nylon pants slowly up my legs or carefully strapping on shoulder pads before pulling a jersey over my head. I'm not a masochist but, side by side with teammates, I even enjoyed the satisfying walk back to the locker room, my burning thighs struggling to pump out the last bit of lactic acid from the end of practice wind sprints. Painfully quiet and reserved, I cherished the playful locker-room camaraderie and banter. I never thought any moment on the practice field, in the weight room, or in the locker room was a burden or sacrifice. For me, these were the simplest and purest of pleasures.

While the physical training of football became a lifelong habit, I instinctively gravitated to the mental preparation. At the beginning of the season the coaches gave each player a playbook. By the end of the first week of practice I'd memorized the entire set of plays for my position. By the end of the second week I knew what each teammate was supposed to do on every offensive play. By the third week I knew what each teammate was supposed to do against every various defense. Instead of burying my head in a math or history textbook I was moving plastic players from my electric football set on the dining-room table, mentally rehearsing every play from every possible angle. The biggest difference in my mental preparation was the powerful tool of visualization. Using an intuitive mental process I couldn't have explained, I spent hours lying in bed or sitting in class imagining each play as if it were a Friday night under the stadium lights.

I've never been artistic in the classical sense. Except in the privacy of my shower I can't sing a note and even struggle to hear the words while listening to the radio. I've never had any interest in being an actor performing in school plays or musicals. Not only can't I paint a landscape, sketch a person's face, or sculpt a clay figurine, I can barely draw a recognizable stick man. What I could do was paint a picture of perfect athletic movement in my mind. Slowly building a heavily textured gesso, I mentally created the detailed ridges and brush strokes of oil on canvas, but my pictures weren't two dimensional or static. My artwork was a multidimensional movie of kinesthetic feelings. Frame by frame, each subtle movement exploded into a vibrant collection of colors, sounds, and smells.

I imagined the distinct smell of cigar smoke from the stands wafting down onto the field. I had a perfect image of our quarterback, Bruce, forcefully calling a play in the huddle as I gazed at the freshly cut grass between my cleats. I pictured walking to the line of scrimmage purposefully looking into the eyes of the opposing players as beads of sweat silently slid down their faces. I imagined the feel of spring-loaded muscles and tendons fully warmed up, ready to explode on the next play. When the ball was finally snapped, I saw each play unfolding in tiny, minute actions.

Blasting out of my stance in slow motion, my arms wrapping around the beaded leather ball, I focused my vision beyond the blur of linemen struggling for position to the players I had to evade: the linebackers. I even created scenarios where if I couldn't mentally evade a tackler, a slight twitch of my shoulder creating doubt in his mind, I'd imagine how it would feel bursting into him during the tackle. I mentally rehearsed multiple variations and formations of every play hundreds of times. By the time the real game began I had a slow-moving, frame-by-frame movie burned into my nervous system. Most importantly, I believed in the movie, never doubting how it would end. It was déjà vu into the future.

My constant mental focus on football might have been called daydreaming, pointless wishing, or even naïve fantasy, but it was much different: I was creating. Vividly imagining my upcoming performance down to the smallest detail, I was tearing a hole in the ethereal fabric of time, laying a deliberate foundation of pure expectation. I wasn't precognitive but could see the performance so vividly that by the time the game was actually played, my focus was so strong that I had a sense of what was going to occur long before it happened. It was as if the movie had been playing in the theater of my mind for weeks and I'd finally taken my seat to enjoy the show.

Although I was physically prepared from daily practices and hundreds of repetitions in the weight room, I spent twice as much time mentally preparing with the playbook, visualizing what I expected to happen. My preparation for games culminated in an emotional escalation that began in the basement bedroom of one of my best friends: Steve, the center on our team. Getting out of school early on game day, I would drive to his house to sit with him in his black-light-illuminated bedroom, listening to heavy metal music.

235lbs vs 170lbs. *Size is just a number*

As each beat of the drums and bass reverberated through my ears, into my brain, and down my spine, my focus increased to a restrained simmer just below boiling. Two hours later, when we'd return to school to board the team bus for the game, I was in a hypnotic trance, my five senses at their competitive peak. Football is a game of emotions. When the bus finally arrived at the field, I was impatient, unafraid of anything or anyone, ready for the intensity and violence of the Friday-night competition to begin.

My three years of high school were magical. I achieved all the goals I'd privately set in junior high, from making the varsity as a sophomore to making All-City and All-State as a running back. I was on a state-championship team, was the city's leading rusher as a junior and senior, and became the first in school history to rush for over a thousand yards in a season. I was invited to participate in the 1975 Nebraska Shrine Bowl and started my Division I football career as a walk-on at the University of Nebraska. The early success was great, but I didn't know it was only a beginning. I also didn't realize that for each achievement in life, the step up the ladder to the next set of challenges would be exponentially more difficult.

A rare time I enjoyed being the center of attention

I'm privately proud of my individual accomplishments and awards but playing sports was never about acquiring a trophy. If I simply wanted a trophy, I'd just go buy one and put it on the shelf. In the rare times I reminisce about my success in football I don't think about what a sportswriter wrote in the weekend paper. The first few times I saw my name in ink was exciting, but it was more of a validation of the hard work. It wasn't that I didn't care, but I was ambivalent, almost indifferent to the written words. The words were about the past. My focus was always on the future. How to improve.

I had similar feelings returning home after Friday-night games. Our living room was often full of neighborhood parents excited to talk about the game and how well I played. Like the sportswriter's Saturday morning newspaper commentary, I appreciated the sentiments, but I always felt awkward, almost embarrassed, because I didn't know how to respond other than to say, "Thanks." Although pleased by my performance, I wasn't surprised. I never said it but always thought, *Well, of course. What else could have happened? I've been working with my teammates, preparing and visualizing this performance for years.* I had the same reluctance to speak to sportswriters. What was I going to humbly say? "Well, thanks. We were just lucky." No, we weren't lucky. We were prepared.

Conversely, although I never asked for their feedback, I desperately cared about what my coaches, teammates, and competitors said. Usually over in a second or two, never to be recorded in a newspaper, those comments are deeply cherished memories. After scoring an eighty-yard touchdown in our first game of the year I quickly forgot the next day's newspaper write-up or the cheering fans, but the memory of a shared celebration with our quarterback still resonates today. He had chased me down, sprinting after me all the way to the end zone. Grabbing my jersey, his face mask pressed against mine, he was incoherently screaming at the top of his lungs. That celebration was a thousand times better than any birthday party because we'd worked for that moment together.

Even the smallest memories when I wasn't the center of attention are important. Instead of scoring a touchdown against a crosstown rival I'd made a crushing block on an important play. Unsteadily walking back to the huddle, my eyes watering from the collision, our fullback who carried the ball exhorted, "Way to block Danny Cass!" He had been following me into the hole, close enough to witness the violence of the impact. The play, and my block, would be run and rerun in the next day's film review, acknowledged by the coaches and appreciated with the whoops and hollers of my teammates. But neither the newspapers nor flickering film had recorded the importance of his one-second comment to me.

Jim Rohn, the famous motivational speaker, once said, "Each person is an average of the five people they spend the most time with." The teammates I spent most of my time with would eventually become a partner in a law firm, a maxillofacial surgeon, an F-14 pilot for the Navy, and many highly successful businessmen. My teammates became the brothers I'd never had. Hidden beneath their fierce competitiveness, they were men I could trust. I've always felt that in a crisis, I could call any of them for help. I hope my parents, coaches, and teammates understand how deeply their influence affected my life.

Outside of coaches and a few close teammates, most of my relationships in a class of six hundred had always been distant. Although I knew the names of hundreds of classmates, the social aspects of school confused me. Although aware of the loud, chaotic activity around me, I was content not to be the center of attention. I certainly wasn't the most popular, voted "most likely to succeed" or the homecoming king. That might have been nice for a moment or two, but those titles would have required an enormous amount of social interaction and distractions. I much preferred being alone in my rich inner world of competition, dreams, and goals.

It was completely different within the structure of sports and in the locker room. The locker room was a social outlet for me, a place I could express myself—most of the time without saying a word. I was comfortable amid the playful banter of competitive young men and usually hung out with Steve, whose calm demeanor made me look like a bubbly debutante. Like two women who can spend all day shopping together without buying anything and still consider it a great day, we could ride around in one of our muscle cars all evening, barely speaking, and have a great time. I also hung out with David and Tim, both social, outgoing teammates. With the newfound freedom of driver's licenses, we all spent too much time at a local shopping-center parking lot eating popcorn or cruised around town, listening to music and wondering aloud about young women.

Although interested, I had absolutely no idea what to think of the strange species of humans carrying matching chromosomes. As a sophomore I dated a few girls, but usually they were juniors or seniors and had always approached me. Although only a year or two older, the difference in maturity levels made them seem worldly and sophisticated, but on dates or in the school hallways, I was never sure of what to say or do with them.

My life as a man completely changed when I felt the overpowering chemistry of falling in love for the first time. She was gorgeous, with almond eyes, long brown hair, and an infectious laugh. She also had a curvaceous figure so perfect that it seemed that when God was pouring water into her, filling out her feminine curves, with a knowing, inward grin, she'd purposely forgot to say "When." A year younger than me, she attended a small high school outside of Lincoln, but we met while working weekends at a local buffet restaurant. After a few weeks we began to speak as we passed in the hallways but I was too stupid and aloof to understand she was flirting—basically shouting at the top of her lungs for me to ask her out. After a few more weeks of cluelessness, Cupid in the form of a female co-worker came to assist, frustratingly suggesting the obvious: "She wants you to ask her to the upcoming high-school dance."

What? She wants me to ask her to the dance? Really? She's stunning. She's way out of my league.

A few days after gathering my courage to ask such a simple question, "Would you like to go to the dance with me?" under a full autumn moon, I found myself driving to pick her up. Living a second at a time, letting new emotions arrive one by one, I had no plan of romantic seduction or clever jokes designed to make her laugh. I had no idea what I was going to say for an entire evening but everything turned out great. Extremely comfortable talking with her, I was able to relax and just be myself. There was only one awkward part of the evening.

After arriving at the dance my new friend became the center of attention of my male friends. It made perfect sense. She was a gorgeous stranger from another school. What didn't make sense was my first exposure to the hidden competitive nature of women. Before that evening most women in school had shown absolutely no interest in me. I'd been in the hallways and classrooms for three years, ignored—or tolerated, like a stray dog. At the dance, the palace of infinite puzzles called women became obvious, even for me. While my date sat beside me on the wooden folding stands in the school gymnasium converted to a dance hall, previously disinterested girls, one after the other, began taking turns sitting next to me. They were flirting and laughing, but it didn't take long to understand the flirting wasn't about me. It was competition with my date. They were trying to claim me as theirs, like a purse on sale.

After surviving my possessive female classmates, I drove my date home wondering how we'd end the evening. I was nervous when we pulled into her parent's gravel driveway. I was tense when I opened the car door to let her out. I'd kissed girls before but those kisses were mostly physical curiosity with little chemistry. After sharing we'd both enjoyed the evening, I stepped closer to her to kiss her goodnight. I didn't think about it. I didn't wonder if she'd accept my advance. It just happened. Perfectly. Her perfume mixing with the sweet smell of her hair, with one unbelievable kiss, she became both a dream and a curse.

Until I met her I'd always hid behind a thick emotional layer of boyish aloofness. With her, I discovered I was more than a one-dimensional robot. I could move from the extreme competition on an athletic field to the gentleness of brushing her hair as we watched a movie. Instead of living in my head, a million thoughts and ideas competing for attention, I could let go of my protective shell and simply feel her energy. A couple of months after we met I told her I'd fallen in love. I didn't want to be in love; it just happened. I wanted to be next to her. I wanted to hear her sultry voice. I was ten times stronger than her but she could drain my masculine energy with nothing more than a sideways glance and an almost imperceptible smirk. She was a refuge, warming me from the inside out and in some way I'll never understand, I'm probably still affected.

We were together for almost a year and a half but I was too young to understand the drug like rush of falling deeply in love for the first time would slowly wear off. Maybe the timing was wrong. If I'd fallen in love before, perhaps I'd have understood. Maybe it would have been better to have met her when I was in my mid-thirties. Like a drug user's futile journey chasing the dragon after the first ecstatic use of heroin, I'm not sure anyone ever gets over their first love and the dull pain of "I wonder what could have been" has followed me for years.

CHAPTER ELEVEN

I've already been in a skydiving plane

Courage is resistance to fear, mastery of fear, not absence of fear.
—Mark Twain

"**What are you doing**?" There's no rational reason for my trembling hands or the drops of anxiety forming on my forehead because I wasn't doing anything more than sitting in the safety of my familiar home. With gentle music playing on the stereo and a glass of wine in my hand I was reading a book explaining how to skydive. Instead of the simple pleasure of reading and learning, fear insisted on flooding me with useless, negative commentary. "Skydive? By the time you turn fifty-three? Leap into empty space from an aircraft door with only a few hours of training?" My ego in protective overdrive, the thought bubble above my head screamed, "Don't do it! You might get critically injured—or, worse, you could die! This is stupid!"

I've been here before too many times to count: overwhelmed and afraid of the unknown. With no idea how to put on my boots, click into the bindings or ride the chairlift, I was extremely nervous the first time I went to a ski mountain. As heavy northeast trade-winds pelted me with sand, I rigged a sail on Maui's north shore full of the same apprehension. As a white belt, I was anxious and unsure stepping onto a Tae Kwon Do floor the first time. I didn't even know how to bow or tie my belt correctly.

I should be nervous. If I weren't, I'd be naïve, overconfident or both. This is a new activity, but I was reacting with blind emotion, regardless of my ignorance of the skydiving process. I had no understanding of how the equipment worked, the physics of flying in freefall, or the remote probabilities of failing. I didn't even have a mental picture of the sweet adrenaline rush of success. No different than the hundreds of books I've read, simple black ink on white paper with instructional photographs, graphs, and diagrams, this inanimate object was torturing me with fear.

Bursting with inspiration, the night after arriving home from my breakthrough weekend at the Cliff, I went online, purchasing half a dozen skydiving books. Each night after work, I'd read a chapter or two before retiring to bed. Armed with pens and highlighters, I'd do the homework, preparing to perform with confidence. After reading the first book, studying the other books would reinforce my understanding and build my confidence. I've used this learning approach when I began using multiple textbooks after struggling through college calculus courses.

Overwhelmed and confused, sitting in huge classes of indifferent, hung-over students, my mind often whispered, "Maybe you're not smart enough. Maybe calculus is too difficult for you. Perhaps the comments junior-high teachers made were true: math and science aren't your best subjects." After too many frustrating study sessions leading to awful exam results, my first thought was to blame everything outside of me. My protective ego on full display the first thing I did was blame the heavily accented graduate assistant. His teaching didn't match my style of learning even though I had no idea what approach best suited me. I'd never considered a professor's approach might not fit my style of learning. Then my blame shifted to the textbook: the author's explanations seemed circular and indirect. I'd mistakenly assumed if someone had authored a book, or had a Ph.D. after their name, they must be able to simplify, easily communicating difficult concepts with words and pictures. Finally, it was my busy schedule of practices, the weight room, and curvy women scurrying around campus distracting my attention.

It would have been convenient but I couldn't continue to blame someone or something else indefinitely. I wasn't living in a deterministic world. The reality was if I didn't want to learn, nobody was going to force me. Simple but sobering, it was only when the feelings of helplessness showing up for exams unprepared became greater than my excuses that I made a decision and changed my behavior. Deciding to shoulder 100 percent of the responsibility for my grades, the only question was how.

A penniless college student with barely enough money to buy a Saturday-night round of beers, I wondered whether a different author could explain calculus concepts in a way that clicked for me. It was a last resort. After purchasing and studying the new book my revelation wasn't that I was beginning to understand calculus. It was new insights into learning and communication styles. The new book was indeed written in a way that was easier to understand. Once I grasped the specific concept, I reread the first book to understand how that author presented the same material in such different ways.

A light was going on. I used to think I was a slow learner and while that may be true, I realized my style of learning was to read and re-read, doing problem after problem until the details weren't details. They become concepts, their truths obvious. I wasn't memorizing so much as assimilating: structures, data and patterns. The specific learning process usually ended when the thoughts, *how did I miss that concept? It was right in front of my face,* arrived on the scene.

I also changed the way I studied. Armed with the syllabus for the semester, I knew the week-by-week content of the lessons. Instead of showing up for class unprepared, my mind a blank slate assigning all responsibility to the instructor, I studied ahead as far as possible becoming familiar with the new terminology and concepts. These changes in approach, preparation, and accountability helped me move from barely passing to honors level grades.

Even with the intellectual understanding of how I learned most effectively, my current emotional challenge, my new skydiving books still waited for me on the coffee table. I've chosen to put myself in a situation where a mistake means dying, not failing a calculus exam. It's unnerving, but statistically more people die in car wrecks on the way to the jump site than in a skydiving mishap. Similar to my experience with beginning Calculus, I suspect most people who decide to skydive arrive at the jump school completely unprepared.

I'd read that my first jumps would overwhelm my senses. I'd heard the term "pure sensory overload" often used to describe a first jump—people can barely remember what happened. All they know is they jumped and somehow safely reached the ground. Although I'm often a slow learner, needing significant amounts of time to make mistakes, repetitions, and refinements, I don't want to arrive at the jump site hoping the instruction will be presented in a way I could understand. I don't want to be in the middle of the jump, the surface of the earth rushing towards me at 125 miles per hour, and my mind freezes because I received too much classroom information in a short period of time. I'm preparing to perform under pressure.

The plan is to first make a tandem skydive. The preparation for a tandem jump only requires about thirty minutes of instruction because a professional will be strapped to my back handling all the risk. I'm mainly along for the excitement of the ride doing little more than staying out of the way. The day after the tandem jump I'll begin the Accelerated Freefall (AFF) course, a series of six skydives with increasing levels of difficulties and tasks to perform. The classroom part of the course lasts about six hours; the extended time necessary because a professional won't be strapped to my back. Although two instructors will freefall next to me, I'll be jumping with my own parachute, responsible for everything including emergency and safety procedures.

During the AFF jumps, three insurance policies ensure my safety. The first is my training and ability to perform. After jumping from the aircraft, free-falling in a stable body position to a designated target altitude, I'll release the pilot chute into the wind which pulls the main canopy from the container pack. Statistically opening correctly 999 times out of 1,000, the main canopy is designed to deploy within three to six seconds. If I do something stupid, such as forgetting to pull my ripcord, one of the instructors flying next to me will pull it for me. After the canopy is deployed, rapidly slowing me down to thirty-five miles per hour, I'll have to fly the canopy to the ground—alone.

If the canopy doesn't open, or open correctly providing enough stability to land, I must immediately invoke the second emergency procedure, releasing the main canopy before deploying the reserve. I'll only have four to seven seconds to execute this critical backup procedure before reaching an altitude of twenty-five hundred feet. The third insurance policy is the automatic-activation device. If I freeze, doing absolutely nothing and the instructors are unable to help me, the AAD, an altitude sensitive device installed inside of the container, will automatically deploy the main canopy at 2,500 feet.

I'm learning the procedures, but it's entirely different knowing I'll have to apply them for real. Immersed in skydiving books full of terms such as *downwind, base*, and *final*; *holding*, *running*, and *crabbing*; and *square*, *stable*, and *steerable*, I wanted to understand as much as possible before arriving at my first day of jump school. Concerned I'd be overwhelmed with the amount of information necessary to survive, I mapped out the sequence of my first skydive on paper. I've done this type of preparation thousands of times. It was just another football play or a technology project plan.

As I studied my plan broken down into smaller blocks of information and activities, I saw that even with a detailed plan or structured process, I miss things—especially when fear is part of the equation. I get distracted, forgetting the patterns and experiences of my life. I've been here before. I've already been in a skydiving plane wearing a parachute.

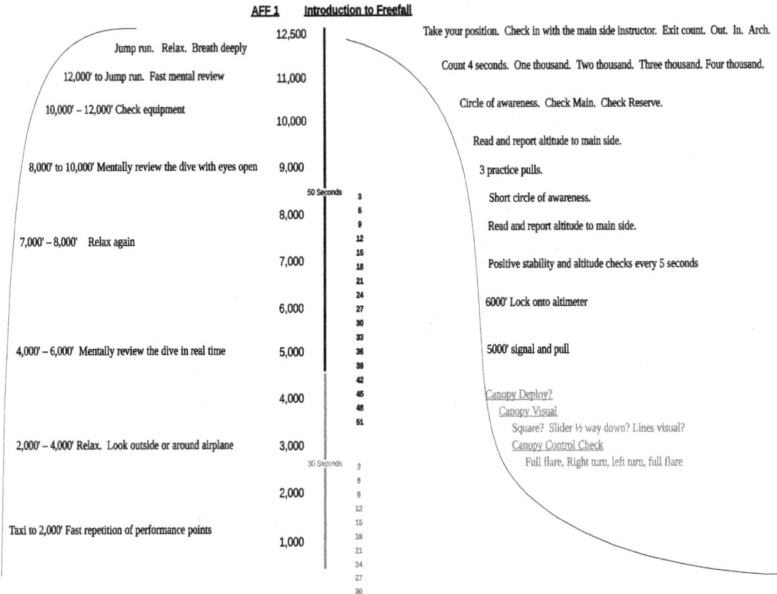
AFF 1 Introduction to Freefall
12,500
Jump run. Relax. Breath deeply
Take your position. Check in with the main side instructor. Exit count. Out. In. Arch.
12,000' to Jump run. Fast mental review
11,000
Count 4 seconds. One thousand. Two thousand. Three thousand. Four thousand.
10,000' – 12,000' Check equipment
10,000
Circle of awareness. Check Main. Check Reserve.
Read and report altitude to main side.
8,000' to 10,000' Mentally review the dive with eyes open
9,000
3 practice pulls.
50 Seconds
Short circle of awareness.
8,000
Read and report altitude to main side.
7,000' – 8,000' Relax again
7,000
Positive stability and altitude checks every 5 seconds
6,000
6000' Lock onto altimeter
4,000' – 6,000' Mentally review the dive in real time
5,000
5000' signal and pull
3 6 9 12 15 18 21 24 27 30 33 36 39 42 45 48 51
4,000
Canopy Deploy?
Canopy Visual
Square? Slider ½ way down? Lines visual?
2,000' – 4,000' Relax. Look outside or around airplane
3,000
Canopy Control Check
Full flare, Right turn, left turn, full flare
30 Seconds
2,000
Taxi to 2,000' Fast repetition of performance points
1,000
3 6 9 12 15 18 21 24 27 30

At the same time that I was struggling with college calculus, a couple of my teammates decided skydiving would be a good way to spend some free time away from football. Unaware of my problem with heights, they invited me to join them. I agreed, but too embarrassed to tell them the truth, I lied, telling them I didn't have enough money for the jump but I'd enjoy hanging out with them for the day, safely on the ground.

As my teammates sat in classrooms mostly learning not what to do, I walked around the airfield thankful I wouldn't be in any danger that day. I was wrong. When the classes were over and my buddies began entering the plane, the jumpmaster casually mentioned another customer had canceled his jumps for the day leaving an empty seat in the plane and asked if I wanted to come along for the ride. "Really? Don't I need some training?" "Legally, we'll have to put you in a parachute because the aircraft will have an open door, but you'll just sit and watch." It sounded simple enough, but what he hadn't shared was where I'd be sitting or what I'd be asked to do when we arrived at the jump altitude.

Providing an excellent view of my friends falling to earth, my seat was an empty space on the floor where the right front seat had been removed. With my back to the control panel we began the long climb to the jump altitude. As I studied the excited faces of my buddies stuffed into the back of the small plane I noticed a twinge of envy as they shared the experience, their grinning faces stretched wide in anticipation. Twenty minutes later the engine noise dramatically decreased and the plane leveled off, signaling that the jumps—and my terror—were about to begin.

The roaring engine made talking impossible so the pilot reached over and tapped my right shoulder before pointing at the closed jump door. He then made a twisting movement with his hand and wrist, mimicking the procedure necessary to open the door. *I had a job to do? I hadn't expected to do anything but watch.*

With no training or cautions from the pilot, I grabbed the latch and twisted, thinking I'd have to push the door open. A microsecond after the latch turned to the unlocked position, the door ripped open, violently yanking my upper body out of the plane. I wasn't wearing a seatbelt or holding onto anything except the handle of the door. Instantly going from relative safety to inches from doom, I was looking straight down at the ground. I had zero understanding how to freefall. Not only didn't I have any training on how or when to pull the ripcord, I barely knew where it was. I wasn't remotely aware of the physics necessary to fly a canopy safely to the ground. If I had fallen out of the plane, most likely, it would have been to my death. After pulling my shaking body back inside the aircraft, the pilot, unaware of the danger he'd just put me in, nonchalantly gave the thumbs-up hand signal to my buddies, and one by one, I watched them fall into oblivion.

My first skydiving experience was a perfect storm for a tragedy, resulting from a lack of knowledge, training, and preparation. Too naïve and trusting to have any thought of self-preservation, I stupidly allowed the world to roll the dice of probability for me. To put a cherry on top of a sundae of negative possibilities, I was surrounded by indifference and incompetence: a random survival-of-the-fittest theory in all its glory. I've learned to accept mistakes and failure are necessary components of learning and growing, but I'm not making the same lack of preparation mistakes this year.

CHAPTER TWELVE

I'm not a freak of nature

The greater danger for most of us is not that our aim is too high and we miss it, but that it is too low and we reach it.
—Michelangelo Buonarroti

It took some time after breaking up with the first love of my life but I eventually began dating again in college. The problem wasn't the lack of available women. They were everywhere. It was fear. I'd tasted magic and when I realized it wouldn't fall in my lap again so easily, I began to worry that I'd never experience those addictive feelings again. I'd always been burdened with the fear of heights and had a new fear about emotions, but I'd never been afraid on any athletic field. Ever.

It was only during a short, hormone-filled growth spurt in the eighth grade when I shot up past my teammates that I enjoyed being the largest and fastest player on the field. I grew so quickly that the only jersey that fit me was for an offensive tackle, so I wore number 75, as a quarterback. After that physically dominating season I was usually one of the smallest players on the field.

Combining fearlessness and passion with a small physical frame was a recipe for injuries. My lengthy collection, both in and out of football, includes three broken arms, four broken ribs, two separated shoulders, a shattered big toe, at least four concussions, and dozens of collisions where the end-result was 'getting dinged'. I also survived two broken noses and dozens of sprains, strains, cuts, and bruises. Recently, a disbelieving chiropractor held an X-ray of my spine up to the bright ceiling light in his office, somberly sharing that statistically, I should be in a wheelchair. Using his ballpoint pen to carefully highlight a dark-gray line across the C2 vertebra, he asked me, "When did you break your neck?" I had no idea, but it was probably in football.

In 1974, the year before I graduated high school, the NCAA reduced the number of scholarships offered by universities from seventy-five to forty-five, greatly reducing the likelihood a major university would take a chance on a player with my small stature. I could have accepted scholarships to a smaller university offering better opportunities to play, but in 1975 I walked on at the University of Nebraska, one of the great programs in the country. I wanted to be a part of its history, its culture of character, and its commitment to winning the right way.

I spent summers working construction jobs to help pay tuition. I even worked one summer on a tree-removal crew, spending many nerve-wracking hours forty feet in the air in the bucket of a high-ranger truck. The only reason I didn't freeze up was the men on the crew. I told them on day one I didn't like heights, but none of them ridiculed me. I was being supported. They acknowledged the emotion of fear as normal but expected me to get on with the task. The necessity of work came before fear.

After spending an entire day performing manual labor, I practically lived in the weight room, trying to get bigger and faster before fall practices began. Even though I was a running back in high school and played the same position in the 1975 Nebraska Shrine Bowl, after a few practices the coaches moved me to defense. New to the position of cornerback, I depended purely on athletic ability and mental preparation, becoming a starter on a freshman team that went undefeated. I was in the exceedingly good company of tremendous, dedicated athletes and coaches. Of the twenty-two starters on that team, eleven went on to play in the NFL. I wish that number would have been twelve.

Redshirted my sophomore year, I was placed on the number-one redshirt unit, practicing against the first- and second-string varsity teams. My fall afternoons were spent competing against Vince Ferragamo, the quarterback who led the Los Angeles Rams to the 1980 Super Bowl. For my freshman and redshirt years at Nebraska, I was in my element. I loved practice, the weight room, and the locker room banter and felt like a contributing member of the team. The locker room was my fraternity.

One of the most memorable moments at Nebraska was the first varsity game of my redshirt season. Although redshirt players couldn't play, NCAA rules allowed us to suit up and stand on the sideline during home games. Shoulder pad to shoulder pad, tightly packed in the tunnel leading from the locker room to the field, the players build off of each other's competitive focus. The escalating emotions quickly turned into a feeding frenzy when we heard, and then felt the roars exploding from the fans in the stadium.

1976 University of Nebraska Photo Day

The pulsating flow of excitement reached its climax when Coach Osborne led ninety-five crimson-and-cream uniformed players out across the field. After sprinting at full speed across the Astroturf, when I arrived at the sideline, all I remembered was the feeling of floating two feet above the ground on a pulsing river of adrenaline. In high school, I'd commonly played before ten thousand fans at Seacrest Field on Friday nights, but nothing could compare to the surreal experience of an eighteen-year-old running into Nebraska's Memorial Stadium in front of seventy-six thousand roaring fans.

After my redshirt year, it quickly became obvious I wasn't being groomed for a starting role. Bigger, faster junior college players had transferred in and even a wingback from the offense was moved to my position. It was the first time anyone had ever said, "While you were a great high-school player, at this level your discipline and intensity are not enough to overcome your lack of size and speed." It was a bitter, sickening pill to swallow. I was angry, hating the physical reality: the raw emotion of my desire was imprisoned in a body too small and too slow to compete at this level—or the next. Although I didn't like it, I was forced to accept that at five feet nine inches and 170 pounds, running a 4.7-second forty-yard dash, unless I became faster, I probably wouldn't be the key to success at Nebraska as a sophomore, junior, *or* senior. I wasn't fast enough, period. The difference between a 4.6 and a 4.7 forty is only a tenth of a second, about a yard on a football field—but that yard is critical for being in position to make a play.

The difficulty with my improbable if not impossible dream was reinforced when an NFL scout showed up to watch a practice. Even though the odds of anyone playing in the NFL are miniscule even with the requisite size and speed, I shared with the scout my astute personal insights and the cliché, "size is just a number and doesn't measure the heart of a player." While he agreed with an understanding smile, he offered me the cold reality of the situation. "Dan, in the NFL, we're trying to find freaks of nature. It's not normal or natural for a man who is six foot three and two hundred thirty pounds to run a 4.4 forty or have a thirty-eight-inch vertical jump. It's even rarer for someone to have the desire to run at full speed colliding into another man of the same size."

If I wanted to play at Nebraska or in the NFL, I'd have to face adversity and prove the coaches wrong. Because of the immense talent levels at Nebraska, I'd do my best every day, mentally preparing to be the typical walk-on redshirt player contributing by working hard so I might eventually start as a senior.

It should have been one of the great periods of my life. Even if I wasn't destined to be a starter, I was part of a group of young men playing Division I football at Nebraska in the Big Eight conference. Instead, it was awful. When my redshirt season ended in 1977, Monte Kiffin and Warren Powers both left Nebraska for head-coaching opportunities at other universities and were replaced with a new defensive coordinator and assistants. The new graduate assistant coach for the defensive backs was a former player at Nebraska who had transferred in from a junior college with a six-foot-three-inch, 215-pound frame of God-given size and speed. At Nebraska, he hadn't been a respected leader on the field, in the weight room, or in the locker room. He'd done just enough, the minimum necessary to get by. An underachiever, the phrase "Nothing in the world is more common than unsuccessful people with talent", described him perfectly.

I grew up at the dinner table listening to my parents and grandparents talk about character, politeness, and doing the right thing. In junior high, my coaches preached the virtues of hard work, personal discipline, and teamwork. I devoured sports stories in the newspapers, underlining and highlighting motivational phrases before taping them to my bedroom walls. All of my coaches—Bob King, Hop Cook, Dean Cell, Bob Els, Barry Alvarez, Tom Osborne, Monte Kiffin, Mark Heydorff, Bob Thorton, Claire Boroff and Terry Renner—shared the same types of inspiring messages.

I didn't like or necessarily agree with all of my coaches or teachers, but I trusted their passion and competence. That was all I needed to give everything I had. I looked up to them, believed in their messages, and could feel their commitment to us. I would have run through a brick wall for them because they loved being on the practice field and the day-to-day grind of the work. Most important, while they practiced tough, consistent discipline, I could feel that underneath the constant yelling and prodding, they cared deeply for me and the other players.

Like all the other coaches I'd played for the grad assistant would yell at us to work harder, not make the same mistake twice, and do our best play after play. I understood the meanings of his words, but couldn't reconcile them to the empty, hollow, and demotivating lack of passion with his past efforts on the field. On a daily basis I could feel his continual lack of effort and commitment. I didn't respect his work ethic. Most important, because he had wasted his natural gifts of size and speed, I didn't respect him as a man. He was going through the motions exactly as he had as a player. I could respect his position of authority only up to a certain point, but without respect for him as a man, his title wasn't enough. The need to respect someone leading me would be a theme that would follow me throughout my professional career. If I didn't respect a person, working for them or with them would always prove difficult. Without respect, personal relationships were impossible.

I vividly remember the exact moment I decided to leave the team. Waiting for a stoplight to turn green driving into a Saturday-morning practice, I was indifferent. For the first time in my life, I didn't care about football. I had no desire to practice, working to improve my skills as part of a team. When I concluded I was also going through the motions, not caring whether a coach respected me or not, leaving the team wasn't difficult. It probably helped that I was a walk-on player. If I had been on scholarship, the financial pressures might have been different. I might have felt trapped in a miserable situation, spending three years playing for a position coach I didn't respect so that later in life, I could tell drunk strangers in a bar, "Yeah, I made the team at Nebraska." The thing is, I could already say that.

The hardest part of leaving the team at Nebraska was telling my father. But I shouldn't have been surprised by his reaction. The night I told him I'd left the team, he reacted with grace and understanding. All he asked was, "If this is what you want, your mother and I will support you." I knew it surprised him, but I also knew how rare it was to have supportive parents, even in the most difficult situations. Although I'd soon transfer to another college, I never felt it would disappoint or embarrass him if I didn't play for Nebraska.

CHAPTER THIRTEEN

Accelerate the failure

Our deepest fear is not that we are inadequate. Our deepest fear is that we are powerful beyond measure. It is our light, not our darkness, that most frightens us. We ask ourselves, who am I to be brilliant, gorgeous, talented, and fabulous? Actually, who are you not to be? You are a child of God. Your playing small doesn't serve the world. There's nothing enlightened about shrinking so that other people won't feel insecure around you. We are all meant to shine, as children do. We are born to make manifest the glory of God that is within us. It's not just in some of us, it's in everyone. And as we let our own light shine, we unconsciously give other people permission to do the same. As we are liberated from our own fear, our presence automatically liberates others.

—Marianne Williamson

It was subtle, especially for a guy who often misses signals from the opposite sex, but I couldn't ignore the emotion in her voice. As she closed the heavy plexiglas door at the end of her flying session, I asked if she was a skydiver. With a mischievous but understanding grin, she paused before gently saying, "Don't do it."

"What do you mean, 'Don't do it'? Don't do it because it's dangerous?"

"No," she said. "Don't do it, because you'll become addicted to it."

This fascinating woman proceeded to share her newfound addiction to skydiving. Like me, she had begun to skydive to challenge her fear of heights. We were at iFly, an indoor skydiving facility in Union City, California. She was here to practice free-fall skills, maneuvering, twisting and turning her body eight feet above the ground instead of eight thousand. I was here to learn how to fly, utilizing the wind tunnel as part of my learning process. The entire concept of iFly is designed around a wind tunnel blowing a 125 mile-per-hour hurricane of vertical wind providing the sensation of free-falling at terminal velocity.

For my first session at iFly, I paid for ten minutes of flying time in five two-minute blocks. My instructor for the day was great, teaching me body position and where my eyes need to be focused to fly well and stay in control. In the beginning, like breathing underwater while wearing scuba gear for the first time, trying to float on a blast of vertical air was a foreign experience.

If I followed my typical pattern—trying too hard, rigidly forcing everything with effort—I tired quickly, floundering around in the wind flow like a kite without a stabilizing tail. When I began to use patience and relaxation, letting the technique come to me, it began to make sense. I learned to use my body as an airplane wing. I learned that physics would surround me with enough high and low pressure to stabilize me in the air.

It was an interesting, enjoyable morning, learning a new skill, but I wasn't nervous. I'd already been in a skydiving wind tunnel. My previous experience had been in Las Vegas, but at the time it was simply an interesting novelty. In contrast, this activity was focused preparation, which is far more interesting. I've been consistently preparing for skydiving by doing my homework. I've developed a rudimentary skydiving vocabulary and understand what techniques to use while floating on a cushion of air. I've studied how a body will react at terminal velocity, after watching dozens if not hundreds of skydiving videos on YouTube. On recent business flights, I've tried to get a window seat so when the aircraft is ascending to about ten thousand feet, I can get a sense of what that relative height looks like in the open door of a skydiving plane.

The difference with today's preparation in the wind tunnel is I want to fail. A lot. I need to build repeatable fundamental skills under varying degrees of stress. This is Skydiving Freefall 101, helping me build my associative understanding but I'm not trying to be careless, making mistakes at random. I can accept the mistakes but only if I learn from what I did wrong. It's essential to make as many structured mistakes as possible, learning how to recover my position into a controlled flight. Instead of avoiding mistakes trying to protect my ego from embarrassment, I want to get into as many awkward, out-of-control body positions in the tunnel before recovering into a position of flying stability. This is exactly what I'll have to do when I jump out of a plane. In these early stages, it's important to remember I'm a novice, not worrying about embarrassing myself in front of complete strangers I'll never see again. The critical mistake I'm training to avoid is simply showing up at the jump site, overconfident but underprepared, winging it all on a hope and a prayer.

I like the phrase "accelerate the failure" in both my private and professional lives. I'm comfortable with the concept of making mistakes. In the professional environment, I've taught numerous large staffs and a few select peers the calculus of early failure. When "accelerate the failure" is first introduced people usually think I'm crazy, incompetent, or have an ulterior political motive. It's exactly the opposite. I'm removing their fear from the equation.

I want them to understand with a calm, sane clarity we're human and imperfect. We generally learn by making mistakes—teaching us what not to do. I've worked with far too many well-educated people hopelessly burdened with the expectation of instant perfection, myself included. Expecting perfection from themselves, they smother everyone around them with unrealistic, practically impossible expectations: a proven recipe for driving out the best and brightest staff members. My most successful staffs have learned how to accept early failure and move on, improving day by day.

The key with failure has always been *when* and *how.* Humans will fail, so the only question is when. Failing early, when the consequences are low giving time to regroup, is smart. Delaying failure to the eleventh hour, when consequences are catastrophic and expensive is just stupid. The '*how*' of failure is just as important. Failing within a planned structure provides a context for learning.

One of my most talented staff members reinforced my belief in making mistakes early when I asked him how an important development project was progressing. As the head of our software Quality Assurance group he astutely shared, "We should have more bugs in the software at this point in development. Something's very wrong."

My first day at iFly was great. I made dozens of mistakes on the "vertical bunny hill of wind". It was a successful, satisfying first step in my process. I learned a tremendous amount in only five two-minute flights in the wind tunnel. Of course the initial flights were awkward but I left feeling confident I was learning not only the techniques but also starting to visualize falling through the air fully in control.

The plan is to continue practicing in the wind tunnel each weekend from now until the end of January, which will give me at least an hour of free-fall flying time. Considering that the average freefall from a skydiving plane averages ninety seconds at best, in theory, I will have had forty-five jumps before setting foot in a plane. Forty-five jumps will provide the necessary repetitions and arm me with a fundamental understanding of how I'll perform at terminal velocity.

I've spent the last three months immersed in books and videos, studying the technical aspects of skydiving. I've skied this winter in more dangerous and precarious situations on the mountains. For the next three months, I'll continue escalating the intensity, pushing against fear in an environment I've been especially comfortable my entire life: water. I've scheduled a weekend excursion to the Farallon Islands, twenty-five miles west of San Francisco, to sit in an underwater cage waiting for great white sharks to swim by considering the day's possible appetizers and dinner menu. I've also planned a few weekends to water-ski and scuba dive, but the main water-based activity will be windsurfing.

CHAPTER FOURTEEN

My life's dream is over, at twenty-two

Do not let your fire go out, spark by irreplaceable spark, in the hopeless swamps of the approximate, the not quite, the not-yet, the not-at-all. Do not let the hero in your soul perish, in lonely frustration for the life you deserved, but have never been able to reach. Check your road and the nature of your battle. The world you desired can be won. It exists, it is real, it is possible, it is yours.

—Ayn Rand

After leaving the Nebraska team most rational people would have set football, and particularly the obsession to play in the NFL, aside. The odds against *anyone* signing an NFL contract are staggering; many bigger, faster, and stronger players who'd started at Nebraska for three years didn't make it. So what made me think I could? My reasons? A few NFL players were only ten pounds heavier and only two-tenths of a second faster in the forty-yard dash. Even Louie Giamonna, the nephew of the Philadelphia Eagles head coach Dick Vermeil, was playing at 5'9" and 180 pounds. My dream was possible.

More importantly, I'd never learned how to let go. I was Don Quixote on a quest, content to be alone in an imaginary world of wooden swords and imposing windmills. I'd been carefully protecting my dream since the sixth grade so I couldn't just give up, passively accepting the finality of defeat. To continue the journey, after researching smaller local schools with more opportunities to play, I transferred to Kearney State College, now called the University of Nebraska at Kearney.

When I joined the team, football became satisfying again. I was growing as a player, as a teammate, and most importantly, as a man. I still made mistakes on the field and got yelled at more at KSC than I had at Nebraska. Our fiery defensive coordinator, Coach Renner, was always engaged, using every fiber of his being, constantly driving each player to become better. He was disciplined and focused but always fair. The key difference accepting Coach Renner's constant, haranguing critiques was I was now being corrected by someone I respected as a man.

I spent three years searching for the magical combination of training, diet, and recovery to increase my weight and decrease my forty-yard-dash time. The problem I had, and still struggle with, was the concept of balance. I over-trained every day, performing thousands of full squats, deadlifts, and power cleans. When I should have been recuperating, trusting my body to repair itself before growing stronger, I ran stadium stairs until my thighs, pumped full of blood and oxygen, couldn't move another inch. I sprinted in the soft sand of a local lake, wearing a thirty-pound weight jacket until I almost passed out. If I had any excess energy on a scheduled rest day, I used it to train. In a perverse way, it was masochistic self-sabotage.

Other than football, my priorities were sleep, food, the weight room, schoolwork, and finally, women. Supremely confident, bordering on arrogance when competing on any athletic field, I was the polar opposite with women. Late in junior high, when I was being flooded with the powerful hormones of male adolescence, I promptly ignored my father when he delicately shared his thoughts about the difference between physical sex with a woman and intimacy with a woman while in love. I was too young to understand and far too stubborn to accept his wisdom. He might as well have tried to explain what an apple tastes like.

I wouldn't appreciate the subtle taste until college, where being a football player provided ample opportunities to invite curvy women back to my apartment. Searching for the emotional chemistry I had felt with my first girlfriend, a few nights per week I ended up in smoky college bars forcing the flirtatious small talk necessary to pick up a strange woman before sharing experimental evenings of physical lust.

Although the roar of the room gave me a convenient excuse to put my face next to freshly washed hair and perfume, my sophomoric attempts at flirting usually went unrewarded. More exhausting than spending two hours in the weight room, I always felt I was missing an important clue or was doing something wrong. If the women were showing any interest, I often missed every feminine signal, no matter how overt.

Night after night I'd watch teammates leave with an endless queue of women, but because I found most conversations tiresome and with little captivating content, I was usually indifferent. It felt like a lie chatting up a stranger with the only goal being an hour, or often less, of physical pleasure. Not only was I not in love with these women, I didn't know who they were—which made it difficult to even like them. I didn't know what or how they thought. I didn't even know what they wanted from their lives. Not only did I feel like I was on a different planet from most women, I wasn't even in the same galaxy.

My indifference to emotionless sex became crystal clear one evening after leaving a crowded bar with a woman. She had approached me and after a few too many drinks and awkward mutual flirting we ended up at my apartment. She was stunning, but as the bedroom door clicked shut, I could barely remember her name or anything she'd said at the bar. Instead of a passionate encounter, it was clumsy and empty, and when it was over, I wanted her out the door as quickly as possible. Fortunately, she felt the same.

Using alcohol to lubricate my indifference, I continued to force the genetically driven hunt for women until it became a burden and chore. Some women were beautiful. Others were intellectually interesting. Rarely did I meet a woman with the unusual combination of both. Except for the four or five seconds of *la petite mort*, "the little death," sex with a stranger was little more than physical small talk and just as unsatisfying. I certainly wasn't a pickup artist trying to validate myself as a man competing to conquer the most women. An acquaintance of mine would actually return to the bar the same night after a pickup with his trophy—her panties in his pocket—ready for his next conquest. I tried having two girlfriends at the same time and found the complications necessary to juggle schedules, expectations, and duplicitousness, overwhelming.

I wondered what the hell was wrong with me. Was I really that weird? Why couldn't I chase after every woman with a heartbeat like many of my teammates? One of the most notorious, tall, dark, and handsome, he was wildly successful with women. Add in the attributes of being a jock, outgoing, and funny, everything with women seemed incredibly easy for him. Although I wasn't envious as he walked out every night with a new woman on his arm, my curiosity had been piqued. How did he do it? What did he get out of it? The shocking answers were revealed at a weekend house party.

Hanging out alone in the kitchen to escape the frantic roar of the party, I was seriously contemplating another escape out the back door to the peace and quiet of my apartment. Before I could make another surreptitious, early exit into the night, he came into the room asking if there were any more beers. I'd known him for a couple of years but he was more of a daily acquaintance in the locker room than a close friend.

After clicking the sweaty necks of our beer bottles together and giving him a teammate's nod of friendship, I decided to uncover the secrets of his success with women. There were only two of us in the kitchen, which meant I didn't have to compete with interruptions, so I asked, "Can I ask you something?"

Taking a long, slow sip of his beer, he studied my face before cautiously replying, "Sure…"

"How do you do it?"

"How do I do what?"

"Pick up so many women?"

I didn't know if he'd had too much to drink or was exhausted from carrying a heavy load for so long, but after a long pause while he carefully looked around the room, he finally said, "Can I tell you something?" The tone of his voice implied he had a dark secret waiting to be shared.

"Of course."

"I don't know why I do it. When it's over, I hate myself and particularly every woman I've ever taken home. What's worse is I never speak to them again except in the cruelest of ways."

I was stunned. "Really?"

"Yeh, I'm dead serious."

"What are you going to do?"

"I don't know."

Amazed and shaken, it was the first time a man had removed his emotional armor in front of me. I didn't know what to say or why he had chosen to trust me with his admission. Maybe it was because I rarely spoke in the locker room, and if I did, I rarely spoke about other people. As we stood there, awkwardly letting the silence consume us, I could see he was lost in his problem, wondering what to do. Before that evening I'd never felt overt compassion for another man except for my father. He was a teammate, not even close to being a trusted friend, but my respect for him had changed.

Lubricated with alcohol or sober, it didn't matter. Like him, I'd slept with women I didn't know, but every encounter had ended the same way: an unfulfilling, dark cloud crushing me with deep feelings of emptiness. We'd both walked the same path, searching for something either in women or ourselves, but perhaps I had come to the painful realization sooner. The real difference between us was that I chose not to do it any longer. The emptiness wasn't worth it.

Although my external frame of reference had changed, I continued to struggle with women. When I shared with a disbelieving girlfriend that during the fall, I only spoke with my parents once per week—when they came for weekend football games—but during the spring semesters it was at most once every other month, she said, "You don't call them every day?"

"Of course not."

"Don't you want to know about their life?"

"I lived with them for eighteen years. I know their life. If something important happens they'll call me."

"Don't you feel guilty you don't want to talk to them every day?"

"No. I don't need a daily phone call to be part of their life." As she looked at me incredulously, calculating how quickly she could get away from the bizarre alien standing next to her, I bluntly asked her, "If you speak with your mother every day, what exactly do you talk about?"

Bewildered, frustrated, and probably frightened, she snapped, "I don't know. We just talk!" That exchange was the typical end of another short relationship.

Less than a week after another woman vowed never to speak to me again, I'd found a quiet nook in a popular bar where I could drink alone. While I was seriously contemplating the pros and cons of becoming an ascetic monk, a woman sat down next to me and began talking like she'd known me for years. In one moment I'd been wallowing in self-pity, debating whether to commit to a life of celibacy and in the next, I was looking into the eyes of a lovely woman.

Puzzled, trying to comprehend how my feelings could switch from one polar extreme to the other, I gave in, simply accepting it felt good being next to her. It was that simple. We began a relationship, and for whatever mysterious reasons, I liked our chemistry together—

enough that she would eventually become my first wife. She was a bubbly extrovert and in the beginning the relationship worked well, but maybe that was because she lived four hours away in Omaha. When she drove to Kearney every other weekend she had my full attention: romance, dinners, flowers, and long conversations late into the night.

I'd observed glimpses of the concept before, but was beginning to understand how easily I could compartmentalize my life. When she returned to Omaha, my priorities shifted. I could return to my isolated mental bubble, recharging alone. Although I'd fallen in love with her, I didn't think about her every second and certainly didn't call her every day until she returned. I'd just spent three days concentrating on every syllable, attentively watching for hidden meanings in each twitch of an eyebrow. The weekends were great and I always looked forward to the next one. My life was looking up. My numerous, awkward failures with women aside, I was in love again.

I graduated with a degree in business and for a normal person, it all should have been enough. But my NFL dream was still alive, as it had been since the sixth grade. I thought about it every day, every hour, for twelve years. I was never happier than during those years of absolute focus. Although idealistic and improbable, the best part of the journey was that everything in it was mine.

I'd just finished a college sports career, starting three years on teams that went to the national playoffs my sophomore and senior seasons, finishing 3rd in the national rankings. But instead of beginning the process of finding a job, over Coach Renner's objections, common sense, and reason, I pleaded, coerced, and begged him to send letters of introduction to all the Canadian Football League clubs so I could try out. I thought the CFL would be a path to the NFL. I wanted the opportunity to run a few 4.5-second forties before moving to hitting drills. I was depending on the coaches recognizing the intangibles of my passion and ability to hit while overlooking my size.

Of all the CFL teams Coach Renner contacted only the B.C. Lions extended an invitation letter but I wasn't mature enough to know what to do about it. Teams in high school and college had always pursued me, making arrangements for me to try out. I waited for them to call with reservations for plane tickets and a hotel room. I didn't realize it was my responsibility to get to Vancouver to take the one-in-a-hundred-thousand chance to get what I wanted. Of course the Lions never contacted me a second time. Heartbroken, forced to accept I'd never realize my goal, I joined the gigantic army of young men whose boyhood dreams of being professional athletes would never be fulfilled. I didn't achieve my goal, but every second of work had been worth it.

It was time to wake up from my beautiful NFL dream.

Forever.

CHAPTER FIFTEEN

Who's your Daddy?

Having a dream you don't pursue is like buying an ice-cream cone and watching it melt all over your hand.
—Frank Papasso

Comfortable in water since my parents signed me up for annual summer swimming lessons when I was five, my enthusiasm for windsurfing began twenty-two years later on the island of Maui. Like many tourists new to the island I'd planned to make the daylong drive on the curvy Road to Hana. While sightseeing trips around the island are a beautiful distraction, for an intensity-seeking athlete they're not particularly stimulating. Fortunately, on a random day on a tiny island halfway around the world from my home on the barren flatlands of Kansas, the universe grabbed a handful of synchronicity, mixed in a dose of fate, sprinkled in a smattering of opportunity, and served a new meal of adventure that has nourished me with pleasure ever since.

If my trip had happened a week earlier I would have missed it, but on that day the Road to Hana took me past Ho'okipa Beach Park where the O'Neill Windsurfing World Championships were being held. I pulled my convertible rental screaming "clueless mainlander" into the red dirt parking lot just long enough to realize a new door was opening. The electricity buzzing through the crowd of tanned, flip-flop-wearing locals was fantastic. Dazzling colors of windsurfing equipment strewn along the white-sand beach highlighted world-class athletes performing spectacular jumps and twisting upside down loops on bone-crushing waves. I typically loathe the passivity of being a tourist or spectator but within the span of four hours I was hooked, each cell of DNA screaming, "I need to learn this new sport!" Three days after returning home to Wichita, a new windsurfing board, boom, and mast sat in my garage.

Windsurfing seemed impossible, but unlike this year's well-planned skydiving progression, I attacked it with reckless abandon. Facing an incredibly steep learning curve, I took a few introductory lessons on Cheney Reservoir just outside of Wichita. I went through the usual beginner's misery. Balancing on a wobbly board pulling a heavy sail out of the water with sore hands and an aching back, every session was a marathon of frustration. Too stubborn and overly burdened by my gender, I fought the sport for weeks until a few glimmers of progress appeared. As a beginner, everything happens at slow speed, and while enjoyable, it's not addictive. Everything changed in a split second when a timely gust of wind sent the board, my sail and me chattering across the water. I only sailed for thirty or forty yards before crashing, but once my head broke the water's surface, my ear-to-ear grin signaled this was the beginning. Sailing at least forty days per year since that infamous day I'm now using windsurfing to help build on my new relationship with fear.

As soon as the snow-skiing season ended, I began ramping up the intensity of my project another notch preparing to return to Maui. Constantly checking my wind-forecast pager, I had many windsurfing locations to choose from in the Bay Area. If the wind was good, I was out of bed at 5:00 a.m., rushing to dawn-patrol sessions at the nearby Rio Vista Delta. If I didn't have important meetings, I'd leave the office for late-afternoon sessions sailing Crissy Field next to the Golden Gate Bridge. When I was desperate for wind I even sailed in the shark-infested waters of Waddell Creek or Tomales Bay. I even flew to Baja, Mexico, spending a week at the remote windsurfing spot Punta San Carlos.

I'd been traveling to Maui for almost twenty years and this trip would be no different. I wasn't going to relax on the beach, sipping on a drink with a pink umbrella. The sole purpose of every trip was to windsurf. Home to the world's best windsurfers, Maui is the Mecca of the windsurfing world because of the strong northeasterly trade winds and consistent waves. In the past I'd allowed the waves and huge ocean swells to randomly choose me, sailing tentatively trying not to get hurt or damage my equipment.

On this trip, with the explicit purpose to challenge fear, I did exactly the opposite. Using a more aggressive attitude I intentionally put myself in harm's way. With an increased sense of purpose, the ocean, and its dangers existed for me. I sailed my usual north-shore beach, Kanaha, aggressively choosing the outer-reef swell. Using these moving mountains of water as ramps, I forcefully launched myself into the air before using the aerodynamics of the sail to gently return to the water's surface.

When the waves weren't too large, I sailed at Ho'okipa beach park. With strong ocean currents, massive walls of water and razor-sharp coral, Ho'okipa is an expert-only sailing site. I've never worried while windsurfing, either from crashes, sharks or the water, but even with an aggressive attitude, in one of my most comfortable settings, my mind can quickly shift into overdrive. While rigging a sail my first day at Ho'okipa, my dark companion, whispered something bad might happen, shook his head *no, no, no*, trying to distract me with uncertainty and fear.

My mind is constantly working. It's on full alert on winding, mountain roads in the Sierras. It's calculating and evaluating, consuming patterns and data at the speed of light two hundred feet above the snow in a swaying chairlift. It wakes me up at 3:00 a.m. with ridiculous observations and dire warnings about things I can't control, influence, or prevent. Even when reading a skydiving book while savoring a sip of wine, my mind is in motion, relentlessly observing, categorizing, and labeling—everything. It's always talking. Not with me, but at me. It's a roaring voice, silently whispering, "be careful" or sometimes shouting, "You're wrong!" It even tries to confuse me with, "Maybe you're not doing it right." But whatever the intent, the voice is always there—a nameless, faceless apparition, haunting me from within.

In today's information-driven society, it's estimated the average person has around fifty thousand thoughts per day. I can accept an inner voice, my ego, trying to protect its existence, but if that voice was external I'd never stand for it. It's easy to imagine an invisible stranger tagging along behind me making relentless, inane comments. Always hiding just out of my peripheral vision, six, twelve, or eighteen inches away, he's shuffling behind me every second of the day. Never confronting me eye to eye, the voice incessantly categorizes things as good or bad, friend or foe, safe or unsafe.

This faceless person, pressed up against my back in line at the grocery store, assuredly repeats what I should eat because a celebrity doctor on a TV talk show host said so. Sometimes he's directly behind me in important business meetings. With an internal smirk, he whispers, "You know, other people around the table probably know more than you do, so it's safer to remain passively slumped down in your chair rather than ask clarifying questions." Constantly trying to keep me off balance, his well-honed tools of manipulation, uncertainty and doubt, silently feed my fear.

The problem is my unnamed fear isn't the hooded, horrific specter of death wielding a sharpened sickle ready to gruesomely slice my head off. This ephemeral ghost of emotion, my ego, isn't a terrible giant, unafraid of anything or anyone in the world. He's the opposite—a tiny being terrified of his own reflection. He survives not by sharing profound truths or eternal secrets hidden from the world but by telling me lies—little lies, big lies, and half-truths, all of them woven into the distorted fabric of my thinking. If this imaginary phantom, shadowing me at every moment, were real, a human of flesh and blood, I'd abruptly whirl around and aggressively confront him. "*Hey! Exactly what is it you want from me? All this whispering, these ridiculous, never-ending comments—what's in it for you? Why are you here? What purpose do you serve? What do you want?*"

It's always been a silent, informal relationship. I've never had a third party politely say, "Mr. Cass, I'd like to introduce you to an old friend called Fear. He's been with you every day since your birth. Furthermore, he'll continue as your constant, intimate companion. Your ego wants to survive, but your soul wants to live. Your ego uses fear as an implement of manipulation, very effectively preventing you from living your dreams. At rare times, he'll help you avoid real danger, but mostly, he'll do little more than distract you with random thoughts of fiction or fantasy. He'll be your personal ball and chain, moment by timeless moment, stealing your joy. I'm sure the two of you will get along famously."

I've rarely had a problem with motivation. I've always used any method or technique I could think of to increase the endogenous energy fueling my discipline. In junior-high, pictures of my favorite football players and teams plastered my bedroom walls. In high school, I read and reread motivational books on goal-setting, character, integrity, and work ethic. My most important motivational reminders were Scotch-taping newspaper articles of opposing high-school players on the back of my bedroom door. Every time I left my bedroom, I read sports commentary about my adversaries, creating the extra incentive necessary to squeeze out more reps in the gym.

Line Steals Thunder From Battle of Backs

By Randy York
Prep Sports Editor

Omaha — Nebraska's two best known prep backs were paired opposite each other here Friday night, but in the end, the battle was won in the trenches.

"Trenches" in football are the offensive and defensive lines. And Omaha Benson clearly had the best of both in blanking Omaha South, 28-0, before an overflow crowd of 5,840 at Bergquist Stadium.

Although Benson used what it calls a Bandit Defense to stifle South all-state back Mike Burton, veteran Bunnie coach Roger Sorensen stressed his line made the difference.

Bobby Bass
Line Gives Aid

"Our line just plain whipped their line all the way across," noted Sorensen. "Every kid carried out his assignment. I can't think of one breakdown."

Keying heavily on Burton, Benson's quick defense checked him to only 35 rushing yards on 14 carries. He carried the ball only twice in the second half as Benson dominated while building on its 14-0 halftime cushion.

Benson all-state back Bobby Bass, the other individual feature attraction, fared better than Burton, thanks to superior line play from his teammates.

Bass accumulated 85 yards rushing on 12 carries. One was a 19-yard touchdown scamper on a halfback delay two minutes into the second quarter. Bass broke three tackles on the effort.

His best run, however, may have been an 13-yard gallop on another delay in the third quarter, setting up Charles Greene's one-yard touchdown on the next play. Bass showed remarkable balance in scooting the distance when it looked like he might be stopped twice for short yardage.

Benson capitalized on a poor South punt to score its first touchdown with 3½ minutes left in the first quarter.

The punt went straight up in the air and landed on South's 21-yard line. Benson needed only three plays to cover the distance with hard-running fullback Robert Woodworth busting 12 yards up the middle for the TD.

Mike Burton
Stopped In Tracks

Although the offense was pleasing to Sorensen, he seemed more impressed with the defensive effort against the usually high-scoring Packers.

"Anytime you get a shutout, it's nice, but especially so when it comes against a team like South," acknowledged Sorensen.

Benson's Bandit Defense, Sorensen explained, calls for one of the Bunnie safeties "to go everywhere Burton goes about every third play.

"It's always been a regular part of our defensive repertoire," he adds, "but we thought this was a good time to emphasize it. We used about six different defenses. We mixed them up well. I'd call it a tremendous job."

My project has been progressing well, but after an unusually trying day at Ho'okipa, why not use the same technique, explicitly creating a name and face of my most difficult competitor? Why allow an unnamed, annoying stranger to whisper irrational, nebulous thoughts that become wasteful, exhausting emotions? I'd never say the same types of things to a person I loved, so why would I allow my mind to say them to me?

So instead of continuing to ignore my internal stranger, denying his existence, or worse, having well-meaning people around me state, "Well, that's life. You'll just have to accept fear is a big part of being human," I decided to name my fear creating a tangible competitor. I'll begin the new competition with a formal introduction to an old, if not ancient relationship. The real challenge was deciding what name to give my relentless background voice of fear?

I love animals and in particular dogs. In the next incarnation of life, it might be fun to be a dog—eat when I'm hungry, sleep when I'm tired, roll in the dirt, and wag my tail, barking at squirrels and birds invading my backyard kingdom. I'd ride in my owner's car, my ears blowing in the wind as the smell of the world got pushed into my wet nose like a turbocharger on a race car. The next day, rinse and repeat. After a week of contemplation, I was watching Cesar Milan's television show *The Dog Whisperer* and decided to name my voice of fear after Cesar's famous dog Daddy. Daddy, a powerfully muscled pit bull, was the perfect metaphor. Like the majority of pit bulls, Daddy is well trained and extremely gentle, but he's still a gladiator breed, able to kill or at least make life miserable. Instead of having my voice of fear off leash, able to come and go as it pleases, free to roam the hidden recesses of my mind, I want him under control. I'll be the alpha dog in my mind's pack.

Cesar suggests a daily, hour-long walk is one of the fundamentals of having a happy dog who knows who is in charge. There are constant opportunities to walk my fear. Doing something every day that either frightens me or is at least uncomfortable is the same as walking a dog. I need constant awareness of my thoughts and feelings that turn to fear. The bottom line: a dog, and my fear, needs structure. Daddy needs to know who's in charge and if he doesn't see me actively taking that role, he'll fill the gap, even if reluctantly. It's the way of nature. An egalitarian approach, while nice in the theoretical make-believe world of ivory towers or politics, isn't going to work. Dealing with my fear isn't a watered-down win-win situation where no one ends up happy or learns from failure. My fear, a screaming two-year-old, doesn't respond well to a time-out, a polite adult-to-child discussion, or rationalization. When Daddy knows I'm in charge, he can relax, become my partner and actually warn me of real, not imaginary, danger.

I've created a yearlong, personal game with fear. Fear has been an unwelcome parasite feasting on my mental and physical energy for years: an eternity of fear and doubt. To fuel my daily motivation, I've given the slippery, whispering voice in the back of my head a name. I now have a new, explicit opponent to Scotch-tape to my bathroom mirror. It's a refined viewpoint and perspective to add to my personal toolbox of growing skills. The first challenging walk for Daddy will be soaring thousands of feet above Lake Tahoe's blue water—in a glider.

CHAPTER SIXTEEN

Being laid off was a blessing in disguise

It was like coming this close to your dreams. And then watch them brush past you like a stranger in the crowd. At the time you don't think that much of it. You know we don't recognize the most significant moments of our lives while they're happening. Back then I thought, there would be other days. I didn't realize that was the only day.

—Burt Lancaster
Field of Dreams

Dejected, lost, and defeated with no idea what to do with the rest of my life, I had moved from Kearney to Omaha, married my college girlfriend and began the process of starting a new project: the rest of my life. I looked for a job but without a long-range goal or even a general direction to go towards, I was unprepared to succeed. Football had been my lover for twelve years and our intimate relationship was over. I'd never considered failure a possibility so it hadn't seemed necessary to develop a set of tools to soften life's crushing blows. The only thing I could say was that although I had failed at reaching the NFL, at least I'd spent the years doing something I loved. Unfortunately, I was soon to find out that I was only at the beginning of a long string of disappointments.

I had an opportunity to divert my attention away from the low trajectory of my passionless life when a group of former Nebraska players asked me to join their city league flag-football team. It might have been fun for a while, and although I'd miss the after-game beer and camaraderie, I had to say no. Flag football wasn't real enough. I could sprint toward an opposing player catching a pass but I couldn't tackle him, my hips exploding through him in a perfectly timed release of kinetic force. All I could do is grab his plastic flag, politely signaling the proxy tackle. Pulling flags would be a constant tease, little different than a platonic dinner with a stunning woman destined to end with a chaste kiss on the cheek. When I realized pulling a piece of plastic would be more frustrating than fun, my football career officially ended with a soundless whimper.

Desperately trying to figure out how to apply the focus from years of sports discipline, I was bluntly reminded of my passionless life at a party with one of my former teammates, a linebacker named John. After graduating with a dual major in political science and criminal justice, he had worked as a police officer for a few years before joining the Secret Service. He'd invited me to join his fellow officers and agents for a few beers and I was looking forward to reminiscing about football, college girlfriends, and too many late-night adventures far past curfew. I'd never been envious of other men, before that moment or since, but my reaction when I saw him talking with his fellow officers at the party was visceral. I immediately understood that football, school, and my soon-to-start white-collar career were poor substitutes for bonding, particularly with men. I was a gaijin, an 'outsider' in Japanese, and no matter how fluent I became in their language, no matter how many stories they shared with me, I'd never be part of John's tribe. I'd never have a partner who depended on me to save his life.

I'd read extensively about men in combat whose bond with each other was closer than those they had with their wives or children. They'd protected one another in the most extreme human experience: war. Although I wouldn't want to endure the horror of battle, I envied the bond and intensity those men shared. I was seeing that bond right before me. I'd always been a civilian, where adrenaline-pumping sports was as close as I could get, but no one was trying to kill me.

Windsurfing on an ocean wave, racing a motorcycle, or jumping into the tight entry of a double-black-diamond ski run are dangerous, but they're artificial. Like my decision to skydive, I'd chosen to engage the superficial, semi-controllable dangers, not the other way around, where danger or death chooses me.

Unprepared and naïve, without the protective structure of goals, I was floundering. Other than the mind-numbing process of preparing resumes, cover letters and practicing interview techniques in the mirror, I didn't have anything to apply my energy to except training at the gym. The gym used to be an environment where I could develop physically to achieve a long-term goal. When I realized that it had become little more than a place to work off tension, I joined a local Tae Kwon Do school. Combining the mental focus of disciplined drills, one-on-one combat with physical consequences and led by patient, but demanding instructors, the martial arts were the closest I could get to the intensity of football. I enjoyed it immensely. It also provided a difficult long-term goal: a black belt.

I eventually found a job in the computer section of a large corporation and was grudgingly adapting to an uninspired life. It was a job that paid my bills and gave me something to do with my time, but I had no idea if it was the first or last building block of a career. I bought a new TV to replace the one that worked perfectly fine. I purchased my first new car, the excitement wearing off as quickly as the smell of the fresh interior. I was doing all the "right" things, but was falling into a dull, predictable routine: Go to work. Go to church. Mindlessly watching IQ-reducing TV at night drinking one too many glasses of wine, hoping to make it all go away, I was becoming a clone for society's assembly line of conformity.

On Sundays after church, I'd go to my in-laws' house for polite but uninteresting dinners. They were a nice couple, and I liked them, but I went purely out of social obligation. I could hide it for a while, an actor struggling with a poorly worded script, but small talk was a foreign language I'd never mastered. After the weather, the banality of a weekly TV sitcom, or a new way to cook a tuna casserole had been thoroughly examined, I learned that introducing any of the million thoughts constantly rambling through my mind was considered inappropriate dinner conversation. My fork dangling over an empty plate, "What do you think about?", "How do you think an economy would function if everyone was rich?" or "What did you think about this morning's sermon?", were questions answered either with exasperated sighs or complete silence. I didn't want to talk about people or things. I wanted to talk about invisible things: ideas. I wanted to hear a question so compelling that I'd be thinking about it at 3:00 a.m. that morning. My awkward failures at polite dinner-table socializing a precursor to my relationship struggles, I learned to restrain myself to conversations matching the monotony of overcooked meatloaf and cold apple pie.

After failing at small talk, too young to understand what it meant, I also failed at my marriage. I certainly wasn't prepared to be in a relationship. Completely unfair to my new bride I was unconsciously asking her to provide the same motivation, intensity, and passion of my football mistress. The tension was further exacerbated because I had little if any, time alone. I was either working with dozens of people in the office or was with my new wife at home. I loved my wife but didn't know how to be with her every day. I'd gone from having days of private downtime at college to none. Other than the time spent fighting human stupidity during commutes to work I had no time alone to recharge. I was suffocating under a heavy blanket of social expectations, a massive problem destined to haunt me in every intimate relationship.

It took me over a year to recover emotionally from my divorce, but at my ten-year high-school reunion, I reunited with a woman whom I'd always felt was completely out of my league. She still lived in a Lincoln, which gave me time alone. While juggling a new girlfriend, going to the gym, and quickly moving up the ranks in Tae Kwon Do, I moved into a new job with another major US corporation. It was an enjoyable time early in my career that challenged me with stimulating, extremely difficult work. My life seemed to be turning around until a surprise announcement: out of 302 people working in the Omaha division, 300 were to be laid off, including me. Life was providing another jarring, early morning wake-up call. I had failed at the NFL. I had failed at marriage. Now I had been laid off.

The only positive aspect was my surprise when I noticed I was enjoying the uncertainty of what lay ahead. The feelings were similar to the tension-filled hours leading up to a sports competition not knowing if my team would win or lose. Circumstances had forced me out of my comfort zone, the familiar, the safe, and the known. I sent my resume to a few companies and worked with a few recruiters, and a few weeks later, a small software start-up in Wichita, Kansas, hired me as a software support engineer. It was a fresh start and was my first move out of my home state of Nebraska.

CHAPTER SEVENTEEN

Glider flight over rolling, green hills

There are thousands and thousands of people out there living lives of quiet, screaming desperation who work long, hard hours, at jobs they hate, to enable them to buy things they don't need, to impress people they don't like.
—Nigel Marsh

I was sitting on the runway strapped tightly into a five-buckle harness designed to keep me secure while performing upside-down loops when I noticed the tiny rope attached to the tow-plane pull tight. I've been in situations like this before. Trying to challenge my fear, I'd sometimes found myself anxiously sitting in a massive amusement-park roller coaster. As the padded safety bar tightly pressed into my thighs, link by greasy link, I could always feel the clanking, clinking sprocket inching the train of cars closer to the summit. Moments before we reached the crest of the steepest section of track, where the last link of chain disengaged, my thoughts then, and now in a cockpit, were the same: *There's no safe way out of this now, Dan. Just relax and try to enjoy the ride.*

Just east of South Lake Tahoe and only an hour from the Kirkwood ski resort, today's challenge in the tiny town of Minden, Nevada, was a huge ramp-up in intensity and fear, the first significant push of my project. I've consistently challenged my mind reading about the techniques of skydiving. I've watched hundreds of skydiving YouTube videos. I've been flying in wind tunnels learning the aerodynamics of lift. Although I'm becoming increasingly comfortable with the idea of jumping out of an airplane, today is a checkpoint designed to evaluate if my aggressive plan is on track or whether I should scale back a little.

Sitting in the tiny cockpit trying to stay calm, each deep breath into my diaphragm expanded into the thick nylon webbing securing me to the plane. While I carefully studied the single-engine aircraft at the other end of the towrope, little more than a crop duster on steroids, Daddy's butterfly of fear returned. Floating on invisible mental updrafts trying to distract me with vague mathematical probabilities of success, I wondered whether the crop duster really had enough power to tow us above Lake Tahoe. Although the most real danger I'd been in all day had been on the drive from the hotel, my fear began introducing thoughts of low-maintenance, shoestring budgets and duct-tape solutions to every mechanical problem.

Thankfully snapping me out of a dangerous imaginary cycle of mental anguish, the glider lurched forward with a jolt. The towrope had stretched tight and we began moving forward, soon to leave the safety of the ground. As the two planes slowly built momentum down the runway, choreographed dance partners for the next fifteen minutes, Jon, my pilot for the day, casually asked over the scratchy intercom radio,

"Do you like huge theme-park roller coasters, Dan?", implying, do I want him to perform upside down rolls and spins.

"Not particularly, Jon," was my immediate, instinctual response. "I just want to be in a plane without an engine and make an easy introductory flight."

Jon spent his career as a military test pilot and helicopter rescue pilot in Vietnam, flying numerous aircraft for over fifty years. Earlier that morning when he approached me in the hangar, I instantly liked him. My intuition rarely fails me when I meet new people. Wearing an oil-stained baseball cap above his weathered, sun-tanned face, Jon had the same calm approach to teaching as Lorne, my ski instructor at Blackcomb.

It was the exact same early-morning energy of farmers and ranchers I'd met in Nebraska's small-town cafés. As a young man, my father and I would share a table eating breakfast with them before hunting ducks or pheasants on their land. Their quiet poise came from experience—not only did they know what to do but also when, why, and how. As Jon watched me sign the first of my many release-of-liability waivers for the year, it was comforting knowing I was putting my life in the hands of an expert with years of experience. What I didn't want to see was a pilot in his twenties who had only been flying for a few years and needed the job just to get more hours in the cockpit.

I had the front seat of the glider which gave unbelievable visibility. Jon had the pilot's seat directly behind me. After averaging seventy-five thousand miles per year over the last ten years, I'm used to bumpy flights, but the lift-off was unlike anything I'd experienced in a commercial jet aircraft. A long, slow pull with both planes straining against gravity didn't create the comfort of being pushed back in your seat by a powerful jet engine on takeoff.

I had prepared for this moment and as we left the ground beginning the slow climb to our release altitude, I fell back on slow, rhythmic breathing, trying to stay in the moment. As the tow-plane gained altitude, slowly pulling us upward in a gentle circle, the plexiglas cockpit provided a perfect view of the airport runways shrinking away.

Although I had tried to imagine what flying in a glider would feel like, I couldn't practice this activity. All I could do was accept what was happening at this unique moment in time. It's in these moments of intensity, either physical or mental, that the past and the future seem to fall away.

After a fifteen-minute contest with gravity, we leveled off, heading west, toward the ridges of Lake Tahoe's eastern shore. This is where Jon had cautioned me that serious turbulence would most likely begin. As we edged closer to the lake, my breathing increased, matching my trepidation, but when the first jolt of turbulence battered our aircraft, an invisible hand sending us off course, I thought, *That's it? This is the out-of-control situation I've been afraid of*?" I've been in far worse storms flying across the Pacific.

After ten minutes fighting the updraft-filled ridge, we escaped into cleaner air, arriving at our release altitude. With the radios crackling, coordinating the release of our tiny umbilical cord, Jon gave the final command, and the tow-plane began falling away from the rope now dangling in the wind. Freed from the constraint of being towed, the aerodynamics of the glider took over, calming me with its agility and control.

The flight was great, and while there was the expected bouncing turbulence, Jon made me feel extremely comfortable. Even when my stomach tried to escape out of my throat as we climbed unseen updrafts or fell through empty pockets of air, I was fine, mostly because Jon seemed completely unperturbed by anything, his composure filling the cockpit. We spent almost an hour flying over the lake, using invisible updrafts to keep us aloft. I even shared with Jon my skydiving goal, and he had some simple words of comfort, stating, "It's really no big deal." Although we didn't do any loops or anything approaching the performance ceiling of the glider—just another basic flight for Jon—I was filled with excitement and wonder.

When it was time to return to the airport, Jon gave me the first and only "Hold on" warning of the day before putting the glider into a steep dive down into the eastern Nevada valley. As we skimmed less than a hundred feet above the side of the mountain, two things surprised me. The first was how loud the cockpit became at this increased airspeed. It was almost a roar. For most of the flight, I had easily been able to chat with Jon in the cockpit without much effort. The second surprise was how much I enjoyed the heavy weight of gravity as we fell through the sky. Signaling an end to the day, our exhilarating high-speed drop in altitude eventually leveled off into a soft, circular glide back toward the airport.

After opening the cockpit and stepping onto the runway unusual feelings flowed through me. Leading up to today's project checkpoint, I hadn't been sure how I'd react to my first serious "push" of the year. As my legs readjusted to walking on the ground, I was relieved and disappointed at the same time. I was physically relieved of today's uncertainty and tension—I'd survived. I hadn't gotten sick or suffered any type of anxiety attack—certainly none that turned into terror. But I was also disappointed because the flying hadn't felt that difficult. Trying to digest my conflicting emotions, I was soon back in my head, scheming and planning to return for another session. I'd fly with Jon again, but ask him to perform loops, spins, and rolls, pushing both the aircraft and my personal limits.

Slowly strolling back to my truck ending the day, I could put a "completed" checkmark next to the green ski-hill milestone. More important than a checkmark, a serene bubble of satisfaction enveloped me. My step-by-step plan is working. Before today, I'd never had an interest in loops, spins, or high-G, end-over-end rolls, but the new thoughts felt familiar, almost normal. I've been on this road many times and know the territory well. The sequence has always been overwhelmingly simple, starting with intense feelings turning into motivation. My motivation then transforms into concrete decisions before becoming detailed action plans. Then my daily actions developed into ingrained habits as automatic as shaving, brushing my teeth, and taking my morning shower. Finally, my habits become rituals, unconsciously fueling my life and lifestyle.

Slowly absorbing the odd mixture of relief, disappointment and satisfaction, I know other emotions, thoughts and experiences are just around the corner. The next challenge of my plan? Climbing.

CHAPTER EIGHTEEN

When is the protective bubble of safety a trap?

If you don't design your own life plan,
chances are you'll fall into someone else's plan.
And guess what they may have planned for you?
Not much.
—Jim Rohn

I moved to Wichita alone knowing only the three men who interviewed me. Although it was painful leaving a lovely girlfriend in Nebraska, moving to Wichita eventually turned out to be a good move. My new job provided the foundation for learning new software and business skills. Outside of work, I spent much of my free time in a popular local health club where I met a fellow Nebraskan. I'd seen him walk in wearing a red Nebraska T-shirt so I struck up a casual conversation about football. He was the most social guy I'd ever met. While hanging around him I wasn't forced to overcome my awkwardness meeting new friends. He did it all for me, introducing me to dozens of other active people and, eventually my second wife.

I had moved to a new city, was meeting a small circle of friends, and my job provided the financial resources to buy all the toys a young professional man could want. Externally, I was living a comfortable life, but internally, everything was exactly the same. Accumulating one winter after another, I was reliving the same day-to-day life I had in Omaha. I wasn't growing as a man. As the days and weeks slipped from the calendar, the trajectory of my personal universe began veering out of control, methodically building to a crisis. It began when a stranger's empty eyes met mine in the bathroom mirror a few mornings each week. When it began to happen more often, I turned to a futile strategy of avoidance, using alcohol to mask my numbness. Eventually, when the stranger's uninspired face indifferently greeted me every morning, I knew I was in real danger. I wasn't living life on the edge. I was existing. Conforming to the well-worn path of a 401(k), two weeks of annual vacation, and a gold watch at retirement, I'd completely forgotten who I was, ignoring every important life lesson I'd learned.

Discounting my father's early advice and my experiences of soulless sex with women in college, I was repeating the masochistic self-torture in Wichita. I'd meet women in neighborhood bars, at the gym, or even in the grocery store. I knew I was looking for something more than a notch on my bedpost, but after a date or two at the most, I'd find some way to get them into bed. It was too easy. I'd often felt isolated and alone in crowded bars, at parties, and at family dinners, but when the door clicked shut ending an evening of awkward, physical lust, the emptiness and loneliness far surpassed any encounters in college. My physical desires had become a trap.

Although I suffered the emotional consequences, I was lucky. There were no unwanted pregnancies; there would be no divorce followed by a twenty-year nightmare of attorneys, alimony, and child support. There were no painful STDs and no false rape accusations to destroy my reputation or worse, send me to prison. I never had to face an insanely jealous ex-boyfriend or husband toting a gun. Thinking it would fill the emptiness in the bedroom, when women offered drugs, I tried them all: pot, cocaine, speed, and hallucinogens. When I noticed that drugs couldn't match the chemical rush of falling in love or the intensity of the adrenaline from competing in sports, I soon quit experimenting with drugs—but not with women.

Using every opportunity to attract their attention, I tried various costumes at Halloween parties. One year, I went as a martial artist, wearing my gi and sparring gear trying to impress them with my ruggedness. The next year I wore a different mask of hyper-masculinity: my football uniform from Nebraska. The following October, I tried cuteness mixed with intellectual humor. After purchasing a dozen stuffed cats, including a large orange Garfield, I arrived at a party in black combat boots, stocking cap, and fatigues, every pocket overflowing with soft, furry felines. The subtlety of my costume didn't work. After too many frustrating attempts to explain my costume was a grammatical pun, 'a cat burglar', I stood at the bar alone for the rest of the evening sharing dark humor and inside jokes with a quiet but sympathetic beer bottle.

One year I went as the exact opposite of a male stereotype. Instead of trying to get clothes off a woman's body, I was putting them on. I could have bought a cheap cotton dress from Goodwill, creating an ugly parody of a woman, but like everything else I've ever done I went all the way, trying to look as feminine as possible. Trying to hide the V-shape of athletic shoulders and a tiny waist under layers of silk and chiffon I was entering a new world completely unprepared. When I can wake up, shave, shower, and be out the door in a suit and tie in under twenty minutes, the time and effort women take to look attractive were shocking. Every step an eye-opening learning experience, especially through eyeliner and mascara, I was surprised by how relaxed I was and how much I enjoyed the process.

I was nervous driving to the party, worried I'd be shamed and ridiculed, especially in socially conservative Wichita. When I arrived, I expected—and received—good-natured joking from my male friends, but the reactions from women were shocking. There was no gray area. A few disgusted looks screamed I wasn't adhering to the expected role of protector and provider, the masculine alpha male. Regardless of the testosterone flowing through me, powdered and perfumed, my presence was perceived as a threat. It was either that, or jealousy, the athletic curve of my nylon-covered legs perched in heels looked much better than theirs.

Most surprisingly I received more attention from women in one night than in the last ten years of Halloween parties combined. They approached me within the safety of a group, usually two or three at a time. Others were bold or intrigued enough to approach me alone. All of them were curious—about everything. As they examined every detail of my outfit, they asked where I bought it and how much it cost. For the first time in my life, socializing at a party was easy.

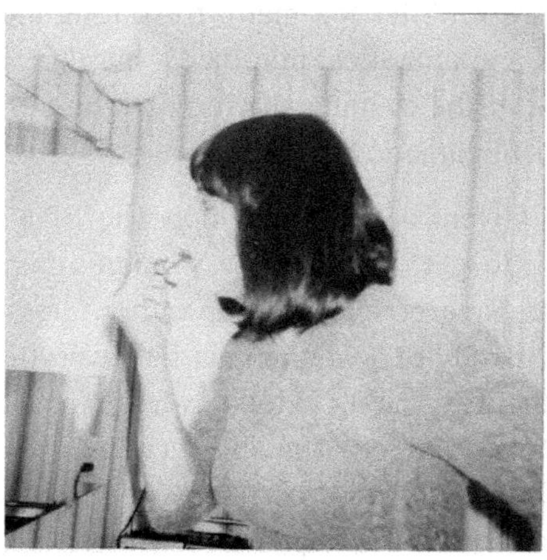

It helped that an unusual lipstick stain was building on my wine glass, but a huge weight had been lifted. I was the center of attention, without effort or tension. Not only was I talking with ease, I was funny, getting the women to laugh when I asked how they could simultaneously drive and gracefully apply mascara in the rearview mirror without poking their eyes out or causing an accident. When I shared the circus of problems I'd had getting ready, they nodded together in shared understanding. I was being accepted into their group.

Everything changed when I told them the effort to stay poised on heels was killing my feet. For a moment, they all laughed, but I'd entered their secret world of feminine discomfort. When the laughter died down, one of them moved closer. Stepping far past the comfortable boundary of personal space, her eyes never leaving mine, she reached out gently touching my arm.

When I'm interested, I recognize the energy of flirting and the signals women use to show interest. Leaning in, fingers twirling a lock of hair, absentmindedly playing with an earring or a nervous bite of their lips. Even the warm blush from inadvertent physical contact. This was different. Fifteen seconds later her hand was still on my arm, gently supporting me in an act of compassion and acceptance I'd never received from a woman. Ever. Often told I'm too intimidating to approach, the gentle power of her kindness was more painful than being punched in the face. It broke my heart. For a gender supposedly more compassionate, empathetic and intuitive, it took mascaraed lashes and sharing a feminine rite of passage—enduring the pain of pumps—for her to see that hidden beneath a protective masculine shield, my heart was as soft and vulnerable as hers.

Two days later I switched from silk and lace to scratchy cotton slacks and back to the monumental effort of trying to fit in. With no impossible goals and fewer personal boundaries, outside of the office, I was becoming what I detested most—the bland nice guy trying to be everyone's friend, passive acquiesce my guiding principle. Inside the office, it was worse. Bouncing from one distraction to the next, a kaleidoscope of cognitive dissonance, I'd become a chameleon trying to wear the dangerous mask of perfection. Every problem of the moment became gigantic. I couldn't put anything into perspective, especially at my new job.

Working for a mathematics Ph.D. and his top two engineering students, I watched them methodically build their start-up. In the beginning my responsibilities were manageable and felt I was contributing to the company. My problems began and ended with competition. If I wrote software with too many bugs, I'd lose sleep. The more I obsessed, the worse it got, especially when I compared my performance to theirs. The problem was I didn't have the experience or maturity to know what I didn't know. Not involved in their code and design reviews, business meetings, or any strategic planning, I rarely saw their inevitable missteps and mistakes. I didn't give them the benefit of the doubt or realize what a gigantic struggle it was to start a company. I thought they were perfect and wanted to mirror them. Now. My insistence on perfection in the office was like shooting a last-second free throw to win a basketball game in front of thousands of screaming fans. Instead of relaxing, my hand and wrist gracefully sending the ball toward the net, my only thought was, *Don't miss!* This created tension.

I'd made the same fundamental mistake in football. After-practice weight-room sessions wouldn't end until I was exhausted, unable to move the heavily loaded bar one more rep. I had a mental picture of a beautiful garden but was too impatient to create a nurturing environment for its growth. Unconvinced that less was usually more, I watered and fertilized every day, my stubbornness killing any possibility that my garden would grow bigger, faster, and stronger. On most evenings when I should have been studying with a fresh mind, I was too tired to do anything but lay in bed trying to recover. My greatest strengths, discipline and passion, were also my greatest weaknesses, and they eventually became a trap.

I was repeating my obsessive habits at work. Instead of focusing on improvement, getting a little better day by day, when the inevitable mistakes happened, I worked harder, trying to force perfection. I didn't know how to step back and regroup, setting the stage for peak performance. Out of misguided pride, I also made a unilateral decision: without my boss's input, I concluded they didn't have enough time for mentoring because they were building a company from scratch. So instead of asking for help, I kept pushing the envelope, working incredibly long hours, further compounding my mental stress with physical exhaustion.

I had been hired to solve a problem: they needed to deliver more software. Patient, generous, and gracious, they welcomed me into the company and their families. I'd spent three years in dawn water-skiing sessions before work with one of the partners. I'd go to their houses for dinners after work. I'd become their friend. In the end, I burdened them: they had to fire a friend, and I could see the remorse on their faces. I would have fired me as well. I had tried too hard. More embarrassed than angry when they relieved me of my position, I felt I'd let them down.

I had barely reached the age of thirty but my life had become an exhausting, daytime nightmare. I'd failed at my NFL dream. Then I suffered through the devastation and uncertainty of a divorce. Soon after that I was unceremoniously laid off. Now I'd been fired. I was living as fast as possible, speeding through the expected motions at 150 miles per hour, not enjoying a single moment. With no internal fire fueled by an impossible goal, I was imploding—dancing to songs whose words I didn't understand and the beats I couldn't feel. Each time a song ended, the words and rhythm a meaningless blur, I was in a hurry to start the next.

The consistent thread permeating all my failures was "nothing had happened *to* me". I wasn't a victim of random circumstance. A deterministic universe wasn't conspiring to keep me down. No one had forced me to do anything, an emotional gun at my head, threatening me with hot bullets of guilt or ridicule. There wasn't one gigantic mistake I could point to but rather thousands of tiny, unseen thoughts, ingrained habits, and decisions, one-by-one compounding over time. I was responsible for every decision, significant or not, leading to my present situation. I owned them all. There was no one to blame but the confused stranger reflected in my bathroom mirror.

At weekend dinner parties a common conversation starter when meeting a stranger is, "What do you do?", implying "What is your job?", "Where do you work?", "What easily understood label can I judge you by?" I had many labels to answer the "*What are you?*" question, the easiest was simply to answer Software Programmer which most people interpreted as antisocial techno-geek. If someone had asked, "*Who* are you?", I might have answered with my name.

In the unlikely event I was speaking with someone insightful enough to get past the predictability of superficial chitchat he might have responded, "No, Dan, I wasn't asking what your parents named you at birth. I don't care about your vocation. Tell me what defines you. I loathe the predictability of parties like this. Surprise me. Share an interesting idea or anecdote. What are your dreams? What were the best sixty seconds of your life, your greatest, most passion-filled moment? What mistakes have taught you the most? What do you want from your life? How do you express who you're becoming as a man?"

If I'd stumbled upon someone bold enough to ask such thought-provoking questions I couldn't have answered. I might have unconsciously regurgitated society's default placebo, "I just want to be happy." Maybe I'd have blandly answered, "I just want a simple, easy life with no stress, like I had as a child." I might have shared what I did for fun. For most of my life, driven by outrageous goals, I'd been defined by what I could do on a field of competition.

Since graduating from college I'd been defined by my job, my relationships, my possessions, where I went to school and what I had studied. I had a great apartment, a shiny new Porsche, a ski boat and a truck to pull it. Excess savings I called my bag of "fuck-you" money—enough to live on for two years without working—sat unused in my bank account, patiently waiting to be spent. I'd arrived at a zip code of material success, but without a set of explicit goals, I'd never been more miserable. At best, one shallow breath at a time, I was merely existing. If my life was a piece of art, I certainly wasn't creating a masterpiece I could be proud of.

How did I get to a point where the addictive feelings of purpose and motivation had slipped through my fingers like a dream upon awakening? When had my discipline and decisiveness, once an unstoppable flow of energy, evaporated like raindrops in the sun?

I'd become entangled in the world, allowing irrelevant outside distractions and poorly chosen responsibilities to slowly chip away until I couldn't remember *who* I was. I'd been indoctrinated, but not because I'd been arrested and sent to a 're-education camp'. It wasn't necessary. I went to the mental gulag voluntarily. Every morning I addictively consumed two or three newspapers trying to keep up with world events. I read every syllable from the shouting headlines of doom to the anguished cries of the angry, but impotent mob of self-proclaimed experts in the letters to the editor.

After work, I ingested TV propaganda from sociopaths posing as politicians and puppets masquerading as journalists. Each time I pushed the remote's power button the daily specials on the menu were the same. "Hello again, Dan. Welcome back! Here's a hot mug of frustration. Enjoy a bittersweet bowl of disinformation. Please help yourself to a smorgasbord of victimhood." Trapped in the allegorical cave of social engineering, I didn't understand the flickering shadows on the wall were lies and illusions. If I'd been paying attention, I'd have noticed that every time I put down the paper or clicked off the remote I didn't feel any more knowledgeable or empowered. It was exactly the opposite. I felt hopeless, frustrated, and angry. Submissively allowing the stifling veil of fear to be pulled over my eyes, I was being controlled as effectively as a ventriloquist's dummy.

It was tempting though. If I accepted the subtle but persistent conditioning, doing what the outside world thought was best, I wouldn't have to think for myself. If I didn't have to think, I wouldn't be forced to make my own decisions—which meant I couldn't be held accountable: my happiness, safety, and life were in their hands. "Dan, just be a good boy. Realistic, safe, and practical are best. If you surrender a tiny bit at a time, it won't hurt as much. Unconsciously conform to the relentless messages of our planned world. Submit to the faceless crowd. Most people do. You won't really be happy, but you won't be sad either. Don't pay attention to the hollow feelings gnawing at you from the inside out. It's only your soul whispering you're not living on the edge of your passion. Better yet, deny the emptiness, pretending it doesn't exist. Anesthetize your existence with alcohol, drugs, strange women, and mindless entertainment. Pull out our well-designed script, repeat the insignificant lines we've given you, and get on with it."

Lost and floundering, trying to grasp the hollow shell of who I'd become, an hour after the trauma of being fired I was on a treadmill running until my lungs burned and my legs screamed in pain. As an introvert, most of the time I live in my head, the three-pound organ between my ears relentlessly observing and categorizing everything around me in minute detail. Often the only respite is intense physical activity; the feelings permeating my body dominate my mind, forcing it to submit. The gym, dojo, or even a steep mountainside are my sanctuary, church, and refuge—places of mental peace and quiet.

Not that day.

As the lactic acid burned my legs, despair and disbelief floated on raging mental waves. *What had happened? What was the quality of decisions I'd made that had led to getting fired? What poor habits had I unconsciously built up over time? What could I do to turn it all around?* My cup has always been full. Before graduating from college I was focused and driven but at ease, the top half of my cup filled to the brim with impossible goals and dreams resting on a half cup of optimism. The clarity of my goals, my inner compass, had always been my power and protection. After graduation I tried to be normal, but I had no idea how to do it. I didn't know who I was becoming, where I was going or even what direction I was headed. My goals at the top of my cup had been replaced with society's lies, dirtying the water, making everything seem complex and hopeless. Naked, lost, and vulnerable, I was in terrible danger. I was a tourist, little more than a spectator watching men of action in life's arena. For the first time in my life I didn't like who I was. I'd reached the bottom with nowhere to go, but as painful feelings of defeat were released in each drop of sweat, I remembered.

The best decisions I've made in life have typically come from competition, sometimes with others, but mostly with myself. Sometimes the reason for taking massive action was either from disappointment, an overwhelming level of frustration or someone telling me I didn't have the ability to do something. Most often, I was inspired by Sunday-afternoon heroes or charismatic characters in movies or books. It was during these bursts of goal setting, motivation, and visualization that I felt I could change the world—and if I couldn't do that, at least I could change myself.

When I previewed the painful images living the next ten years on the treadmill of an average, normal life, I knew exactly what to do. I made the decision to reclaim everything, becoming the screenwriter of my life again. The first thing to do was write an opening scene of deliberate, ice-cold murder. The pathetic role I'd been playing since college had to die. If I didn't do it symbolically now, in ten years I'd do it for real. The pertinent question of the moment was, how?

I thought about a ritualistic Japanese death using the world's greatest sword, the Katana. I considered the efficiency of a gunshot to the head or my body's frantic struggle for survival if I hung myself. I entertained the uncertainty of a drug overdose. I even considered leaping from a building, giving my fear of heights a half-the-peace-sign final salute as I fell through the air. After careful deliberation I knew the best way to kill the uninspired actor living my life was starvation. I'd remove the world's fables, myths, and lies—all the poison floating at the top of his cup.

The most dangerous lie? The Gordian knot of "I'll be happy when….." That lie has many variations: "I'll be happy when I'm married. I'll be happy when money isn't a problem. I'll be happy when I save the world. I'll be happy when I make the NFL." The problem with "I'll be happy when…" is that the address kept changing. It was exciting buying a new car, but the excitement wore off as quickly as the new-car smell. It was rewarding to purchase a new home until the reality of yard work and maintenance began stealing my time. It was great getting a new title on a business card, but the title meant the work was magnitudes more difficult, not easier. It was all a colossal cosmic joke I'd been playing on myself.

After a final look in the mirror at the pathetic character I'd been playing, without pity or remorse, I consummated the murder, tipping my cup to the side. As the liquid lies of the world, especially "I'll be happy when…" poured to the ground, I knew I was free again.

With new room in my cup I began to create difficult, if not impossible, long-term goals again. More than just having a series of random, fleeting thoughts, I wrote down every idea no matter how crazy it sounded. My new goals weren't about acquiring things—especially money, fame, or comfort. They certainly weren't about being perfect. My goals were about becoming. Learning. Growing. Expanding. What am I capable of as a man?

I wrote down goals in one, three, five, and ten-year increments. One of the best ideas was, "I'll begin a new life of adventure, living all over the world working in international banking and technology." I didn't know where the thought came from. I definitely didn't know how I was going to do it. What's important is I didn't discount it as a naïve fairy tale or look externally for validation. Separated for far too long, the audacity, curiosity and wisdom of the ten-year-old boy had returned.

Until I wrote it down as an explicit goal the possibilities of living and working overseas were remote. I didn't speak a foreign language or have a degree in International Business. My family hadn't paved the way serving overseas in the military or foreign embassies. The odds of living and working overseas were much better than making the NFL, but I had to take action. Working overseas only meant I needed education and a desire to assume more risk. I began taking Japanese-language and international-finance courses at Wichita State University. I also began another creative-visualization process, imagining exactly what I'd wear and the sensation of sitting in a plane flying over the world's oceans to overseas assignments.

Within three weeks of being fired, I found a new software-engineering position with a large regional bank in Wichita beginning what was to become the main focus of my professional career: technology in the world of banking and finance. The bank was replacing its antiquated software with a state-of-the-art platform. Assigned to the upgrade project I worked closely with the business helping them move to the improved functionality. Unfortunately, the project wasn't going well. With significant cost overruns and scheduling delays, questions about what had happened, how to fix it, and most important, whom to blame began to emerge.

Without the heavy burden trying to be perfect, my mind began noticing the structure and patterns of the project and how people were interacting. The main problem was the stifling fear of change. Comfortable with the old system, the business units were recreating every archaic business process on the new platform. Prior to being fired, if asked for my opinion I tiptoed around the obvious truth thinking I was being politically astute, but the real reason was safety. I wanted to keep my job. But by trying to be safe I was part of the problem, enabling the dysfunction to continue. After replacing perfection and safety with the goal of constant, incremental growth, I began taking calculated risks, accepting the inevitable mistakes and confronting the unknown. It was also easier. If asked a question I couldn't answer, I simply responded, "I don't know. Can I get back to you?" That was far easier than dancing around some half-truth and then trying to remember what I'd said.

My career officially took off near the end of a two-hour marathon meeting comprised mostly of frustration, circular dysfunction and avoidance. Relatively new to the company and the project, I was silent for most of the meeting until the leader asked, "Before we end for the day, does anyone have anything to add?" With a new attitude toward risk, I waited, looking around the room for someone, anyone, to state the obvious. Senior managers, consultants, and staff surrounded the table, but everyone was silent, eyes glued to the table or floor. Beat down, they were praying the misery would end so they could escape to the safety of their desks. I would have preferred for someone else to state the obvious, but when I couldn't bear the internal tension any longer, I raised my hand, rhetorically asking, "I don't get it. I don't understand what we're doing."

His tone of condescension implying 'you're the new guy, who the hell do you think you are?', the vice-president running the meeting responded, "What do you mean?"

"I don't understand what specific problem we're solving?"

Pausing to make sure the entire room was watching, with a well-practiced, perfectly coordinated roll of his eyes and a heavy sigh of sarcasm, he snapped, "It's obvious. We're putting in a new banking system!"

I wasn't having it, especially from the guy leading the dysfunction. "That's true, but that's a solution. What problem does putting in a new banking system solve? Since you avoided answering my specific question, I'll ask it again in a different way. Who is going to explain to the chairman and the board they were talked into spending millions on new software, but with one change request after another, we're forcing it to look and perform *exactly* like our old system? Why spend millions recreating our cumbersome, antiquated business processes on a new platform?"

The opposite of a radical thought, it was simple, screaming to be said. We had purchased a technologically sophisticated Ferrari to replace our twenty-year-old pickup truck but were putting the truck's analog dashboard into the new car purely to avoid the discomfort of change. The problem was who was making the critical decisions. Operational staff told passive software engineers how they wanted the software to work. It was Burger King's "I want it my way". No middle or senior management were involved to insist on achieving the long-term, strategic platform goals.

Two things surprised me after the meeting. The first was the number of people pulling me aside in the hallways to say, "Thank you. I've always thought the project was on the wrong track, but I was too afraid to say anything." The second was my growing comfort speaking in public, particularly about difficult subjects. I could tactfully explain my thought process, unemotionally letting the facts speak for themselves. Although it was disconcerting to many people, saying exactly what I thought was incredibly liberating.

My career seemed to be back on track. My social life was improving as well. I'd met and married an adorable woman, a Science and Physical Education teacher who possessed a gentle soul. We had a lot in common and I promised myself I'd do whatever it took to keep us together. But I still hadn't learned. Trying for perfection in a marriage was simply a variation of trying for perfection everywhere else in my life. The next in a long line of critical mistakes, I didn't realize how easily I could lose myself while trying to love another person.

I worked on the flatlands of Kansas living a typical Midwestern life until a snowy November-evening phone call. It had only taken three years, but the universe had responded to my impossible written goals: I was moving overseas. A door to a new world was opening. It was an extremely exciting time. In addition to the Japanese and international finance I was studying, I'd soon be exposed to other cultures and languages. What I didn't know was I'd also be exposed to new languages of fear, in and out of the office, again.

CHAPTER NINETEEN

I'm ten years old again

If it's important to you, you will find a way.
If not, you'll find an excuse.
—Andy Bailey

I've slipped through a portal in time, but I'm not the military commander devising elaborate strategies for a squad of G.I. Joe action figures in daring backyard missions. I'm not the gentle boy spending hours alone in my basement bedroom meticulously painting electric football men in NFL team colors. I'm certainly not the inspired young man setting the impossible goal to play football at the highest level. The feelings of anxiety, dread and panic permeating every cell, I'm the terrified ten-year-old paralyzed in another tree fifteen feet above the ground. Again.

I was at an indoor climbing gym learning to climb and rappel. Although it was nice developing another tool for my backcountry-skiing toolbox, the main purpose of the day was to challenge Daddy with another walk into fear. After spending an hour absorbing the instructor's basic introductions to the gear and climbing techniques, I took my first attempt on the wall. Assertively scaling the first ten feet, each purposeful step of sticky rubber climbing shoes coordinating with confident handholds, forty years of fear and anxiety seemed to fall to the ground like the chalk from my fingers. Methodically climbing another five feet to the halfway point, I stopped before evaluating my next move.

The top of the wall patiently waited twenty feet above me but the next handhold was a few inches past my comfort zone. Technically I was safe. My belay partner on the ground was carefully monitoring the tension on the safety rope. As a backup, the instructor was attentively monitoring us both. In the remote possibility they both screwed up and I fell to the padded mats, at most I'd sprain an ankle or maybe break a leg.

As I calculated the effort necessary to stretch out to the next handhold the first glimmer of self-doubt began building momentum. Regardless of the statistical safety, as soon as my hand left the wall reaching out for the next handhold my reptilian brain engaged, signaling I was in imminent danger. Already loaded with cortisol and adrenaline, milliseconds later my nervous system joined the party paralyzing my muscles with dopamine. The rough bark of neighborhood trees had been replaced with the smooth climbing surface. My face was pinned to the wall and I couldn't move my arm an inch. Every emotion of the terrified ten-year-old boy trapped halfway up an oak tree had returned. With a vengeance.

Playing my game, purposefully walking Daddy into dark neighborhoods, I've been learning how to manage the mental and physical sensations of fear. Developing confidence for freefall, I've been learning how to fly in a wind tunnel. A few weeks ago I achieved an exciting milestone silently soaring thousands of feet above Lake Tahoe in a glider. I've windsurfed Maui's north shore, attacking the waves with reckless abandon. Day after day, block after block, after each momentum-building step, my confidence continued to grow. Boldly advancing towards the intensity of a skydive, my meticulous plan has been working as expected—until today.

Only a few months away from achieving my goal I'd run into a well-known block of fear as cold and hard as a piece of smooth, black granite. Worse than a barrier I can't go around, over, or through, the granite wall had tipped over, crushing me with the massive weight of its indifference. I want off the wall and I want to stop confronting fear. Now.

Unfortunately, before I could quit my project, I had to do something. My partner and instructor were patiently waiting below me. With a deep sigh of futility and resignation I managed to pull my head back from the wall, shouting down, "I've had enough!" and would be coming down. That was when the day became even more bizarre. As soon as I leaned back into my climbing harness, I felt comfortable, safe and secure. Seconds before, I had been frozen in failure at exactly the same height. Now I was fine. How could that be possible? For a second I thought about regrouping, waiting for the tension to dissipate but I wanted off the wall and began rappelling down. The instant my feet touched the padded floor I depressingly began wondering, *what happened?*

I should have asked a better question. "What didn't happen?"

For weeks prior to arriving at the climbing wall I'd spent dozens of hours in the office with senior architects and engineers, painstakingly analyzing high-availability database cluster scenarios. What would happen in this circumstance? How do we test and confirm the servers are synchronizing correctly? What happens if we lose this network segment? We identified hundreds of Use Cases, interspersed with dozens of possible failure points, the probability of occurrence and the anticipated costs of an actual failure. After careful written planning, we created and repeated each scenario in test environments until every possibility was fully understood.

My detailed plan for the climbing wall? Nothing. I wasn't prepared. I hadn't done any homework on climbing. Not only didn't I have a structured plan for what I'd do if I froze up on the wall, I didn't even have an expectation of how many times I'd climb it. I hadn't prepared for possible moments of terror or panic. I loathe the phrase "90 percent of success is just showing up," but I can be the consummate hypocrite. I'd showed up to play an important football game on a vertical field. Instead of detailed planning and relentless preparation, my game plan was to wing it, randomly drawing plays in the dirt as the game played out. Of course I got my ass kicked.

I didn't have any type of plan to accelerate the failure. I didn't try moving up a little bit at a time, getting more comfortable with the increase in height. I didn't know how it would feel slipping off the wall falling a few feet before being caught in the climbing harness. I could have practiced, climbing a few feet up working with my belay partner learning what a six-inch and then a twelve-inch fall felt like. I didn't plan or effectively utilize that process either. I didn't ask, "How many times am I willing to fail at this before I succeed?"

If I'd planned better, or even at all, building a matrix of probabilities and expected outcomes, I could have stopped, gathered my emotions, before trying to move up another step. I could have regrouped, thinking, *Yup, I'm here. I planned for this possibility.* Instead, I had tossed every opportunity to learn and grow to the side, wanting off the wall as quickly as possible. I didn't trust my belay partner or the instructor. I didn't trust the equipment and I certainly didn't trust myself. I wasn't in control of anything, especially my emotions.

Residing in my primordial brain, my primitive beast of fear is far beyond logic, intelligence or any learned experience. My fear was of the unknown. I've never fallen from anything, especially trees. I was never hurt leaping from an Olympic swimming-pool tower. Without any previous experience where a severe injury imprinted my brain with deep memories of pain: my fear is completely imaginary—nothing more than the vagueness of negative expectations pulsing through me without boundaries.

My entire project is now at risk, the momentum lost because I showed up stupid and naïve. Not only haven't I vanquished Daddy with process, planning and patience; he's returned in all his glory, gloating and stronger than ever. His mocking laugh only lasted a few moments, but the mental gymnastics I carried out of the gym were exhausting. Worse than my emotions on the climbing wall were the constant rationalizations on the drive home. An explanation became a reason, and a reason became an excuse. Finally, the excuses became justifications: foundational pillars for the type of life I don't want to live. That sequence of thinking is from the fear of a ten-year-old boy. Not a man.

If I imagine every rationalization chiseled into my book of life, I'd be extremely careful about how each thought affects my motivation, willpower, and discipline. Perhaps a better visual than a book is to imagine family members at my gravesite reading an engraved tombstone. My spirit, gloriously free from the restrictive container of a human body, I'd watch my family silently weep over my passing. I'd also weep, knowing my massive collection of excuses could have been brushed away as easily as a small child sets aside a toy. Etched into the supine slab facing up for both the heavens and the world to see is:

Here lies Danny Nelson Cass

Born in sublime innocence and unlimited potential
February 4, 1957–
Died with regret
In the month of "I can't"
On the day of "It's too hard"
In the year of "What if I fail?"

Instead of living a life of passion, intensity, and satisfaction, he became an expert collector: of excuses. Constantly adding to his enormous book of elaborate reasons for why he couldn't do something, he knowingly dragged its soul-crushing weight behind him every moment of his life.

A partial list of his many excuses were:

I'm afraid, but I don't know why.
I don't have enough time in the day.
It's too hard to be disciplined.
I wasn't born into the right family.
I don't want to risk being alone.
I don't have enough money.
I couldn't get into the right school.
I'm not attractive enough.
I'm not smart enough.
What will people say if I fail?
Life isn't fair!
What if I die?

Not only did he have an endless list of readily available excuses, he persistently searched for distractions instead of focusing on his goals. He didn't know how to let go of the excuses defining him and his life. He was a private, intense man with a deep reservoir of untapped ability but used a tiny fraction of it, only when it was convenient and easy.

Engraved under this tombstone, facing down for Dan to view for all eternity, is the private list of dreams he never achieved because he was afraid.

Dan, Julie, Kae

Father, son, and dog

Unprepared for public speaking

Comfortable within the safety of the group. No one was talking.

Speed at 22 Off / 32 mph

Lanai Cathedrals, Maui

British Columbia

Pebble Beach

Czechoslovakian Aero L-39

CHAPTER TWENTY

Leaving the illusion of a safe, predictable life

We don't stop playing because we grow old;
we grow old because we stop playing.
—George Bernard Shaw

Complete darkness enveloped me. I couldn't see a thing, but instead of being overwhelmed I relaxed into the moment, ninety feet below the surface of the legendary and mysterious Bermuda Triangle. At night.

I was a member of the Bermuda Sub-Aqua Club, a large scuba-diving group on the island made up predominantly of white-collar expatriate workers from dozens of countries around the world. On a windless July evening under a full moon and millions of stars, our large dive boat had taken twenty of us through the complicated and dangerous reef system surrounding the island. A mile offshore from Bermuda's pink-sand beaches we arrived at our dive site, the *Hermes*—a 165-foot long, 254-ton ship sunk in the Bermudian waters in 1985.

I've been immersed in water since my first year in grade school when my parents started me on summer swimming lessons. Intrigued watching weekly TV episodes of Jacques Cousteau exploring the world's oceans, I eventually began scuba diving in college and have been diving ever since. I'm extremely comfortable in water but the Atlantic Ocean's fabled Bermuda Triangle has captured the human imagination with mysterious unexplained disappearances of ships, planes, and people for centuries.

Choosing to step off of a dive boat into Bermuda's daytime water is one thing. Weightlessly descending, meter by meter, my handheld dive light straining into absolute darkness is another. My dive partner for the evening was no more than five feet away, but the only way to ascertain my relative position in the water was to constantly check my depth gauge or watch my exhalation bubbles rushing to the surface. As we continued our descent, I was confident the piercing rays of my dive light would eventually meet an object, either the rusting metal hull of the *Hermes* or the white sand of the ocean bottom. Until then, all of my senses were dramatically reduced.

Constrained to the dive light's narrow beam piercing a few feet out into the dark water, eyesight, my predominant human asset for determining physical safety, was extremely limited. Exacerbating the problem, my mask also eliminated any peripheral vision warning me of possible dangers from the side. I certainly couldn't rely on my hearing: sound doesn't travel well underwater especially under a thick neoprene hood. My closely related senses of taste and smell were limited to the acidity of rubber: the smell of the mask tightly encasing my face and the taste of the regulator obtrusively filling my mouth. Finally, my balance and innate sense of the earth's gravity were reduced as I weightlessly fell to the bottom of the sea.

The fundamental human attribute that hadn't been reduced was the staggering capacity of my imagination. Making up for the significant reduction of sight and sound, my creative mind shifted into overdrive, instantly building and scanning a ridiculous checklist of every possible danger, real or imagined. As the rhythmic sound of my regulator comforted me I descended into the darkness, past mental shadows of hungry sharks, curious moray eels, sleek barracuda, and gray aliens from other worlds. Unlike my paralyzing struggles with heights, as quickly as each illusion entered my mind, I let it go, releasing each thought as easily as the exhalation bubbles racing to the surface.

Descending through imaginary creatures with empty stomachs and razor-sharp teeth our dive group finally arrived, our lights reflecting off the reassuring safety of a physical object—the *Hermes*. After gathering together on the expansive deck, the eerie shape of its twenty-ton cargo boom looming over us, our dive leader instructed us to turn off our high-powered lights. Effectively blind, bathed in suffocating darkness, I couldn't see the inside edge of my mask or even my hand six inches in front of my face. I was still calm, but as my pupils fully dilated a fantastic surprise greeted me. The night's piercing moonlight had penetrated all the way to the bottom, illuminating the excited faces of my dive mates. Although regulators blocked their physical smiles, twenty pairs of excited eyes wordlessly shared the emotions of wondrous adventure.

As I adjusted to the magic of being able to see ninety feet below the surface of the ocean at night without battery-powered light, the dive leader moved in front of us gently swirling his hands through the water. As if waiting for a cue from an orchestra conductor, thousands of phosphorescent plankton instantly exploded into a symphony of light, creating an underwater Aurora Borealis.

After our group settled down from the excitement of the moonlit phosphorescent fireworks show we got back to the real drama and purpose of the evening: swimming into the dark interior corridors of the *Hermes* where the reassuring illumination of moonlight couldn't reach. One by one we cautiously entered through the cramped steel doors of the ship. Inside of the ship the ocean water seemed colder and darker, but it wasn't spooky or frightening. It was a great evening, ending with celebratory cold beers and huge smiles, but I wondered how I could be completely calm inside the rusty hull of a ship ninety feet below the surface of the ocean at night but be paralyzed with panic fifteen feet above the ground in a neighborhood tree in broad daylight? It's a mystery that continues to unfold.

The answer to a different mystery was revealed a few weeks later during the Thanksgiving holidays when I'd flown back to Lincoln to attend an informal reunion of high school friends. A quiet neighborhood bar was the venue for sharing my new world of scuba diving at night, international banking, wearing Bermuda shorts and knee socks with a blazer while driving a scooter on the English side of the road. The evening took a turn when a distant school acquaintance and I clicked the narrow top of our beer bottles. That's when he said it.

"I'd give anything to have your life."

"What?"

"I'd do anything to have your life."

I couldn't believe he'd said that, because it wasn't true. His words were as effective as a "Life Isn't Fair" bumper sticker on a rusting car. I didn't say anything, but his answer instantly explained the mystery. Why did I constantly avoid him in high school? I hadn't disliked him; it was just that it was uncomfortable to be around him. Now I knew why. I could feel it. It was his energy. It was exactly the same from school. He hadn't changed or grown. Led by his guiding principles trying to stay comfortable by looking cool, he always did just enough to get by, never giving much of anything.

I had to give him credit though. He was as lazy with his thinking as he was with his actions. Still empty of passion, curiosity and insight, he wasn't paying attention to the exact meaning of what he was saying. He should have said, "I'd love to have your life as long as I don't have to risk too much or work too hard. I'd try it if I had a guarantee, an insurance policy or at least someone to blame. If it doesn't work out, I want a safe, soft landing to return home to." Because he wouldn't prioritize his life with a set of goals, he's still where he's always been for most of his life—safe, comfortable, and bored, but he has no idea why.

Although I was blessed with athletic DNA, I wasn't given an extra dose of genetic courage. My brain isn't larger than his. He has the same numbers of hours in a day as everyone else. Nothing has been easy and I've always had fears and doubts. I *was* afraid when I decided to move overseas. Already laid off, divorced, and fired, moving to a new country certainly didn't guarantee *'worldly success.'*

Overcoming my self-preservation instincts, leaving everything safe and known, making the decision to move was difficult. I had many late night internal conversations staring at the darkened ceiling of my bedroom. My silent battles were an impossible combination of vacillating thoughts, *'What if leaving is a mistake'* and *'What if staying is a mistake?'* Adding to the opposing thoughts, dull vagaries oscillated: "Why can't you settle for what you have? Why can't you be more realistic?" At the top of its lungs, my ego was screaming about the (false) sense of security my material possessions provided.

The reality? Those 'things' *had* me. I didn't have a home—because I was responsible for the monthly payments, the mortgage had me. The house was simply a place constructed of wood and nails, barely more than an inanimate object designed and built to hold other material things. My car and other physical possessions insisted on a safe, dry place to live, meaning I had to provide, *for them*. I was a slave to my possessions.

Eventually my nightly monologues of anguish came to an end when I woke up one morning to the thought, "I can't do it. I can't stay here any longer." Pacing back and forth, slowly dying in an invisible cage of safety and dull contentment, a feeling I couldn't articulate compelled me to go. I had to explore the world, but it was really just a way to explore myself. When I shared I was not only leaving Kansas and my job, but also the country, many friends told me I was crazy or delusional. I listened to their judgments masquerading as advice: "What are you doing? You're out of your mind. Maybe you should talk to a professional…a psychiatrist. You'll regret it. Who do you think you are? You're not better than us. You'll come crawling back." Although many did try to be helpful, most of the comments were projections of their fear.

I knew if I listened to the voices coercing me to stay safe, external or internal, I'd regret it for the rest of my life. It was simply time for me to leave, even if it would hurt my career. The Midwest is full of great people. It's a solid place to raise a family with good school systems, morals and values. Generally, the work ethic is without question, the people possessing an approach to personal character and integrity that isn't a situational convenience or legal technicality. I left good friends, a great job where I was respected, a comfortable home in the suburbs, a sports car, a boat, and all the other trappings of external success. I didn't leave the Midwest or the United States because they were bad, but to enter the realm of the unknown. I was curious.

A month before leaving the country my wife and I had a "Moving to Bermuda" sale. Instead of a typical weekend garage sale where neighbors come over to say hi and satisfy their voyeuristic curiosity, it felt like an estate sale, but we were still alive. We sold everything except clothes, my library of cherished books, and sports gear. Purging physical possessions was extremely freeing. It was my life's version of a spring-cleaning garage sale. Leaving the deceptive feelings of safety and security behind, I wondered if I'd ever return to Kansas.

I arrived in Bermuda the weekend of the Queen's birthday. With the haunting sounds of bagpipes as background music, I was thrilled watching the Bermudian Regiment proudly marching through Hamilton uniformed in kilts. I was finally living overseas, experiencing a different culture.

Adapting to Bermudian life, my wife and I lived in a classic pink cottage with a white roof in Warwick, only a couple hundred yards away from Bermuda's pink-sand beaches. Commuting to work every day on an 85cc Honda Scoopy, I was quickly becoming immersed in the island's culture of test cricket, Dark 'n' Stormy cocktails, and saying "Good morning" to complete strangers while walking to the office.

My contract position with the bank was relatively easy. Technology, with its numerous three-letter acronyms, was merely another foreign language to learn. Accounting, finance, and law also have similarly arcane languages, but they're fairly simple when broken down into the functional basics. My difficulties centered on people. I thought the business and technical environments in Bermuda, a major international banking and reinsurance center, would move so quickly I'd have to be at the top of my game working incredibly long hours just to keep up. I couldn't have been more wrong. Beautiful, exotic accents from all over the world echoed through the office hallways, but the distinct emotional verbiage of fear in all its forms—uncertainty, avoidance, and doubt—crossed every cultural, demographic, and gender barrier.

Throughout my career, I've watched exceedingly talented people struggle not only with the difficulties of decision-making but specifically with the task of prioritization. Even getting people to make a simple recommendation was met with trepidation. From first-year engineers to senior executives with advanced Ivy League degrees, I've watched extremely confident, outgoing professionals struggle to prioritize short lists of projects. The emotion of uncertainty overwhelming their logic, the priority and importance of each problem was the same regardless of Return On Investment, resources available or timing. It didn't matter if ten or a hundred projects were on the list; they all had the same irrational priority: "We have to get them *all* done as soon as possible! It doesn't matter how!"

In one infamous, tension-filled meeting, I suggested to a struggling member of the legal team that I knew his favorite Crayola crayon from grade school. He responded with, "What? How do you know? What does *that* have to do with our project?"

With piercing eyes softly padded by a gentle smile, I shared that his favorite color was gray. Nothing in his legal world was black and white. Every decision was a slippery, evasive legal target designed to protect the business from lawsuits. I acknowledged his professional dilemma and fiduciary role, but I told him my software engineers and architects didn't have an "If-then-else, notwithstanding the foregoing" conditional in their software skillset to monitor the constantly shifting bureaucratic perceptions of the legal and regulatory world. I wasn't asking him to notarize a contract in blood, but for the time being, he had to transcend his paralysis or the project would quickly grind to a halt.

My struggles outside the office were worse. Bermuda is a very social island where nightly after-work pub visits are expected, and weekend get-togethers are the norm. I had hoped moving overseas would be a stimulating change but of course the problem was me. I was still the same, foolishly thinking conversations with an expat population who had assumed the substantial risks of moving overseas would be full of depth, open to differing opinions or perspectives. I couldn't have been more wrong or disappointed. Tickling my contempt or piquing my disinterest, with the sophisticated smugness of Fabian socialists most weekend conversations began or ended with statements determined only to confirm whether I was a member of *their* group.

I was already an outsider, an American, but I was tired of conversations consisting of statements without thought and single syllable responses without questions. I wasn't shy. I was lonely, desperate for open-minded discussions about subjects without easy answers. If I were curious or drunk enough to risk social banishment, I'd sometimes ask how a conclusion had been reached. I wasn't challenging the opinion or the status quo; I just wanted to understand the thought process. The problem was there wasn't one. The conclusion was usually based on feelings that someone couldn't—or wouldn't—articulate.

For the sake of my now-struggling marriage I tried to fit in. I resorted to keeping my mouth shut while politely nodding which only exacerbated the impression of the shy tech guy with nothing interesting to say. Bermuda, a tiny island of conformity and mundane social expectations, was as intellectually stifling and conservative as Kansas. I was suffocating in every possible way.

When I wasn't awkwardly fidgeting at a party, I tried to recharge by windsurfing, golfing, and scuba diving—activities where I could be alone. It didn't work. I wasn't any more social on Bermuda even when I was rested. After too many discussions and arguments about why I couldn't be normal in every way, the stereotypical outgoing boy next door, I moved to a new apartment as my soon-to-be-ex and I began the divorce process.

During the painful relationship separation, I was offered a new consulting opportunity in Lisbon, Portugal. After leaving Nebraska and then Kansas, it was easy moving to another continent. First, I understood what was necessary to be successful in the banking and technology world: extremely hard work combined with clear communication skills. I also had the innate ability to make difficult decisions, moving projects along, most of the time with little information. Most importantly, because I'd returned to the world of internal competition, becoming more and more comfortable facing the unknown, I was willing to go almost anywhere in the world to live, work, and play.

CHAPTER TWENTY-ONE

Knight takes bishop, at 125 miles per hour

Should I be afraid?
For a man like you?
—Meet Joe Black

Until last week my process for challenging heights has been working. Incrementally learning and growing, day by day my momentum was building. One encouraging accomplishment after another, I could feel the unfolding expansion of possibilities. Today? The entire project has collapsed into failure, sharp pieces of broken glass scattered across the floor.

Since the demoralizing defeat on the climbing wall every day has been a tasteless stew of physical and emotional exhaustion. Searching for a way to move forward, I had many thoughts, most of which were little more than rationalizations. The most dangerous thought was to quit my project, leaning on the convenient but hollow excuse, no one would know except me.

The worst mistakes in my life have typically come when I was tired, empty of motivation. Instead of ceding to fatigue, I retreated, surrendering into a couple nights of restless sleep. As difficult as it was, I also took a few days away from the physical grind of the gym. I needed to recharge, allowing the feelings of disappointment to slowly dissipate before deciding how, or even if, to proceed.

As I stared blankly out the aircraft window during another uneventful business flight back to the Midwest I wondered how it would feel to abandon my project, adding one more entry to my pages-long list of failures. For the first hour of the flight I gazed indifferently at blue skies and puffy white clouds, my mind a blank slate. A relaxing flight with no unexpected turbulence to startle Daddy, it wasn't until a flight attendant offering refreshments brought my attention to a passenger watching a movie on his laptop.

Across the aisle, within the small confines of a thirteen-inch laptop screen, world champion Valentino Rossi's knee scraped the asphalt at a hundred miles per hour, his leather glove calmly rolling on the motorcycle's throttle. The longer I watched, the more intrigued I became. As each flickering frame of video flew by my mind began boiling with excitement, each idea percolating to a surface of new possibilities. Why was watching a DVD across the aisle on a routine business flight so inspiring? How could my emotions change from the stale emptiness of defeat, indifferently staring out an airplane window, to the well-known feelings of purpose and motivation?

As the braking-point of the next turn, a high-speed encounter with massive deceleration, gravity and physics, reflected in Valentino's mirrored visor, I had my answer. The DVD, or at least its subject, was a solution around my failure on the climbing wall. I wasn't only fighting heights. I was fighting Daddy, in all his forms. Instead of forcing my way through heights, stubbornly confronting my vertical opponent, I'll recapture the momentum of my project in an environment I'm comfortable with: speed. I'll put my motorcycle on a racetrack, riding at speeds three times faster than on the street.

Always enjoying the pull of acceleration, I loved the feeling of explosive power sprinting out of starting blocks at high school track meets or from a three-point stance in football. I enjoyed the muscular neck strain, the weight of my head forced rearward, as my right foot mashed the accelerator to the floor in my first muscle car. I became addicted to whipping back and forth across a boat wake water-skiing, putting my ski on edge in anticipation of the instantaneous rope pull from the ski boat. I love speed, but a significant problem with my new idea to challenge Daddy with speed was I'd never been on a racetrack, on four wheels—much less two.

My first time on two wheels was in Bermuda after purchasing an 85cc scooter to commute to work. With a maximum island speed of 50 kilometers per hour, the only concern I had was sliding off the scooter on oily roads during seasonal Atlantic rainstorms. My unlikely introduction to the allure of high-speed sport bikes began when I left the tranquility of Bermuda for the short consulting assignment in Lisbon, Portugal, in 1994.

A few weeks into another major system conversion at one of Portugal's largest banks, one of my Portuguese banking friends invited me to join him on a five-hour drive to the city of Jerez in southern Spain to watch my first professional motorcycle race. Trying to be a good consultant and guest, I kept my indifference to watching motorcycles boringly circle a track to myself, but I should have known racing at the highest levels would inspire me.

The MotoGP event, often described as the Woodstock of European motorcycle racing, begins a week before the race when a quarter million sport bikes from the continent descend on Jerez. After four amazing days and nights overwhelmed by the smell of burning fuel, hot tire rubber, gorgeous European women dressed head to toe in skintight leather riding gear, and the intoxicating Spanish thirst for living, I was hooked. A few months later when my contract in Lisbon ended I had an opportunity to work in Vancouver, British Columbia. Within a week after arriving in Canada, I purchased my first sport bike—a Honda CBR 600F2.

It was thrilling to make the huge jump from an 85cc scooter to a 600cc sport bike. I enjoyed riding the twisty mountain roads of British Columbia and the suburban streets of Vancouver, but eventually the luster of riding faded. Constantly on watch for distracted drivers, riding had become an unsatisfying, tedious chore. It was the same after moving from Vancouver to San Francisco. After fighting San Francisco's filthy third-world roads full of potholes, broken asphalt or oblivious drivers turning in front of me, I came home after every ride exhausted from the effort of defensive driving. For the last three years my bike sat in the garage collecting dust. Watching Valentino Rossi in the tight confines of a flying aluminum bus changed everything.

After landing in South Dakota I rushed to my hotel excitedly searching the Internet for a racetrack near San Francisco. I discovered that Infineon Raceway, at the southern edge of the world-famous Napa vineyards, was only forty minutes north of my home. Infineon was home to the Jim Russell Racing School and periodically offered the California Superbike School.

I more or less taught myself to windsurf, snow ski, water-ski, and golf. Each learning effort was a long sequence of trial and error with generous helpings of bumps, bruises, and significant expense. Falling on water from a windsurfing or water-ski crash is one thing. Falling while snow skiing hurts more, especially on hard packed snow or ice. But falling from a sport bike onto asphalt, at any speed, would be painful. Physical injury is likely, damage to the bike is practically assured and death a waiting specter. The difference with speed on a racetrack is I'm leaving my "I can learn it alone" ego at home. This time I'll be paying for world-class instruction.

Instead of being a bulldog with a bone, my competitive ego forcing me onto the motorcycle first, I also decided to create a mini-process within this year's project plan. Breaking it down into three parts, I'd begin my initiation into the world of motorsports with high-speed go-karts. After getting comfortable with karts, I'll move up the ladder of intensity driving open-wheel Formula 3 cars. Finally, after learning to race on four wheels, I'll enter into a new dimension of speed and danger: a high-performance sport bike on a racetrack.

I began learning the hands-on skills of head-to-head racing my first day at the Jim Russell Karting School. I've driven twenty-five-mile-per-hour indoor go-karts and forty-mile-per-hour Malibu Grand Prix cars. I'd even driven retired Formula 440 cars on a scaled-down track in Tsawwassen, British Columbia, but those activities were recreational. Driving Jim Russell's high-speed karts was thrilling, but it wasn't recreation. It was extremely demanding. Two inches off the ground, a high-performance kart delivers twenty-eight horsepower to the rear wheels—enough to accelerate to sixty-five miles per hour in three seconds. It's a rocket ship. With no suspension to smooth out bumps, turning a kart at high-speed is brutal. I returned home every day physically and mentally drained.

Learning to race a kart against other students was an interesting challenge. I loved the competition, but I wasn't prepared to perform well. I hadn't visualized a kart inches in front of me. I didn't have thousands of laps to let my eyes relax into the flow of the track. Impatiently trying to apply the lessons from the classroom to the racetrack, I was making one mistake after another. I expected errors in my racing technique, but I was making the same type of mistakes I'd made in the gym, the office, and my relationships: I was trying too hard.

Unafraid of the speed, I'd accelerate as fast as possible, chasing my competitors before slamming on the brakes trying to make the next turn. Forcing everything with competitive will, I was fast into the turn and slow out, an extremely inefficient technique. In motorsports, inefficient means frustratingly slow. As soon as someone passed me coming out of the corners, my foot would instantly crush the accelerator trying to catch up. The more I was passed, the harder I pressed. Without a strategy for driving the track smoothly, the head to head competition with the other drivers distracted me, my competitive ego blocking the way.

I didn't have a plan. I hadn't spent any time mentally rehearsing the racing line, my braking points, the apex of each turn or the track-out points. I hadn't thought about where my eyes should be focused. Without the discipline of preparation to fall back on, instead of focusing on where I wanted to go, I was spending all my seat time fixated on the kart directly in front of me.

My toolbox of skill, ability, and aptitude is huge: Planning. Observation. Strategizing. Discipline. Many of the tools are well-honed, sharpened and refined through meticulous practice. On the track, I could have pulled the rarely used tool of patience. I could have grabbed the scalpel of logic, applying it to the problem of the day. Instead, I unconsciously grabbed my favorite, well-worn implement: the sledgehammer of brute-force effort.

My pattern across all activities is usually the same. I've always been fighting, forcing everything with effort and desire. More of everything, except patience and balance, was always better. I did it water-skiing: after making a turn I'd fly across the wake, but arriving late at the next buoy I'd drive my ski into awkward, inefficient positions just to make the turn. I still do it on the golf course trying to crush the little white ball like it's my most hated enemy. I've done it in almost every relationship, trying to make everything perfect.

The track was another blunt reminder my greatest strengths, discipline and willpower, were also my greatest weaknesses. I've been here too many times to count. Why can't I learn from my mistakes? Why do I continue to forget and remember? I still wouldn't allow life, or the racetrack, to come to me. Why is learning the delicate balance of surrendering to the moment while living inside a fiery bubble of competitive intensity so incredibly difficult? Answers to some of my questions appeared in the F3 racing machines.

Even after the humbling exposure to the lightning-quick acceleration and physicality of karting, driving a Formula 3 racecar was a massive jump up the performance ladder. Jim Russell's three-day racing school uses FJR-50 open-wheel cars able to accelerate to 125 miles per hour on the short Infineon track, the same speed I'll reach at terminal velocity after jumping from a plane.

I quickly realized formula racing was an entirely new world the first morning while being fitted for the car. After struggling to squeeze into the tiny cockpit the pit crew began cinching down my five-buckle quick-release harness. Tightening and retightening, one of the crew finally asked, "How does that feel?" My grunting "I can barely breathe" response was met with, "Good; we're almost there. Just a few more tugs." I was soon to find out why being tightly restrained, a bizarre form of race-car bondage, was necessary. Easily pulling 1.5 Gs in turns and 2 Gs under braking, the FJR-50 is a machine designed to do one thing: race. The necessity to mentally focus for extended periods at high-speed, braking with unbelievable, almost violent deceleration and then doing it lap after lap, turn after turn, was punishing. The FJR was intimidating, taking me the first full day just to get a feel for some of its capabilities.

The difference between my indoor-climbing-wall and karting mistakes? I was learning that patience and acceptance were not weaknesses. Leaving the sledgehammer of my ego at home, I hadn't shown up to drive the FJR stupid and overconfident. Mimicking my process visualizing a football game, I began long evening sessions visualizing Infineon's racing line, hitting the exact braking-point on each turn before smoothly flowing through the apex. The mental preparation dramatically changed my performance on the track.

When I kept my vision up, looking down the track through the other drivers to where I wanted to go, everything slowed down. It didn't matter that other cars were only meters away, I could relax, patiently letting the track come to me. It was as if I were sitting in a stationary car as the track flowed under me. I'd been here before. Passing a competitor coming out of the Carousel, Infineon's turn six, I was back in high school again. The front wheels of his car slipping behind me out of sight, the race cars, soft objects in the periphery of my vision, were football tacklers from my past.

I know how to look through obstacles and barriers, visualizing where I want to go. I do it during every-day driving, scanning the road ahead predicting and avoiding possible accident situations. I do it skiing, particularly on mogul runs. If I look six or eight moguls ahead, focusing my vision on where I want to go, I relax into a smooth run. If my vision drops to the snow directly in front of my skis, each mogul becomes an unpleasant surprise. Skiing moguls, driving a race car, or playing football with my vision focused directly in front of me is exhausting. When I'm reduced to reacting to every distraction, big or small, I'm not creating a flow. The distractions start in my mind and quickly reach my vision, which sets the stage for physical tension and fear.

Incrementally moving up the speed sub-process is working well. My karting mistakes reminded me to prepare better, re-focusing my vision to where I wanted to go. I applied those lessons in the FJR's cramped cockpit, dramatically improving my driving. In addition to my satisfying improvements driving a racecar, I've also been preparing to put myself on a racing motorcycle. Each night after work was spent on motorcycle-racing homework: reading books and studying video. I had a good understanding of the terminology, the physics of speed, and racing strategies, but nothing could have prepared me for the anxiety rolling out on two-wheels from pit lane onto the track.

A Porsche GT3 Cup car designed for the track weighs 3,000 pounds, and its 450-horsepower engine develops 1 horsepower for every 6.6 pounds. The FJR-50 I drove weighed 1,200 pounds with 230 horsepower—a weight-to-horsepower ratio of 5.2 to 1. Calculating to a staggering ratio of 1 horsepower for every 3.8 pounds, a four-hundred-pound, 600 cc sport bike delivers 105 horsepower to the rear tire. Power ratios aside, the incomprehensible part of motorcycle physics is that the contact patch of a motorcycle tire is only the size of a credit card.

My first two-wheel foray on the track began as part of Keith Code's California Superbike (CSB) School. Keith has been running his two-day Superbike school around the United State for the last thirty years. The CSB School has a learning process similarly structured to that of Jim Russell racing schools. CSB was incredibly organized; its daily schedule run with the logistics and precision of a special-forces military unit. In the classroom, I learned the techniques of professional motorcycle racing: the racing line, vision, body position, high-speed cornering, and many other skills. The level of professionalism brought comfort and clarity to what I was trying to achieve: challenging myself with a step-by-step progression of knowledge and skill. However, being in the classroom was one thing. Rolling onto the track for the first time was another.

With a cautious twist of the wrist, my leather-encased palm slowly rolling on the throttle, I entered the track, the whining pitch of the engine vibrating up through my racing suit. I was light-years beyond nervous, barely able to breathe. During my ascent towards Infineon's off camber turn number two, the muscles in my neck turned into steel cords trying to rip my chest open.

Although I couldn't breathe, I was lucky. Keith's process protected us from ourselves, forcing us to go slow. Each hour of the day was tightly scheduled and exactly the same. Twenty minutes in the classroom prepared us for twenty minutes on the track, followed by a final twenty-minute detailed debrief. The day's first twenty-minute session on the track was simply "follow the leader" at a boring thirty-five miles per hour with no passing. In the second twenty-minute session, we could pass, but we were only allowed to use fourth gear—but no brakes. Not being able to use the brakes meant that we had to go slow, or go off the track. The next sessions were the same: third and fourth gears only, again no brakes.

As lessons progressed and we moved to faster speeds, I began to use an often-neglected tool: trust. First, I had to trust Keith and his coaches' instruction. One of the first techniques they taught was counter-steering. I'd read about it but didn't fully understand how it worked until I made turns on the racetrack. Counter-steering means that when a bike needs to turn left, especially at high-speed, you direct the front wheel slightly to the right. This is exactly the opposite of how I thought I'd been riding on the street. Pushing, not pulling, on the left handlebar turns the bike to left. Then I had to trust physics and the bike. I had to trust a piece of hot tire rubber the size of a credit card would keep an accelerating motorcycle leaned to the side stuck to the asphalt track.

Finally, and possibly the most difficult, I had to trust myself enough to let go of control. I learned the hard way that on steep ski runs, driving my upper body down the hill toward the danger put me in a much more stable position than leaning back. I learned the same lesson on a motorcycle. As the asphalt rushed by inches from my knee, I was more stable leaning my chest into the turns and into the danger, counterbalancing the forces of inertia.

When I combined trust and the correct techniques with vision, looking as far down the track as possible, I relaxed, feeling the subtle signals coming from the bike. When I allowed the bike to share its messages, each lap became a dance. Instead of strangling the throttle in with tension, I was gentle, like caressing the shoulder of a woman on the dance floor.

I also chose a new performance strategy. Instead of riding as fast as possible, as close to the ragged edge of my skill and emotional limits, I backed down to 85 percent, focusing on staying relaxed and smooth. I didn't care if I got passed. I didn't care about lap times. I focused only on what the bike, my coaches, and my feelings were telling me. Most racing drivers I've read about say that they can't drive all out for more than two or three consecutive laps. Most golfers are taught to swing the club at about 80 percent of their top speed. In track, the fastest runners have the ability to stay relaxed while at the same time giving an all-out effort.

The more I rode, the more I trusted the techniques. The more I felt the perfection of physics at work, the more comfortable I became. Not having to think as much, I could relax into the moment. I was beginning to trust myself. In the beginning, at 85 percent of my ability, I averaged about seventy-five miles per hour on the track. With each lap of patience, I became more comfortable. Before I knew it, 85 percent effort had inched its way to eighty and then eighty-five miles per hour. The more I relaxed, letting the track come to me, the faster I rode. This was immensely satisfying.

Resting in the deep cushions of my sofa reliving a particularly fulfilling day at the race track, I absentmindedly gazed at a forty-year-old wooden chess set resting on my living-room coffee table.

Although exhausted, I was content, reminded of a satisfaction I've known for years. The nouns, verbs, adjectives, geography, and activity of motorcycle racing were radically different, but I've been here before. I was playing chess again, this time on a motorcycle.

My parents spent hours with me as a young boy teaching me the game on the same wooden chessboard. While not an accomplished player, I love the game. I appreciate an opponent devising a strategy filled with a complex series of moves, forcing me deeper into the flow of the game. Riding a sport bike on a track requires the same high level of concentration. Extraneous thoughts, on a bike or over a chessboard, are dangerous. Forced to be quiet, my mind enters the chess match, a moving meditation at high-speed.

What I need from chess or a motorcycle on the track is the same: surrender to the moment. I need the intense concentration, the precious moments, sometimes as short as a fraction of a second, when my mind is completely focused only on the task at hand. It's therapy without talking. I've had those rare moments on a racquetball court, when all my senses merged together with time and movement. For a far too short ten or fifteen minutes in time, everything on the court slowed down. Frame by frame, the match played out in slow motion as if the game were playing me. Immersed in a waking dream, I knew what my opponent was doing and thinking. I knew exactly where the ball was going. When I casually arrived to meet the hundred mile-per-hour ball's three-dimensional rotation through space, it seemed to be moving so slowly I could read the manufacturers label. I had found the zone.

Surprisingly, I've experienced the same addictive moments of peace within the violence of full-speed collisions in football. As the facemask of my helmet drove into an opponent's chest just under his chin, it started and ended with a perfectly timed guttural yell, the same as a martial-arts "*Kiai*." Enveloped in a split second flash of light and silent peace, my hips exploding through my opponent's center of gravity, I was free, in a different state of consciousness, if only for a moment. I've never felt more alive. Even today, thirty-five years removed, I miss football mostly because of the intensity of those moments outside of time.

Like the silent moments on the racquetball court or football field, each corner on a racetrack is a miniature chess match, only at high-speed. Without distractions, able to focus on the purity of the moment, all I have to do is determine my braking and turn-in points, setting up for the apex of the turn, generating the drive and acceleration to the track out point. Each turn requires a clear mind while performing a series of multidimensional calculus, geometry, and physics. Like the squares on a chessboard, each asphalt turn on a track is the same—static and unchanging. What changes are the positions of the pieces on the board and motorcycles on the racetrack. Motorsports, and in particular, chess on a sport bike, reminded me to add patience to my combustible mixture of competitive instincts and intensity.

The day after my first motorcycle-racing course ended, I stood in a long line at the DMV, going through the process of un-licensing my sport bike. I would never ride on the streets again: it was too dangerous. Because the track and the learning process was so addictive, I also continued my education, attending more of Keith's racing schools. I also began attending local track-day events to further develop my new racing skills. After moving through time and space horizontally at 125 miles per hour, it was time to re-engage my vertical nemesis and the next phase of my project: flying upside-down in a combat military trainer dogfighting at twelve thousand feet.

CHAPTER TWENTY-TWO

My fear turns to fun

Following a guy like Murray Ball around Chamonix was a bit unnerving. After all, it was frightening getting here. It was a little frightening living here. It was very frightening skiing here. But the most frightening thing of all was that after a while you got used to it, and before long being scared was fun.

—Gregg Stump

The Blizzard of Ahhs

As the aircraft violently bounced around in the high wind and turbulence, each jarring gust forced the lightweight plane to radically change altitude and heading. Normally in situations like this I'd be terrified, reacting with tension, my stomach making the short journey up to my throat suffocating me from the inside out. It was bizarre but I was enjoying this encounter with heights and for the moment had no idea why. I was in this situation by choice, commuting to work from Vancouver across the Strait of Georgia to Nanaimo, British Columbia, a small city on the southeastern side of Vancouver Island. The difference with this daily business commute was that it wasn't by car, bus, train, or ferry but by a tiny, six-seat floatplane.

After leaving Bermuda for the short contract in Lisbon, I had a new consulting opportunity in the beautiful province of British Columbia. The assignment was to support a large group of credit unions convert to a new banking system. My high-pressure responsibility was to design and support the technical conversion, create all the financial reporting, and develop the post-conversion audit functions for the project. The first credit union being converted was in Nanaimo. On such a critical, high-visibility project, every hour was important. I'd been working twelve to fourteen hours per day, including an excruciatingly slow hour-and-a-half ferry ride both ways. The bank wanted more of my time, so I agreed that instead of the ferry, I'd take the shorter twenty-minute commute by floatplane.

Only hours before my first flight, I woke up from a nightmare at 4:00 a.m., my sweaty hands strangling the bedsheet I imagined was the seat of a floatplane. Still in the foggy dimension before full consciousness, I shakily walked to the kitchen for a glass of water, worrying my first flight would be a repeat of my nightmare. My actual experience was the opposite.

As nearby boats bobbed in the dark green water of Vancouver Harbor I made the early-morning walk to the plane wondering how, or if, I'd survive. I'd only been in a small plane once before—my infamous skydiving adventure in college. The floatplane had six seats: one for the pilot, five for passengers. Not knowing what to expect, I was in full avoidance mode and made sure to be last in line, delaying my boarding process until the last possible moment. As the other passengers politely squeezed into the four rear seats, all that remained was the copilot's seat directly to the right of the pilot.

I'm not a pilot and wouldn't have known what to do in an emergency, but the sunrise flight out of Vancouver Harbor was amazing. Watching the morning sun peeking over the eastern horizon from the front seat was comforting. More interesting than the fantastic views, I was studying the pilot, watching him adroitly moving levers, twisting knobs and speaking to the scratchy voices from control towers. I liked him immensely. He was similar to my Blackcomb ski instructor, Lorne: professional, reassuringly, and calm. Completely engaged and curious about the technical aspects of flying, each day after the first flight, I arrived early at the dock to claim the copilot's seat before burdening my new friend with a deluge of flying questions. I'd never looked forward to flying, but unknown doors of insight were opening into the rooms of my fear.

Outside of floatplane commutes and challenging consulting work, I spent every second of my free time taking full advantage of the Pacific Northwest's limitless opportunities for adventure. Every weekend in the winter, I'd drive up the coast on route 99, the breathtaking Sea-to-Sky Highway, to ski Blackcomb. Every Friday in the summer, I escaped Vancouver and the office, driving south across the US border, continuing through the state of Washington. Seven grueling hours later, I'd arrive in Hood River, Oregon, more commonly called "the Gorge", one of the world's famous windsurfing sites. I even learned how to surf in the chilly fifty-degree waters of the surf spot Long Beach, just outside the small coastal city of Tofino.

My favorite memory was sharing my BC lifestyle with my sister Kae. On her first trip to Vancouver we decided to ski Blackcomb. Over dinner on Vancouver's famous Robson Street we excitedly discussed the twenty centimeters of new snow forecasted for the next day. We also discussed her skiing ability. Spending a week every year skiing in Colorado with her husband Mike, she assured me she was a strong intermediate skier and enjoyed powder. The next day on the mountain, after a few easy warm-up runs, I discovered the snow she normally skied was on perfectly groomed intermediate runs with only an inch or two of dry Colorado snow.

Although she was a manager at a health club and worked out daily, after a few runs in Blackcomb's deeper powder, her legs were tiring. Her normal ski technique was to skid the back of her skis through her turns, which wasn't working in the heavier, lower-elevation snow. I began to worry that we were moving into a situation where she could easily become injured, twisting a knee or worse. After each awkward fall she kept telling me she was fine, but trying to be the helpful brother I made a terrible mistake. I suggested that we go higher on the mountain to the Blackcomb Glacier, where the snow might be a little lighter.

Sitting on the backside of the mountain range the glacier is huge, covering thousands of acres. When the snow is right, it's a skier's dream. When your baby sister from Nebraska hasn't skied deep powder, it's a daunting challenge. After skiing past Blackcomb's famous Blowhole, we started down the glacier's lighter snow. I skied ahead about fifty yards before stopping to catch my breath. Expecting to see her right behind me when I looked back, she was slumped down in the snow barely thirty feet from where we'd started.

Taking the opportunity to rest before she skied down, I took a breathtaking 360-degree scan of the magnificent, snow-capped cliffs. When I looked back again she still wasn't up or moving. In a protective panic of brotherly concern, with images of a torn ACL and the medical complexities of surgery in a foreign country racing through my mind, I clicked out of my skis and began the awkward ski-boot hike up the mountain. After ten minutes of high-altitude hiking I sat down next to her, asking if she was okay, but I already knew the answer. Through puffy red eyes and tears of frustration, she confessed, "I can't ski this type of snow, Danny. It's too hard."

I understood but unfortunately had to share that returning to the top of the glacier would be tough. A better option was for me to become her protective big brother again. She hated the first day of every new school year during classroom introductions when teachers always asked, "Oh. Kae Cass? Are you Dan Cass's little sister?" On the other hand, she took full advantage of it using my name to thwart unwanted attention from boys. "Do you know who *my* brother is? Dan Cass. He'll pound you. Leave me alone!" Instead of shielding her from adolescent boys, today's solution was to ski ahead twenty feet at a time, slowly clearing a path in the snow. It worked. After a few minor crashes and many rest periods, we made it safely off the glacier to groomed runs where she could enjoy Blackcomb. Exhausted but uninjured, a few days later, Kae returned home to Nebraska.

I've enjoyed the roles of protective brother, dependable teammate and helpful co-worker. I liked feeling needed, able to help others with their problems, but with the exception of critical work issues or ski mountain emergencies it's been my downfall in every personal relationship, always coming with a double-edged sword. At work, under the constant pressure of tight deadlines and huge financial consequences, I could focus on architectural solutions with cold, unfeeling pragmatism. I could do the same thing on almost any athletic field. Trying to help someone with a personal problem was never as black and white.

It only took three or four weeks after arriving in Vancouver before people began noticing I wasn't the overbearing consultant, my ego dominating every room or conversation. I spent most of my time observing and listening, asking lots of questions, and taking copious notes. I confirmed and reconfirmed my understanding on whiteboards. Eventually, over a Killer Whale Ale in a Granville Island pub, one of my clients asked, "How come you're so quiet? You never talk about yourself. Why don't you open up a little?"

The ice-cold beer in a frosty mug loosening my usual reticence, I replied, "To who? Complete strangers? Clients with huge business problems to solve? I'm not compelled to share my life. In fact, I'm incredibly particular, almost obsessively, with who I let into my inner sanctum. I'm not antisocial or misanthropic, but I've discovered most people don't care about my problems or worse, many are happy I have them. I often think it's inconsiderate—almost rude—to unnecessarily burden someone with a problem they can't help me solve. If I really wanted help, I'd find someone who had solved the same or similar problem. That way I wouldn't get an opinion empty of experience, or worse, emotional support without understanding. The problem is the people who can help are usually incredibly busy working on their own problems. Conversely, if I talk about my successes I feel it's arrogant, almost bragging. So in a sense I'm trapped into silence—or gossip, masquerading as social pleasantries."

"You don't share much, but you always seem so confident, like you know exactly where you're going and what you're doing."

"Thanks. I appreciate that."

"How do you do it?"

"I have a personal plan—a to-do list of goals—which keeps me focused. It's similar to a detailed project plan at work. I set my intention and then my attention before taking consistent action."

“Sounds like a lot of work. How can you be so sure your plan will succeed?”

“I’m not. I’m constantly reviewing and revising it. There aren’t any guarantees.”

“You’re different. Kind of weird, actually.”

“Yes, I’ve been aware of that fact for a very long time.”

“Maybe you could help me.”

“With what?”

“I’m not sure exactly what I want to do with my life.”

His downcast eyes and slumped shoulders revealing the level of his commitment, I wanted to emphatically respond “Absolutely not”, but politely settled for, “I’m sorry. I can’t help you with that.”

“Why not?”

“You’re not serious.”

“Yes, I am.”

“You’re not. If you were, you’d tell me the specific problem you’re having and how you got to that point. How am I supposed to help with such a broad, generic problem? Do you want me to feel something or do something?”

“I don’t know exactly, but I think about it all the time.”

“C’mon, Brian. You’re undisciplined and completely confused about the importance and sequence, of thought, word, and deed. A slave to your moment-by-moment level of emotional comfort, you’re stuck in a vicious cycle where you skip thinking, dwell in pointless small talk, and seldom take action. You’re a well-educated adult acting like a boy on Christmas morning, hoping Santa will bring you a new toy to keep you distracted for a few weeks. You’re a dilettante, a dabbler in life.”

Someone had called his bluff. But instead of acknowledging the obvious, he dug in. “That’s not fair.”

As he expectantly waited for my tacit agreement, apology or both, I surprised him. “What do you want me to do with that?”

“What?”

“The present you gave me.”

“What present?”

“Full of impulses and emotions, you took your big box of ‘I’m not happy’ before wrapping them in the ‘that’s not fair’ shiny paper of guilt. After that, you slid your problems over to me as an unwanted present. I simply removed the wrapping, returning your gift without a receipt. Enabling you with compassion and empathy is easy. In effect, they’re my emotional ‘get out of jail free’ card. I don’t have to do anything or take any risks. Instead of effusively validating your difficulties, I’m actually doing something to help you.”

Completely bewildered by the strange direction of the conversation, he resorted to attack, handing me the next unwanted present of guilt. “Don’t you have any feelings?”

“Of course I do. I’m not trying to be profound or provocative, but I’m taking a big chance. You’re a client so it would be more prudent restricting myself to business issues but after watching you make a few difficult decisions in the office, I thought using disruption would shake you out of your illusions. Unfortunately, you’re so used to everything sugar-coated and easy you expect me to lie to protect your tender feelings. I’m doing the opposite. You just can’t see the approach.

“Since we’re talking about feelings and emotions, let me explain *my* problems trying to help people like you. The first is that I clearly see what you’re going through. I often wish I could go through life blind or at least indifferent, but when I see you struggle, usually with problems needing little more than a simple decision, my desire to help shifts into overdrive. It’s a curse.

"As I patiently listen to your growing list of excuses, rationalizations and self-created distractions, my problems begin when I start doubting your sincerity. After you insist on complaining without taking even the smallest action, my doubt becomes frustration. Somewhere along the way, when I realize I have more belief in your abilities than you do, my frustration becomes anger. I feel like I've been played for a fool or worse, a sucker. Eventually, when everything has simmered into a bitter stew of contempt and disdain, I have to let you and your growing collection of excuses go, accepting you're an adult with free will consciously choosing to suffer.

"It's taken years of punishing disappointment wondering where I should draw the line to get to this point. At its simplest, my biggest problem is that I'm incredibly selfish. I like to help because it makes me feel good. Why else would I do it? I never help people out of guilt, social obligation, or misguided altruism. When I hold a door open for someone, I want them to acknowledge my kindness. A nod is all that's necessary. It's simple, but it's important to me.

"The problem is that no matter how much time or emotional support I invest, I can only help people as much as they want to change. It was hard, but when I realized I was often alone on the hill struggling to support someone's Sisyphean boulder of problems, I learned to step away. People like you are great teachers. You taught me to detach with an indifferent, insular shrug, coldly saying 'No' without explanation. I also learned the subtle difference between desperately wanting to help and knowing when it's pointless to even try.

"You called me quiet, but that's a misunderstanding. Silence is my protection. I used to carry people's self-created problems and drama with me for days or weeks. With intimate partners, it could be months. Now? I feel like the prophet Cassandra. I've been through it so many times with so many people, it takes me less than sixty seconds to see it coming from a mile away. Since we're being 'fair,' society requires I give you a present in return, but I'll be more direct.

What are *you* going to do to resolve the roller coaster of emotions you put me through in our short conversation?"

Although my question was rhetorical, I already knew he'd never considered his complaining could be a burden to others.

I couldn't detach so easily in intimate relationships though. I'd listen to women I deeply cared for sharing a problem. It was raining in their world and they were getting soaked to the bone. In the beginning I'd indirectly suggest they come in from the rain. It's dry inside. When they responded, the guilt-filled implication I should be more supportive, I'd hand them an umbrella in their favorite color and style. When the umbrella, viciously ripped to shreds was thrown back in rage, I'd reach my hand out into the pouring rain, patiently letting them feel my calm energy. Soon it became crystal clear it was all an impossible test, a form of indirect torture. Until I was standing in the rain with them, empathetically suffering together, nothing I could say or do would be enough.

The longer the relationship lasted, the more my problems were magnified. Weekend dinner parties compounded my social fatigue from the office. If I didn't go, I'd force my embarrassed and increasingly annoyed girlfriend to awkwardly answer the host's inquiry as to my whereabouts: "Oh, well, uh…he's just tired from work."

"Again? Is something wrong with him?"

In the beginning, they'd defend me, but eventually began to wonder if the host was right, I was "weird." If I did go, the tension was just as high because of the monumental effort to bounce around the room exchanging small talk and pleasantries without constantly checking my watch.

Every serious relationship typically ended with some variation of, "You've changed." The worst part? I had no way to deny it. In the beginning, I was new, exciting, and unpredictable, but I was only in the relationship because of my deep needs for emotional intimacy and uncompromising trust. A walking on/off switch, when I finally trusted a woman enough, I opened the door all the way. When I exposed my many vulnerabilities, I was often dismayed that instead of bringing us closer, the openness became a wedge slowly pushing us apart. They would never say it, but I saw doubt in their eyes and hesitation in their voices. I wasn't the unyielding pillar of strength and confidence they could always lean on. I had weaknesses. I had introduced uncertainty into the relationship and they didn't feel as safe anymore.

That was usually when I began settling, wearing a mask of benign acceptance I rationalized as healthy compromise. The primary mask I wore was avoidance. I tiptoed around every delicate subject, skillfully sidestepping any type of adult discussion or emotional quarrel. As a relationship advanced, I never insisted on candid conversations about children, money, sex, politics, religion, marriage, prenuptial agreements or even paternity tests. Discussions on personal goals or how we would grow as individuals or as a couple never occurred. We certainly never discussed how we would handle the inevitable disagreements and fights. My naïve idea of a successful relationship was no fighting or disagreements. We were in love. *Just make her happy.*

Although I loved the tension of explicit head-to-head competition with men, I hated confrontations with women. It was too emotionally expensive for me with little return on investment. Always lingering, hidden like mold, the emotions of previous arguments were poised to reemerge into the sunlight at any moment. No issue was ever fully resolved. The loving things I had done the day before were irrelevant and forgotten. All that mattered were her feelings in the moment. My feelings cycled from confusion to frustration and finally to anger, but I didn't explode. Instead I moved away and became distant, physically and emotionally. When I accepted the obvious that nothing I could do would ever make a difference, I began wearing the masks of denial and finally stoicism. Protecting every emotion by completely shutting them off, the guy they'd first met was long gone, effectively ending the relationship.

The opposite of the stereotypical unfeeling male, after my second divorce, it took over a year of self-prescribed relationship chastity for each painful mask to burn off. I wasn't lonely and didn't jump into bed with the next available woman because my ego needed attention and validation. I knew exactly who and what I was. Instead, I spent the year reexamining all my mistakes in every intimate relationship, matching thoughts and feelings to words and actions. When I finally realized that words and logic were meaningless without understanding the emotional context and current dynamics of the relationship it started to become more clear. The most devastating thing I began to do was questioning something I'd always believed was real: love and intimacy.

Blinded by obsequiousness, soft lips, and intoxicating perfume, I consistently missed the obvious patterns of behavior, believing the tearful apologies, distraught explanations, and sometimes, the outright deception. Once I began reading between the lines, I realized I'd only begun to scratch the surface of female nature and made a new set of personal promises. I'd no longer wear the masks of avoidance, acceptance or settling. I'd share all of my feelings—bluntly—when necessary. I also promised myself that if I ever lost respect or absolute trust for a woman, there was no getting it back. I might forgive, but I'd never forget. It was over. I was slamming a door on the relationship, in all its forms.

I knew I was finally ready to re-enter the dating world after an impromptu reunion with an old friend. Through the thick steam of my morning shower, a lively pair of smiling blue eyes stared back from the mirror. "I know you. You've been away far too long. Welcome back." It took twelve months, but with the suffocating masks painfully burned away, I could breathe again, my lungs filled with renewed optimism. Open but extremely cautious, I began carefully observing whether women's actions matched their words, particularly in the office.

Politics were changing. It had become unprofessional if not outright dangerous to compliment a woman's appearance. Holding a door open, being too friendly, or even eye contact held a moment too long could be misconstrued, leading to a career-ending harassment lawsuit. Not blinded by d'Orsay pumps beneath figure-hugging pencil skirts, I became an amateur anthropologist, voyeuristically studying women's behavior from a distance. When I discovered they were human, with weaknesses just like men and weren't always angelic, coated with sugar and spice and everything nice, especially with each other, I felt like a six-year-old boy after learning that Santa Claus, the Easter Bunny, and the Tooth-Fairy were myths. I was completely disillusioned. It was all a very *Grimm* fairytale.

All through school the competition in practice and games with men had been intense, but there was always a definitive line of respect. Pushed, prodded, and challenged, in the rare times the line was crossed, a slight nod of the head, a handshake or the minor acknowledgement, "Sorry about that. You OK?" was usually all that was necessary. Even with a hated rival. It was similar in the office. Our masculine emotions matching the escalating volume of our voices, we could argue various strategies and approaches, rarely allowing a business problem to become personal. If it did, after a few hours to cool down, it was common to easily repair the relationship with, "We're still on for that beer tonight aren't we?" Usually, my one on one interactions with women worked the same way: respectful, pleasant, and rewarding.

On the other hand, I had a front-row seat during junior high and high school witnessing titanic battles for power and control between my mother and sisters. Master manipulators, both sisters knew that a carefully placed word, designed to impart the most emotional pain, was just as effective as an hour-long screaming tantrum. I thought it was just an adolescent phase, a remnant of youth easily left behind, but after watching women compete against each other in the office, I completely changed my mind.

Most of the time interactions between women were civilized and professional, supporting both their careers and the company's bottom line. However, when an unseen line was crossed, a discussion became an argument instantly escalating to all out, scorch the earth war. From that moment every interaction contained deep layers of animosity and cruelty hidden beneath syrupy feminine politeness. Regardless of effort, situation, or results, vicious and vindictive, they took perverse pleasure belittling each other for every perceived or actual mistake. Completing projects and particularly team building, were of zero concern. There would be no apologetic nods over a beer or sharing a golf cart the next Saturday morning. Narcissistically engrossed with every opportunity to inflict maximum pain, I was witnessing emotional torture. When I noticed the hidden smiles beneath dancing eyes, I knew it was cruelty in the darkest sense. They weren't the kinder sex. They were brutal to one another, which led me to wonder: if a woman could take such immense pleasure doing that to one of her sisters, what could she do to a man—or me?

With a new outlook on relationships I cautiously began dating a stunning brunette I'd met at the gym. During one of our first dinners I tried sharing how guarded I could be in social situations but my explanations confused my new friend. One on one depending on the subject I could be as talkative as any of her friends. The difficulties began as we drove home after a Saturday-evening dinner at her parents' house. Vancouver's rainy streets empty of traffic, my new friend, extremely relieved she wouldn't have to drag me out of a shell shared, "Wow, you're not quiet. My family loved you. They even complimented you, saying you're a great conversationalist. Why do you keep saying you don't like socializing at parties? I watched you talking to them all night."

This was the hard part—where I had to help her understand and also keep a promise to myself. "I wasn't talking. I was listening. You watched a performance—one of my better ones actually—no different from what I do at work. When you saw me talking, I was initiating the topics. After that I carried the conversation, constantly making sure they were the topic and interjected with questions only about them. Mostly, I listened without interrupting. Unfortunately, no one tonight was gracious enough to reciprocate and ask anything about my life which I find incredibly rude. They certainly didn't seem protective of you in any way. They don't know a single fact about me other than I'm some sort of American computer geek dating their daughter. Instead of being a welcome guest in their home I was a convenient, captive audience. They talked 'at me', not with me. All night long. When you asked me to go to dinner I wasn't excited and knew it would be a lot of work, but I went for you trying to be as social as possible. I liked your family's dog though."

"Don't you think that's a little blunt? They're my family. Can't you just accept who they are?"

"*Family* is a loaded word. Are you using it as a noun or an excuse? I am accepting who they are. Exactly. I'm just not lying to myself about it. I'm also trying to help you understand why I don't enjoy most parties. Can I ask you a direct, possibly painful, question?"

Expecting another series of words assaulting her sensibilities or family, she paused. "Sure. I guess."

"Do you enjoy our long conversations lying on the couch until all hours of the morning?"

"You know I do. I love that about us. We can talk about anything for hours. But sometimes I feel uncomfortable, as if you can see right through me."

"Maybe your discomfort is because you're not used to people really listen to you. Instead of impatiently waiting for you to stop so I can resume talking, I'm listening. I'm not clairvoyant and you're not transparent. I'm paying attention, absorbing your words, letting them become part of me. I'm just interested in you. You've been building your career for—what? Somewhere around ten years?"

"Yes."

"Other than your VP title, do your parents or friends know how you spend your days? Do they wonder why you chose that line of work? Have they ever asked what it feels like when you've exceeded your already high expectations for yourself? How many times have you started dialing them, thrilled to share a fantastic new success, but you hung up, because you knew they'd never understand—or, more likely, didn't care?

"Here's the painful question. How is it I know the answer to those questions after only knowing you for eight weeks? Our conversations weren't manipulative foreplay simply to get you into bed. I'm listening. I study your face as you talk looking for clues. When I was a boy, I had an almost photographic memory about things I was interested in like sports. It's the same with you. I'm telling you all this now so you can decide if the attention you get from me in private is worth the difficulties we'll face in public."

It wasn't. Within a few weeks, I was single again. The authentic intimacy frightened her. I stayed single and in British Columbia until my contract ended. My next consulting assignment would be in Toronto where the stress of another large banking project would be huge. What I didn't know was that I was destined to face a new problem with Kae, where no matter what I did, no matter how hard I tried, I couldn't be her protective brother clearing an easy path through the snow for her.

CHAPTER TWENTY-THREE

Look where you want to go

Discipline is simply a function of remembering what you want.
—David Campbell

Every fall since 2000 a woman (who'd eventually become my third wife) and I went to see the Navy's Blue Angels' Fleet Week air show at Crissy Field in San Francisco. Contrasting with the peaceful rolling hills surrounding the Golden Gate Bridge, the blue-and-gold F/A-18s were an unbelievable show of raw power, technology and precision. Looking straight up, our necks straining to keep the planes in sight, we marveled that humans could build machines capable of performing such spectacular maneuvers. It was primal, the roar of the jets shaking the ground like prehistoric dinosaurs walking the planet. After one particularly great acrobatic show my friend casually remarked, "I'd do anything to fly in a jet"—not a commercial Boeing 747 but a military fighter, where she could pull excessive Gs and experience the overwhelming rush of pure adrenaline.

Her birthday was coming up, so my secret plan was to quickly find where I could make a surprise jet reservation for her. I spent weeks searching the Internet, attempting to get her a seat in a military jet but few if any options existed. The US military certainly wasn't in the business of giving joyrides to civilians. The only other option was Russia. A group of resourceful Soviet military pilots had grasped the obvious opportunities of capitalism and were giving rides in refurbished MiG-29s just outside of Moscow. The cost for the flight was an expensive $10,000, excluding travel expenses. After they converted the money to rubles, I suspect the former pilots were handsomely paid, but perhaps US military-style safety might not have been their top priority. So I scratched that option.

After a few more weeks of searching, I finally found Air Combat USA. Air Combat has been providing dogfighting excitement to civilians since 1988. They use former military pilots with actual combat-mission experience from Vietnam, Desert Storm, and the US Navy Fighter Weapons School (a.k.a. Topgun). The only downside was that aircraft wasn't a jet. It was a SIAI-Marchetti SF.260, a fully combat-ready trainer/fighter.

"Aren't you going to do it with me?" We were at her favorite restaurant celebrating her birthday as she opened the gift certificate. She'd be flying upside down, pulling 4.5 Gs at 270 miles per hour and preparing to shoot down another plane with a laser and wanted me to share the thrill. Contrasting her obvious excitement, I responded with a blunt, emphatic, "No way. I *am* afraid of heights." Watching her struggle to mask her surprise and disappointment, I knew my "I am" statement had been reactive. It was a terrible habit I'd developed when facing anything dealing with heights. This was one example where the world wasn't bombarding me with ridiculous messages about safety. I might as well have said, "I *am* a loser." I was doing it to myself and to my subconscious.

A month after her birthday dinner, I watched her exit the plane at the end of her combat-flying day exhausted, dripping with sweat, but with a jubilant smile on her face. I was happy for her, but wasn't paying attention to my reactions. I wasn't connecting the visual dots of her expressive body language or listening to the excitement in her voice. In full-on avoidance mode, relieved I hadn't put my butt in the tiny cockpit, I wasn't curious enough to ask her about the experience. I didn't ask, "Were you afraid?" or, "If you were afraid, how did you overcome it?" I didn't even have the personal insight to change my language too, "Look at the opportunity I didn't take advantage of."

Five years after passively watching my friend from the ground, I was making the short drive to the same airfield in Livermore, California. As part of this year's personal war with Daddy I'd be flying my own combat mission. This weekend was to be my graduation from the blue-hill ski run of my process, but I was extremely nervous. I 'm not a pilot and had no idea how to prepare for this event. Before the glider flight with Jon, as the customer I could tell him I didn't want to do loops and rolls with the aircraft. The point of Air Combat is the opposite, go full out. Loops, rolls and power dives.

Daddy has been busy working overtime, building one imaginary distraction after another. At work, in the gym, or before falling asleep, my mind bombarded me with a thousand negative thoughts: *Will I be able to do it? Will I get airsick after a few upside-down combat maneuvers before dejectedly telling the copilot the sensations are too much and asking him to get me back to the safety of the ground?*

With fear hovering in the background, my early-morning arrival in Livermore began the process of getting ready to compete in a civilian dogfight. Although I wasn't rushed or overwhelmed the program is designed and executed with military precision. Smudge, my copilot for the morning, was a former marine with over twelve hundred hours in the Marchetti. He'd be guiding me through the high-g, upside-down maneuvers.

After the excited introductions to my eighteen-year-old opponent and his copilot, we were fitted for flight suits, helmets and parachutes. We spent the next hour in ground school and mission pre-briefing, learning military-combat maneuvers: high and low yo-yos, vertical and oblique turns, and displacement rolls. While I'm not a pilot, I'm pretty sure those combat techniques are not taught at FAA flight schools.

Two hours into the process, I was squeezed into a tiny cockpit, shoulder to shoulder with Smudge. This was only the beginning of my discomfort. The Marchetti, designed for combat training, wouldn't be a relaxing joyride over Lake Tahoe with Jon skillfully flying the aircraft. While I scrutinized a confusing dashboard of cockpit gauges, Smudge explained he'd perform the takeoff, getting us up to four thousand feet. After that he'd give me the stick and with it, complete control of the aircraft. The aircraft has two synchronized sticks: one for me and the other for Smudge. It's sort of like high-school drivers-education cars with extra steering wheels (and brakes) for the instructors.

Sitting on the runway waiting for the control tower to give us takeoff clearance, Smudge casually mentioned, "Remember, if you don't want to get sick, make sure you keep your eyes on your opponent. Look where you want to go."

"What? Look where I want to go?"

I've been here before. I've heard that phrase at least a thousand times over my lifetime. I learned how to visualize while playing football. After hours imagining every play from every angle, I knew exactly how the play would unfold and where I was going. I did it playing basketball, taking thousands of shots. I've never taken a shot hoping or wondering if it would go in. Every attempt, whether it went in or not, began with a mental image of the ball dropping perfectly through the net. I've skied my best on the steepest hills when I kept my vision far down the mountain, past the immediate danger.

This mental exercise is exactly how I prepared in the martial arts. For weeks before a quarterly Tae Kwon Do test I'd sit in a quiet room at home, creating the upcoming performance in my head. I'd visualize what I would see from every angle of the dojo, sparring or performing my forms. I would imagine my supporting foot riveted to the ground, my kicking foot or hand violently driving through the wooden boards with ease before small wooden splinters slowly floated to the floor. Before arriving on the test day, I'd perfectly executed the board breaking, my form, the kicks, blocks and punches against imaginary opponents hundreds of times. The advantage of the weeks of visualization was that by the time the test arrived, I didn't have to think or worry. About anything.

I've also been using the critical tool of visualization during weekly skydiving practice sessions at iFly. Positioned in the wind-tunnel entrance before each two-minute flying session, I imagined with as much clarity as possible I was in the door of a Twin Otter skydiving plane, getting ready to drop into an empty void of air. To create this type of intense image, I can't simply show up to iFly at 9:30 am casually turning on a switch. Instead, I visualize for days prior to each practice session.

I heard the same phrase in the karting classes and again from the open-wheel FJR-50 coaches. I heard it repeatedly emphasized by Keith Code's motorcycle-racing instructors. "Look ahead to your braking and turning points. Once you begin braking, look through the apex of the turn to your track exit point as you smoothly roll back onto the throttle. At high speeds, the farther you look down the track, the slower it will feel." As we sat stuffed into a claustrophobic cockpit, seconds away from leaving the runway, Smudge reminded me again: "Focus your vision and intention on where you want to go and what you want to do."

As the engines reached full power, we shot down the runway in military formation, the planes side by side on the runway—which was amazing after flying commercial for so many years. My opponent's Marchetti was so close, it felt like I could stretch my arm out of the plexiglas cockpit and touch the gentle curve of its wing. Once Smudge nonchalantly maneuvered us to four thousand feet, he asked, "Are you ready to take the stick?" A first-time pilot, tentatively wrapping my sweating hand around a stick, I was guided with simple instructions as Smudge let me fly the aircraft up to ten thousand feet. I'd reached another satisfying milestone: flying an aircraft. But the next forty minutes would be spent practicing basic flying drills. With Air Combat and Smudge, this meant *combat* flying drills.

The first drill was to fly straight ahead until Smudge gave the command to pull back on the stick as hard as possible. A small movement of my right hand, no more than a couple of inches, caused the aircraft to shoot straight up. Instantly. I had never felt anything like it before in my life. No commercial aircraft turbulence could have prepared me for the feelings of five Gs of force. There was no feeling of danger, but the force was dramatic, almost overpowering.

The crushing physicality of the first maneuver surprised me, but I was alive, I hadn't gotten sick, and Smudge, leaning forward to get a better look at my reactions was grinning at me from ear to ear. After my introduction to the physics of g-forces, we began performing gentle rolls, plummeting straight down before pulling up as we fought the excess gravitational mass of our bodies.

After forty minutes of eye-opening, gut-wrenching moves, when the introductory combat-aviation drills were over, it was time to fight. The setup is simple. The two aircraft approach each other from a quarter of a mile away until their wings pass each other, signaling the fight is *on*! The ideal situation in a combat dogfight is to maximize two variables used to effectively shoot down the opponent: speed and altitude.

To get altitude I pulled back on the stick hard causing the aircraft to go straight up. Once we had enough altitude, I quickly pushed the stick to the left causing us to dive into a steep roll. Setting us up for our next move, the aircraft was pointing straight down as we chased after our opponent. Air Combat has installed laser based gun sights in each aircraft so the idea is to get the other aircraft in the gun sights before pulling the trigger, sending a flurry electronic signals masquerading as hot metal bullets. If I could get my plane in the correct position and pull the trigger, smoke would then pour out of my opponent's plane signaling the kill, ending the skirmish.

Smudge was great, calmly guiding me through each high-speed aerobatic maneuver. During the five missions we flew, Smudge gave precise instructions helping us accomplish our mission. Combat is a zero-sum game without any feel-good rules where no one gets their feelings hurt. I didn't begrudge my eighteen-year-old flying opponent winning three out of the five missions. I enjoyed the competition and didn't need a pretty gold star simply for showing up and participating.

Air Combat is not a relaxing joy ride. It's work. The flying is more exhausting than two hours in the gym. During a few maneuvers we pulled 4.2 Gs in an upside-down position, crushing my 170-pound body with 720pounds of force. After Smudge reminded me to "look where I wanted to go, I relaxed, redirecting my attention away from fear to today's problem: shooting down my opponent. With a specific goal, I didn't get sick or freeze up, staring at the ground spinning below me. The flying was difficult but exhilarating. After an intense hour alternating between grunting and grinning, getting the plane back on the ground was a letdown.

As I accepted Smudge's congratulatory handshake unexpected thoughts surged through my mind. The first was that I had a new level of respect for a high-school buddy who had become an officer in the Navy, flying F-14 Tomcat fighters. With aching neck muscles sending a preview of the next morning's pain, I was relieved to get back to the normal single g of gravity on earth. How could my high-school friend have withstood the punishing g-forces of a Tomcat?

My next thoughts were shocking as they came out of nowhere. *That was fun. Why don't I take flying lessons in the future? I could get really proficient at this.*

What? *That was fun?* Take flying lessons? Those couldn't be *my* thoughts. Where had they come from? Where had they been hiding? I left the airfield brimming with new thoughts and possibilities. The difference between the floatplane experience and this year's aeronautical excursions is that I now have a huge problem to solve and a detailed structure with which to solve it. In school I was asked to memorize facts and formulas, but I had little interest in rote memorization until one of my teachers asked me to apply the formulas. When I could solve specific speed and distance problems I engaged, understanding how the new tools could be used. My fifty-two-week plan is the same. I have a problem with fear to solve.

Today was a wildly successful graduation from the blue-hill phase of my project. My project began months ago when the doorway of fear beckoned me into a new room of uncertainty and adventure. With my hand wrapped around the door's cold steel handle, when I made a slight twist of my wrist and released the door with a soft click, a tiny crack of optimistic light had pierced my eyes. I knew it wouldn't be easy, but every bit of the project would be worth it.

Everything is on track. To continue my momentum, all I need to do now is remember to look where I want to go and avoid distractions. Where I want to go next is up my ladder challenging heights with visualization as an important tool. Next up: Heli-skiing.

CHAPTER TWENTY-FOUR

A reminder of my contract with death

Compassion hurts. When you feel connected to everything, you also feel responsible for everything. And you cannot turn away. Your destiny is bound with the destinies of others. You must either learn to carry the Universe or be crushed by it. You must grow strong enough to love the world, yet empty enough to sit down at the same table with its worst horrors.

—Andrew Boyd

After a great consulting assignment in British Columbia, I'd arrived at a huge, worldwide bank in Toronto, Ontario. Companies rarely hire high-paid consultants except in the most difficult situations, and this contract was no different. The problems are always the same: fear and uncertainty drive a lack of decision-making, leading to constant scope creep, expensive delays and the inevitable rework. I worked six days a week, fourteen hours per day, for an entire year supporting the installation of a new banking system. It's the reality of the consulting business.

Surrounded by dozens of people, most conversations in the office hallways or neighborhood pubs centered on work or hockey, subjects I enjoyed, but I needed something more substantive. Over the course of a few lunches one of my Canadian co-workers shared increasingly thought-provoking ideas about religion, spirituality, and the afterlife. I couldn't imagine attending Sunday church services, expected to introduce myself to fellow parishioners with awkward hugs, so I accepted his offer to join his men's weekly Bible-study group.

I wanted to be surrounded by men in a place where I could ask all the *enfant terrible* questions I couldn't ask at a dinner party. I was curious whether they had similar doubts as mine. I had thousands of questions swirling within a galaxy of different thoughts but didn't expect black-and-white answers. I wanted an exchange of ideas in which the beginning threads wound into a complex ball of new insights. I even wanted exposure to opinions or ways of thinking I didn't agree with.

After attending every Tuesday night for a few weeks patiently listening to the group leader take us through the evening's schedule, I had the temerity to raise my hand and ask, "When are we going to discuss this evening's content?"

"What do you mean, discuss? I'm not sure I understand your question."

Every eye in the room warily turned to the newcomer with the American accent, I continued. "It's actually a very basic question. When are we going to have a discussion? I'm interested in hearing what you and these men think."

"What kind of questions?"

"Well…for example, what about the concept of Original Sin? Does anyone here ever wonder if God sits on a throne, dispassionately sending the souls He created to a binary choice of everlasting torture or heavenly bliss based on an arbitrary sin, regardless of His gift of free will? Does anyone ever wonder when, or even if, their souls were created? What are their views on reincarnation? What do they think of John 10:34, 'Haven't I have said ye are Gods?' What do these gentlemen think of Thomas's writings found in the Gnostic Gospels? If the Big Bang was God's creative idea for existence, does anyone think he was only capable of *one* idea?"

His unspoken, yet well-understood reaction, written in a disconcerted, slightly threatened face was, "We don't want you to think for yourself, we'll do that for you." His polite Canadian response to my dangerous questions was, "Oh, no, we don't do that here. You're expected to memorize the passages letting scholars interpret the meanings." Starving for authentic, stimulating conversation, I'd set my expectations far too high and was paying for it with disappointment. I was trapped in another social event, the expected rules of behavior just as rigid. The only difference? Regurgitating bible scripture had replaced pointless gossip and small talk.

The biblical metaphor had become real. I've literally been walking in the *Shadow of the Valley of Death*. To my right were the fundamentalists, unequivocally convinced their interpretation of God was the one, and only, truth. On my left were the statists and secular atheists, unwaveringly certain that since God didn't exist, they would claim the mantle. Unburdened with troublesome doubts, each group was unyielding, adamant they were right. Unamusing to me, when each end of the extreme political spectrum wrapped around, the shadows of control were indistinguishable and just as dangerous. Competing oligarchies slowly acquiring power to dominate the world, the only differences were their methods to form and mold their collective of slaves.

When a dozen pairs of vacuous eyes shifted from me to the floor, I knew there would be no discussion, rigorous debate, or even disagreement. My seething rage barely contained, I wanted to scream, "Don't any of you have an original thought? You don't have any doubts? About anything?" Scanning the room for someone, anyone, to stand up and join me, I knew it was pointless. Disciples in the religion of fear, imaginative thinking and free speech were no longer a part of their lives. I wanted to eviscerate each one of them and their shared weakness. Instead, without a word I packed my things, put on my coat, and walked out of the room and with it, the soulless dogma of organized religion. Not surprisingly, no one chased after me asking me to reconsider.

I should have waited, but after failing to meet my minimal social needs in men's Bible study, I tentatively slipped my toes back into the dating world. Toronto was bursting with gorgeous, sophisticated women. I'd approach them in bars or at the gym, but many were attached or simply not interested. Like at a job interview, I, and I'm sure the woman, knew within the first two minutes if a relationship was a possibility, our initial chemistry confirming our intuition.

Since my arrival married women in the office, with one in particular, were constantly trying to set me up with their single girlfriends, usually without my consent. I was even covertly set up on blind dates I hadn't agreed to attend. I'd go to a party out of work obligations only to find a co-worker's single girlfriend was with her. Even for me, it didn't take long to understand I was expected to charm their friend, forcing me into the kitchen corner of uncomfortable chit-chat.

When I wasn't being ambushed at a party, I was often surprised at the office water cooler. "You should meet my friend Nicole. She's gorgeous. Slim, green eyes, and reddish hair. You'll love her."

"She sounds great. Tell me about her."

"She's really fun, dresses well, and has tons of friends."

"That's nice. Who is she? What does she do? What does she want from her life?"

"What do you mean, what does she want?"

"Passion. Beliefs. Aspirations? What does she think about?"

"I don't know. She likes trips to Las Vegas."

"How long has she been your friend?"

"At least ten years."

"You've known her for ten years and yet you still don't know what her dreams are? She's not a friend. At best she's a convenient acquaintance. Secondly, you want me to meet an 'I just want to have fun, party girl?' You're kidding right?"

Many dates were short, only lasting long enough to consume a cup of coffee. Some even made it to the polite end of a first dinner. Rarely did one last more than a month. One of the most memorable began its march to a climactic end in a bustling Toronto restaurant. In the middle of explaining my winding journey from Lincoln to Toronto, my date's cell phone beeped, prompting her to begin chatting with a girlfriend, completely ignoring me. She wouldn't even make eye contact.

I was willing to let it go until I realized the conversation was about me. Unconcerned that I was sitting directly in front of her, the flower of her hypergamy was in full bloom. I was 'the potential boyfriend' accessory, a checkmark on a list of things to acquire. Little more than a new purse or pair of pumps, I was a novelty experience and just as easily discarded. Accustomed to being interrupted and ignored in too many social situations, I tried being patient and polite, but I couldn't hide my annoyed facial expression or body language. Unless it was an emergency, I'd never consider taking a phone call while having dinner with someone.

When she finally hung up, she said, "Did it bother you I was talking to Mary?"

Instead of repeating the countless relationship mistakes of my past, always putting on the considerate, understanding face, I held her gaze for three or four uncomfortable seconds before sharing, "Yes, it's incredibly rude to talk about me as if I'm not here. Second, I'm selfish. If I wanted a threesome, it certainly wouldn't include her. Do you want to have dinner with Mary or me?"

Her eyes acknowledged a glimpse of understanding, but with a well-practiced, exasperated sigh, she stood firm. "She was only letting me know about a problem with her boyfriend."

"She always has some issue with him. She revels in her problems."

Signaling an escalation in my expected guilt, her softly rising eyebrows contrasting with the metallic tone of her voice, she snapped, "She's my friend."

"I have friends too, but I don't excuse their poor behavior. In fact, I expect far more from them. The next time she calls, give me your phone and I'll explain that two people are having dinner together and she's not invited."

This woman wasn't used to being challenged, either with or without the truth. As her outraged eyes tried to burn a hole in me, in perfectly whispered restaurant pitch, she screamed, "What the hell is wrong with you? Don't you have any feelings?"

"Of course I have feelings, but, unlike Mary, I think before acting on them. Since Mary knows we're spending an evening together, you don't find it rude of her to simply intrude on us? She might as well show up unannounced, pull up a third chair, and expect me to pay for her dinner. She's still a child, addicted to attention. I'll give you an example. Do you like helping her?"

"Of course. It's a great feeling. That's what *real* friends do."

"When was the last time you helped her?"

"Yesterday, on the phone."

"Does she still have the problem?"

"Well…yes. Sort of, I guess."

"So, how did you help? Does she have any type of plan, strategy, or inspiration to begin solving her problem?"

"I was being supportive of her! She's really trying."

"She's not trying. She's talking. I doubt she's ever had a single minute of quiet introspection. Has she ever *done* anything? Taken action of any type?"

"No. Not really."

"You're obviously a smart woman. You don't find it peculiar that she's always talking about her problems, yet never asks for your—or probably anyone else's—help?"

Her answer, hidden beneath equal parts understanding and denial, was an unblinking stare.

"You're completely confused about the dynamics of the friendship. Instead of helping or even being supportive, you're enabling her, feeding her addiction to attention like a drug dealer. She doesn't want your help. She needs the drama because she gets attention from you and probably every other guy in the world without her boyfriend knowing it. You accept it all to be the supportive friend. Everyone is comfortable because you don't challenge each other to grow. Her only troubles that I'm aware of are her fluctuating weight and her insensitive boyfriend, yet every time you meet, you share a two-thousand calorie dessert to celebrate an evening of commiserating about men. Why don't you actually *help* her one night, sharing that you're trying to watch your weight? Maybe then she could be supportive of you and join in your discipline."

"If I didn't share dessert, I'd feel guilty, as if I were better than her."

There it was. Hiding my disappointment behind an expressionless mask of politeness, I knew the relationship could never work. The incredibly capable woman two feet across the table lived with shifting, situational boundaries. Because she didn't believe in anything, she couldn't say no without feeling guilty. When Mary shared every detail of her intimate relationships, she'd demand and receive reciprocation from my friend. I couldn't allow it. I need privacy. I'd already learned the hard way. Dating a woman often meant that whatever I shared in confidence, no matter how private, would be repeated without a filter. I didn't want to date a group of women: Mary, her girlfriends or her mother.

I'd been through this before with a former girlfriend. A couple hours after arriving together at a friend's crowded house party, I needed a short break, escaping to an upstairs bathroom. Unfortunately, five minutes later my attempt at relaxation was interrupted when I heard a familiar voice. My girlfriend, just outside the door in the hallway, was enthusiastically sharing a laundry list of my many shortcomings with a sympathetic girlfriend. My first reaction was confusion. If she was going to criticize me she could at least do it well. She was missing most of my obvious faults as a man. When it became obvious that the critiques would not be ending I opened the washroom door into the hallway and the sordid conversation.

When I met the downcast eyes of a woman who had said she loved me, my confusion quickly turned to disappointment and then anger. She didn't love me, faults and all. She loved her projected idea of me, which obviously I hadn't been living up to. She would have my back only when it was convenient or if I was standing in front of her. I should have demanded an explanation how she could be comfortable, if not delighted, sarcastically denigrating me with an approving girlfriend. After that I should have ended the relationship, screaming she was too stupid to see my real weaknesses, but instead of believing her actions, I fell for the Academy Award-winning performance: the tearful apology, the specious pleas for forgiveness and the empty promises. It was my first tangible lesson learning about the massive difference between shame and guilt. It's also taken me years of suffering to learn that honesty was the highest form of intimacy. I wasn't going to repeat the same mistake at tonight's table.

How could the woman on the phone be her best friend, yet she was interested in me? I was everything her friend wasn't. Was she a bad judge of character, or was I? As she stared in disbelief, I began the first sentence of the last paragraph of the evening and our soon-to-be-short relationship. "If she's such a great friend, what is it about her you admire and respect? When have you ever left a dinner inspired by her strength? What would she have to do for you to say, 'Because of you, I never gave up?'"

When she realized I was judging her by the character of the friends she kept, she predictably pushed back from the table, grabbing her phone in disgust. As she stormed out of the restaurant, I knew it was necessary to abruptly end the matchmaking in the office.

Early Monday morning, my insistent matchmaker cornered me in the coffee room, curious about my date. I was certain she'd already spoken with my dinner companion but I played along, sharing it hadn't ended well and that maybe it would be better if I met someone on my own. Oblivious, or unconcerned with my uncomfortable body language she shifted into her favorite role: the fixer of the world's problems. Because she was a woman who'd never been wrong, she knew what was best for everyone, whether they liked it or not. Undeterred that she didn't know anything about me other than I had an American accent and wore expensive Italian suits she began describing the next woman she expected me to meet.

My unspoken intent often written between the lines, why does every conversation become a competition where the person who ignores or interrupts the most, talks the loudest or longest, is declared the winner? Unable to listen to my soft-spoken sentences, every syllable and pause deliberately chosen, the only way to get her attention was to shock her into discomfort. Knowing my next few sentences were necessary to snap her out of her bubble of maternal certainty I asked, "Does your friend understand men?"

Surprised by such a silly question she replied, her overt condescension appropriate for speaking to a misbehaving child. "Well, of course. Men are simple creatures. Food, sex, sports, and cars!"

Unsurprised and unamused by her response, my instinct was to simply walk away. She would only hear what she wanted to hear. But she had pushed me into a corner, forcing me to escalate, so after a few deep, unseen breaths, I finally said, "Some of us have a little more complexity and depth. Does she have an edge?"

She wouldn't budge, sarcastically replying, "What do you mean, 'have an edge?'"

"I mean, is she mysterious? Can she be unpredictable? Dangerous even? When necessary, a sleek black panther patiently stalking her prey, every sinewy muscle tensed, ready to spring?"

I finally had her full attention, but still lost, her eyes darted around the room searching for any type of easy answer. "I don't understand what you're trying to say."

"I know you don't, so let me help you. If your friend is the good girl next door with minimal self-confidence and even fewer boundaries, always trying to please everyone around her, she'll bore me to death in less than ten minutes." As she struggled to comprehend, I mercifully drew her a mental picture.

Carefully setting my coffee cup on the counter, I paused, letting her absorb the intention of my unblinking, unsmiling face. "Does your friend have the confidence to stroll naked into a bedroom wearing nothing but pumps and a devious grin, carrying a blindfold in one hand while gracefully twirling a pair of handcuffs in the other?" I didn't take any pleasure watching the blood drain from her face, but she got the message: the matchmaking in the office stopped immediately.

Regardless that my enjoyment of the daily floatplane-commuting experience was effectively balanced out with too many failed relationship attempts with women, life would provide stark reminders putting perspective on what's important.

My reminder was an awful, tear-filled phone call from my mother in December of 1997. Bathed in a dark cloud of bewilderment and disbelief, almost unable to speak in between sobs of agony, she whispered Kae had been diagnosed with pancreatic cancer that had spread to her liver. That announcement began the ghastly process where I watched my baby sister wither away, dying right before my eyes. She seemed to be perfectly healthy in the prime of her life, but something in her body triggered a chemical sequence of events cascading into cancer.

In the past when I found myself worrying too much about things I couldn't control, I'd assuage my angst with the common phrase, "What's the worst thing that could happen?" Usually, that line of thinking worked well. Not now. I was there. The worst thing was happening. Devastated and helpless, I instinctively knew my willpower, discipline, and goal setting wouldn't be enough to prevent Kae's untimely death. Unlike the path through the snow I'd created for her on Blackcomb's glacier, this was a problem I couldn't fix no matter how hard I tried. I could extend my own life with good personal habits, but like my own eventual death, there was nothing I could do to reverse her illness.

A few days later, I was in a protective trance during my flight from Toronto to Lincoln, each leg of the journey bringing me closer to pain and suffering. After picking up a rental car, I was numb, mechanically driving without emotion to the hospital. Even walking across the hospital parking lot was torture, a prisoner's one-way walk to the gallows. The feelings intensified as the doors of the hospital elevator closed, trapping me on my unwanted journey. Reluctantly walking down sterile corridors filled with rooms of dying patients and heartbroken families, I resented grade school for teaching me the math to understand the sequence of numbers on the doors bringing me to her room. Worst of all was the moment when I turned her door's handle, wondering what I'd find inside. I didn't know what I was going to say or do. Fortunately, her body wasn't yet feeling the devastating effects of cancer. She was still Kae, as stubborn and determined as ever.

For six months I flew back and forth to Lincoln having long discussions with her about God, life, death, and family. While her death was a tragedy, it was also the most beautiful time of my life. The honesty permeating every conversation with family and close friends brought us much closer. Everyone's masks had been set aside, allowing deep vulnerability to shine through. I also felt needed. Working in Toronto I'd frequently receive phone calls from her girlfriends that always began, "Danny, she needs you to come back. She knows you're incredibly busy, but she just wants you here." On the day of my returns, I was told that every hour she'd wake up from her painkilling, drug-induced sleep and anxiously ask, "Is Danny here yet?"

It wasn't necessary for me to do much. All I had to do was arrive as requested, hold her hand, and gaze into her eyes with a soft smile. I didn't have to put on an act; nor did I have to parrot the socially accepted phrases that anesthetize instead of comfort. Being needed was gratifying, and it put me at ease. I could be myself. We talked for hours, usually about nothing, but our small talk had a purpose. Sometimes I'd laugh with her or because she needed the comfort of feeling normal again, I'd laugh at her as if we were back in junior high.

Lacking any real understanding of the mysteries and hidden beauty of life our discussions were unusually simple. We weren't blessed, or burdened, with profound spiritual revelations or philosophical comforts. Before her illness, I'd spent many hours contemplating four fundamental questions of life without any definitive answers: *Who am I? Where do I come from? What is my purpose? What happens to me when I die?* At an odd time or two during our conversations I became aware of explicit feelings of longing and curiosity. I waited for a few trips, but when the flow of our conversations provided an opening, I shared that a part of me envied her. I didn't envy the physically debilitating process ravaging her body or her losing the remaining dreams of her life, but I envied that she'd soon slip through the veil to where answers to my questions might be found.

Although I wasn't the person dying, her illness forced me to traverse my own version of Elisabeth Kübler-Ross's five stages of grief: denial, anger, bargaining, depression, and acceptance. I passed through denial only after strangling myself with a thousand thoughts: *This can't be happening, especially to Kae. She's too healthy. There must have been a misdiagnosis. If the diagnosis was accurate, surely there had to be a cure to save her. This is 1998, when medical miracles happen every day.*

After the shock of denial, I spent a lot of time dedicated to the emotion of anger. I was furious at Kae. She'd ingested carcinogens into her body, smoking with her "cool" friends since she was fifteen. I was incensed with myself for not forcing her, or the rest of my family, to quit such a stupid habit. I was frustrated with the world's research scientists, who hadn't yet developed a cure for her cancer. In particular, I was enraged at God. Unable to comprehend his indifference cruelly sending my sister, parents, and brother-in-law on a pointless journey of suffering, I was beginning to doubt the possibility or the reasons for His existence.

When I couldn't continue maintaining the poisonous levels of anger any longer, I moved to bargaining a place where actions replaced emotions, often leading to tangible solutions. Comfortable believing in a world of right and wrong, good and evil, the black or white chess pieces winning or losing, I was convinced every problem had a solution. The only problem was I'd never negotiated directly with God.

From the outside, I can seem quiet or shy. On the inside, I've always had a constant inner dialogue with dozens of simultaneous conversations. This time I'd shift my focus to a single conversation. With God. With nothing to lose but the emptiness of despair, I indignantly offered my soul in exchange for the power to perform a miracle. I wanted to save Kae from death and free my parents and brother-in-law from their suffering. All problems solved—or so I thought.

If I could bargain for the power to save my sister, why not go further eliminating all pancreatic cancer around the world? Permanently. Surely God wouldn't mind someone taking up some of his slack? I'd use the new power, metaphorically placing my hands on every pancreatic patient around the world. Riding a seductive wave of helpfulness, it wasn't difficult to move from curing pancreatic cancer to ending all cancer everywhere. After that, it seemed logical that if I could end every form of cancer, why not end all disease—even the common cold?

One after the other, my tsunami of solutions quickly washing away the world's problems, it seemed heartless not to end all forms of pain and suffering. Skipping evolution's slow, drawn-out cruelty forcing the world to suffer through eons of adaptation, I'd remove anger, greed, and envy from the human experience. Disagreements, or even the slightest tension of differing opinions, simply wouldn't exist. Not only would I use my new powers to create a perfect world safe from disease, poverty, accidents and war, I'd do everything, once and for all, today. The lure of simplistic power had become addictive.

After iterating through hundreds of strategies to save the world, the ultimate goal was to smugly stand before God, arrogantly sharing my elaborate plans for fixing His mess. That's when my ego's plans for a world without suffering began a descent into depression, a bottomless pit of darkness I'd never imagined and couldn't escape. Each time I rehearsed a talking point, variation of logic or reasoning, my depression deepened. Every day, I had thousands of silent discussions with God, each one ending in a frustrating quagmire of cause and effect.

All of my ideas to save the world began to fall apart one day when He silently asked, "Why would you steal the joy of so many people? Especially without their consent?"

I was indignant, defensively snapping, "I'm not stealing anyone's joy, I'm helping! Removing a problem is always a good thing! I'm eliminating the problems *You* allow! If You or your Son are so powerful, why doesn't one of you fix everything and end everyone's suffering?"

Gently sidestepping my insult masked as a question, He probed deeper. "Fair enough, Dan. But after you've ended all disease, what are doctors, nurses, and the millions of others dedicated to helping others going to do with their lives?" Blinded by feelings of self-importance, I became despondent, spiraling toward suicide. My misguided helpfulness would extinguish the meaning of life and joy for millions. An emotional thief caught red-handed, I quickly changed the subject, sharing that in my perfect world, the hopes and dreams of every person would be filled immediately, without the need for effort or struggle.

"That's kind of you, but I hope you don't mind a few more questions. I need more information before I can fully appreciate the ramifications of your plans for the world. So if a woman longs to be the world's greatest soprano, your idea is to eliminate her arduous but rewarding journey? Without overcoming the insurmountable obstacles and adversity, how is she going to experience her private moment of unspeakable joy and satisfaction — 'I did it!'? You don't find it particularly cruel to take that from her? You're comfortable being Santa Clause, treating her like a child, but what is she going to do the day after Christmas? Not only is the joy of helping others impossible in your world, but with instant gratification, you've removed tenacity, persistence, and maturity built on patience. Really?"

The moment He asked, "If disease and suffering don't exist, does anyone die in your world?", I knew I'd been exposed, my simplistic ideas abruptly stopping at every solution's sentence-ending period. I felt better every time I eliminated a problem, but a new one, usually magnitudes worse, instantly filled the void. My childish ideas were effectively a desire to change human nature. Fear, jealousy, anger, and greed would be gone, but so would hope, compassion, empathy, and forgiveness. With zero critical thought, unable to connect more than two dots in a row, I was creating a world lobotomized of human emotion, a perfect dystopian hell on earth. I'd infantilized the planet creating an entire world of eight-year-olds needing to be protected, fed, and cared for. That power, and burden, would all have been on me. Everything crystallized into perfect balance when I wondered, *what would I do,* after I'd fixed the world?

I couldn't see that without up, there could be no down. Left was only relative to right. How could masculine exist without feminine? They weren't in opposition. They were complimentary. Necessary even. Without up or down, or left or right, what did that mean for right and wrong? The duality and relativism of life were ironic. I like the feelings I get from helping people, but to do that, another person has to have some type of problem, large or small. Perhaps the Gnostic Gospels were correct and the Kingdom of Heaven *is* spread upon the earth. Unable to see the synchronistic design of life's perfection, instead of helping, I, and particularly my misguided ideas for saving the world, were incredibly dangerous.

Long ago I'd read Nicholas Sparks' quote, "Without suffering, there'd be no compassion." I'd grasped the cause-and-effect simplicity of his logic but not its deeper meaning. I'd felt sorry for my parents before, even twinges of empathy trying to imagine the struggles they went through in life, but it wasn't until squarely in the middle of death, helplessness and suffering that a hidden reservoir of emotion began to open. I'd loved them as parents, but I'd never approached how much I loved them now as beautiful but fragile human beings. For me to experience the beauty of human compassion at its most sublime, the bitter truth was that Kae had to die and my parents and brother-in-law had to suffer, unbearably. Although terribly painful, even horrific, the problems of the world exist *for* us.

Before her cancer I thought I could control, manipulate, or at least influence every part of my life, but I've been a fool. I hate quitting and despise giving up, but I've never been in control of anything. It wasn't until my illusions of control burst into flames during a family tragedy that the door to understanding and acceptance began to open, ever so slightly. Without the deepest emotions, especially compassion, forgiveness, and empathy, what's the point of human existence? Not only did I have to accept my sister was going to die, I had to embrace and accept that my illusions of control were just that: illusions. I knew it would be difficult, but it was time to begin learning a new skill: surrendering to acceptance.

I wasn't with her, but I know the exact moment she died: July 4, 1998, at 3:30 p.m. (PST). I was taking a shower after a long windsurfing session in San Francisco. Hands loosely holding onto the chrome showerhead above me, my forearms rested against the shower wall supporting the weight of my body. Head slumped down, my chin resting on my chest, the stream of hot water massaged my aching muscles when something unusual began to happen. I felt something, but it wasn't the heat from the water. It wasn't the mist rising from the shower's floor. It wasn't even a strange sound.

It was Kae.

I could feel her, but not with my skin. I could hear her, but not with my ears. Without understanding how it was possible, the energy of her soul had wrapped around me, surrounding me in a supernatural cocoon of ineffable compassion. In one moment, I was alone, my mortal body relaxing into the simple pleasure of a hot shower. In the next, I was transformed, tears of ecstasy streaming down my face.

Her presence only lasted for five or ten seconds, but it was as timeless as the universe. It was her goodbye present, helping me release the last six months of helplessness and turmoil. In a final act of sibling love, she ripped me out of my five senses of human awareness. Wordlessly whispering she was safe, happy and would see me soon, I was overcome with a peace and acceptance I never knew existed. For twenty minutes of bone wracking sobs and salty tears, I wept in pure release. Ten seconds alone in a shower confirmed what all the church sermons and religious texts in the world hadn't been able to convey. We are all blessed, with nothing to fear.

Moments before joining me in the shower her life ended in Lincoln surrounded by love. She'd left the hospital to live her last few weeks at home under hospice care. She wanted to enjoy the simple pleasure sitting in her backyard in a chaise lounge, feeling the warmth of the sun caress her face as she enjoyed a beer with friends and family. It was a time to wait before finally letting go of her ravaged body. For the last few days, in and out of consciousness, she had struggled, her body fighting for survival. Finally, her day of release had come. In her last hour, her husband had gently held her tiny, emaciated hand as my mother sat quietly in the corner of the bedroom. Everyone had been waiting, but it wasn't until late afternoon that Kae began to stir.

With a violent cough, she suddenly sat up. For the first time in days, her beautiful eyes were clear, the gray, hazy fog of drugs replaced with a serene lucidity. She could see again, but she wasn't paying attention to anyone in the room. She was staring and smiling at something at the foot of the bed. As her last smile stretched into her famous dimples, she reached out in joyous anticipation, drawn to something unseen. Finally letting go of her last breath, her lifeless body fell back on her pillow. She had gone home.

I flew back to Lincoln the next day. As I'd anticipated, over five hundred friends came to say farewell. Even her hospice nurses had fallen in love with her and attended the funeral. The day went as well as could be expected, mostly because of Kae. She had known exactly what she wanted, planning everything down to the last detail: the type of flowers, which photos of her to display, and even what types of comfort some of her close friends might need. We spent hours together discussing what I'd say during the eulogy, whether the attendees would understand, and trying to make the message simple but impactful.

Terribly sad and emotional but not nervous, I had no problems giving the eulogy in front of five hundred people. I wasn't performing though. I was helping everyone in the room. Although I'd known them only indirectly, it was difficult to see her closest girlfriends suffer. But it wasn't until meeting a member of her gym that I appreciated the full effect of Kae's kindness. A frail man in his late seventies, he'd waited until I was alone to share his condolences and thank me for the eulogy. He had tried to be strong, but as he shook my hand and shared that she'd always treated him with respect and compassion, vulnerable tears streamed down his wrinkled face.

Robotically moving through the rest of the final goodbye, I didn't want to be a victim selfishly crying in agony and impotence, "it's not fair." She had lived a great life with innumerable friends and great adventures. While her death was a tragedy, a part of her still remains with me as a daily reminder. I often hear her distinctive voice whispering, "Danny. Don't take your life for granted. Don't wait to be happy, don't worry and please don't be afraid. Live!"

CHAPTER TWENTY-FIVE

I'm not an adrenaline junkie

The more a man is playing his real edge the more valuable he is as good company for other men, the more he can be trusted to be authentic and fully present. Where a man's edge is located is less important than whether he is actually living his edge in truth, rather than being lazy or deluded.

—David Deida

The Way of the Superior Man

"By helicopter?"

Only at Mike Wiegele's heli-skiing operation in Blue River, British Columbia, does a waitress in its rustic dining hall answer the question "How far is it from Blue River to Revelstoke?" with that particular response. I was sitting in the beautiful dining room, enjoying a cup of coffee anticipating a day of heli-skiing flying up and down the Cariboo and Monashee ranges of the Canadian Rockies. Being dropped on a steep mountain peak by a helicopter was another way to challenge fear while enjoying a week of backcountry skiing.

I fell in love with Canada and its people during my consulting work and was thrilled to be back. I made the short flight from San Francisco to Vancouver Friday morning. Not surprisingly, after landing my bags arrived at the bustling luggage carousel long before I did, even on the opening-day chaos of the 2010 Winter Olympics. I know of only two countries in the world where checked bags consistently arrive at the luggage carousel before you do: Japan and Canada. While I don't believe any country in the world can surpass the service levels in Japan, the Canadians are just as sincere in their desire to be good hosts.

After a short commuter flight from Vancouver into the sleepy logging town of Kamloops, a Saturday-morning shuttle to Blue River turned into a two-and-a-half-hour homecoming. British Columbia welcomed me back to its rural, rugged beauty. Away from Canada for over ten years, I wasn't surprised how much I missed it or how much I felt at home.

My week of heli-skiing officially began with an abrupt wake-up call: the helicopter's first landing at the heliport. I thought it would safely land in the distance before an expert guide opened the door shuttling us in one-by-one. My expectations couldn't have been more wrong. Huddled together, kneeling to avoid getting blown over, the helicopter hovered directly above us, the *thump, thump* of rotor blades violently shaking the ground. Seconds later—in the middle of a blinding snowstorm, —the helicopter landed less than five feet in front of us.

I started the week unsure but watched my apprehension become positive anticipation when I realized the Bell 212 helicopter was more stable than a floatplane over the Straits of Georgia or even a large commercial jet. As we roared over another snow-capped peak, I wondered if the stability of a helicopter is similar to that of a high-speed motorcycle. The stability of a motorcycle comes from the counterbalancing rotational force from of a pair of gyroscopes: its two wheels. The faster you ride, the more stable the bike becomes. A helicopter has a main blade and a tail rotor which provides the stabilization forces.

Fundamentally, the helicopter functions as a high-speed chairlift with almost unlimited access to the mountain. The daily ski routine consisted of quick flights up the mountain to remote landing zones where excited exits from the helicopter led to more runs through untracked, waist-deep powder. At the end of a few thousand meters of thigh-burning perfection, the helicopter waited to transport us to the top of another snow-capped peak. Under blue skies on pristine glaciers of dry powder, the stillness of the mountains disturbed only by the distinctive noise of the returning helicopter, it was a week of skiing heaven. Even the non-skiing parts of the week were great.

Every day at 11:30 a.m. we stopped for sandwiches, hot soup, bananas, and flavored tea. As we shared lunch on the tops of remote, isolated mountains, the wordless grins of adventure seekers permeated our temporary camp. My internal smile a mile wide, I knew I wouldn't have been surrounded by skiers from the United States, Canada, Austria, Venezuela, Argentina, Germany, and New Zealand if I hadn't made the decision to challenge the Sudan fifteen years ago. I was also surprised at how comfortable I felt. Almost social.

When I arrived I didn't know a single person. I was expecting a week of skiing surrounded by strangers, their eyes hidden behind goggles, but I was completely wrong. After the first day I knew a dozen people and they knew me. They asked where I was from, what I did for a living, and where I skied. Validating their own ski journeys, they even asked why I'd made the decision to heli-ski. It was thrilling to have two-way conversations with adults outside the office. Showering after a long day on the mountain before heading down to the dining hall, I was shocked when I found myself looking forward to spending a social evening with over a hundred people. I was even more surprised at how disappointed I felt when the evening began drawing to a close.

Sitting shoulder to shoulder at a rustic table strewn with empty plates, this was the time of night when the aroma of the last sips in the wine glass surpassed the taste. I was ready for bed but couldn't excuse myself from passionate discussions about soccer in a half-dozen accents. Trying to pull me into the conversation, my new friends wondered, did I play soccer? "No, I've never played. Sadly, all I see are seven-year-old boys in adult bodies randomly chasing after a ball."

Coming from a country where soccer had barely existed when I was in school, I was half expecting to be ridiculed, but one by one around the table they explained how important soccer had been to them growing up and in adulthood. I didn't understand soccer and couldn't appreciate the subtle beauty of the game, but I recognized their passion. When every Venezuelan at the table set aside nationalistic rivalries and solemnly nodded in respect after one of the Argentinians said, "Lionel Messi was a genius," I realized I'd already met my new friends.

My new friends were all from different countries, but I knew their character and curiosity for life. I'd sat with them in football locker rooms. Some spoke broken English with a charming accent, but I'd already discussed racing suspensions with them at the track. I'd even rigged a sail next to them on Maui's north shore. I was sitting with another group of people who enjoyed difficult personal challenges. Heli-skiing wasn't a weekend novelty, something to pass the time, alleviating boredom. It was a difficult activity, dangerous even, requiring years of work and perseverance. Like characters from a few favorite books I've reread dozens of times, my new friends were members of a tribe I knew well. It was one of the very few times in my life that I wanted a social event to continue.

The challenges of my social awkwardness a background whisper, the only issue of the week was extreme avalanche danger. The week before my arrival the weather had been warm and sunny, creating a surface layer of hardened ice and snow, while each night for the last three or four days, fresh dry powder had accumulated on the mountain. This set the perfect conditions for waist-deep-powder skiing. It was also a textbook scenario for a potential avalanche.

On the third day of the trip, I witnessed the uncontainable violence of an avalanche when our lead ski guide performed a ski cut to check the stability of the slope's snow. As our group stood in a safe zone twenty or thirty feet above him, we watched him carefully ski from left to right, making small jumps until the snow suddenly broke free under him. Fortunately, he was able to ski out of danger, but the entire side of the mountain, a meter deep and fifty wide, was gone. Only a class three avalanche, the destructive power of nature was a vivid eye-opener. Although watching a slab of snow the size of a football field disappear was humbling, I was more mindful than afraid: I understood exactly what had happened. I also knew that our guides had kept us safe. We were skiing on the correct terrain far away from the thirty-eight-degree slopes, or steeper, where the avalanche danger was severe.

It was incredible to feel nature's power while the mountainside fell away, but I've never been an adrenaline junkie seeking risk for the sake of risk. I'm certainly an addict, but my drug of choice is intensity. The feelings watching tons of snow slide off a Canadian mountain were exactly the same as watching an engrossing movie. For two riveting hours the outside world slips away. Hidden in the darkness of a theatre, I'm part of the cast, following the twists and turns of the plot, anticipating the next scene, completely oblivious to people sitting around me.

I have similar feelings playing chess. I'm not moving, but the concentration is the same. Mentally, my hair is on fire as I intensely study the flow of the board before moving a piece to a new strategic position. I've had the same single-mindedness in the quiet of a living room, absorbing every syllable, sentence, and paragraph of a book I can't put down. Playing football brought me the greatest highs of intensity and focus. Deep inside the physicality of football, hidden within the pages of a book, or hunched over a chessboard—when the past and the future don't exist— I could find peace, surrendering to the intensity of the moment.

Intensity is my cocaine, but it's always come with a huge post-high letdown. I loved playing football, but win or lose, when the final second ticked off the clock the competition was over forcing a return to everyday life. The beautiful bubble of intensity had burst, making me wait impatiently for the next game. When I've closed the last page of an extraordinary book, I've often sat on the couch for hours, overwhelmed with the empty emotion of "it's over", wondering what to do next. I'd invested hours developing relationships with the book's characters, entangling myself in their adventures, but without another page to turn, it was like breaking up with a lover. It's the same with an engrossing movie. They always end with crushing disappointment. I enter the theater knowing the experience won't last long, but as the ending credits begin scrolling, unspeakable feelings of resignation return. I feel diminished, reluctantly strolling back to my car and into the glaring harshness of day-to-day reality.

The final scene from this year's movie, the last page of my mystery, and the final tick of the game clock will all soon arrive. I'm satisfied I've prepared well. Although I'll eventually have to answer the question I've repeatedly asked, "Now what?", it's been a fascinating year full of ups and downs watching Daddy's subtle but constant attempts to influence me.

Next up on this year's journey is the climactic weekend jumping out of an airplane.

CHAPTER TWENTY-SIX

Alone, unemployed, homeless

It is not the critic who counts: not the man who points out how the strong man stumbles or where the doer of deeds could have done better. The credit belongs to the man who is actually in the arena, whose face is marred by dust and sweat and blood, who strives valiantly, who errs and comes up short again and again, because there is no effort without error or shortcoming, but who knows the great enthusiasms, the great devotions, who spends himself for a worthy cause; who, at the best, knows, in the end, the triumph of high achievement, and who, at the worst, if he fails, at least he fails while daring greatly, so that his place shall never be with those cold and timid souls who knew neither victory nor defeat.

—Theodore Roosevelt

During the last six months of Kae's shortened life, my consulting contract ended and my Canadian work permit expired. I would have loved to stay in Canada enjoying her natural splendor and people, but it was time to return home to the United States, at least for the short term. The question on the table was where? My current interests were snow skiing, windsurfing, technology, martial arts and the Japanese language, so while Nebraska and the Midwest in general had been a great place to grow up, it was also a great place to be *from*.

Although I'd never been there, I chose San Francisco. The Bay Area had strong winds in the summer for windsurfing, the Sierra Mountains provided great snow skiing in the winter, and the dot-com technology explosion was well underway in Silicon Valley. I've been in this situation before: I didn't know a single person, I didn't have a job or even a permanent place to live. The blunt reality: I was unemployed, single, and homeless, completely alone in a metropolitan area of five million people. Terrifying to many of my more risk-averse friends, after moving to new cities around the world starting new life chapters a number of times already the move to the Bay Area was uneventful.

After my 1992 moving-to-Bermuda sale I still hadn't reacquired many possessions except for a few business suits, more sports gear, and a new motorcycle. Excitedly stuffing everything into the bed of my truck, I headed south across the Canadian border. I stayed in a hotel for a week while exploring the beauty of the Bay Area and eventually discovered the tiny town of Larkspur hidden fifteen minutes north of the Golden Gate Bridge. After taking a few months off to unwind from the office I began to miss the day-to-day grind and pleasure of solving problems in the work environment. I was missing the mental challenge working with interesting people solving difficult technical problems. Most surprisingly, I was also missing the social aspects of leading a team in a challenging work environment.

As a senior executive or consultant I'm responsible for setting the direction and activities of my teams. Although hundreds of variables all compete for limited resources I can prioritize projects with ease, quickly deciding which direction to move. With the responsibility of a large staff it's often necessary to be socially outgoing, even gregarious. Probably because of the specific technical objectives and concrete business goals, I'm able to enjoy the social environment of the office, guiding staff and peers, smiling with the simple pleasure working with others. The contradiction is that out of the office I can happily go for days where the full extent of my daily vocabulary consists of five words: "Small Americano, please. Thank you."

I recognize that for many people speaking in public is a huge fear. Some even half-jokingly say that after public speaking, death is number two on their list. Regardless of the excruciating shyness of my childhood and my continued adult reluctance to convert into a bubbly social extrovert, I don't mind standing on a stage sharing thoughts and insights from my technology and banking career. I don't seek out speaking opportunities, but I'm comfortable in front of people, either on stage or in the office. In the beginning I was often surprised as words flowed from my lips until I realized my comfort came because I was well prepared and the speech had a specific purpose. It's a performance, part of my job. I'm in control of the topic as well as the ebb and flow of the conversation. It wasn't mindless chitchat about nothing; it was directed extroversion: a structured conversation with a meaning and purpose.

Conversely, at a crowded post-speech cocktail party, I find interacting with others difficult to the point of social ineptness. Lost and bewildered, shuffling from foot to foot, I'm often awkwardly fidgeting with the stem on my wine glass or unconsciously peeling a wet label off a perspiring beer bottle. I've been too lively neighborhood parties and felt isolated. I've been in huge auditoriums filled with hundreds of people and never felt more alone. Trapped in loud smoky bars, I've tried feigning interest in the obnoxious chatter of half-drunken strangers who didn't really care if I were listening or not. I've even tried asserting my existence, loudly talking back at a faceless stranger until I noticed they weren't listening, only impatiently waiting for me to stop so they could continue to rattle on.

I can feel the energy of people almost instantly. If they're calm, their attention in the moment, I can connect and chat for hours. If they're unfocused, diffused in a myriad of circling thoughts and worries, constantly glancing around the room, I have to get away. I understand the utility of small talk but to survive an entire evening, mostly where I'm assigned the role of designated listener, I have to make sure I've had plenty of rest, usually days of private downtime to recharge, before subjecting myself to the overwhelming roar of a crowded room. In the beginning my introversion protects me, a thick exoskeleton shielding me from the roar, but eventually the mass of people becomes a painful sponge literally sucking the life out of me.

Without a rested body and mind I have no tools to protect my energy other than escape. As familiar feelings of anxiety slowly increase, I either retreat to the washroom for short, ten-minute refreshers or find some way to discreetly but politely escape the event. I often inwardly joke it would be easier going to a convention of ravenous vampires uninterested in conversation, my blood type tattooed on my forehead, so they can ease my suffering by ending my evening with a violent bite to my jugular. I know others around me feel awkward trying to include me in their conversations. If it's any consolation to them, I feel just the same or worse. I've often left parties wondering how I can be a semi-extrovert in the office and a borderline hermit outside of it. How is it possible to be two completely different people—a chameleon in human form?

To answer that question, between long hours at the golf range refining the nuances of my swing I used the time off to prepare for new career opportunities. Instead of relying on my strengths of cold logic and long-term strategy, I wanted to explore and improve my weaknesses. I took two personality assessments. The first was a DiSC behavioral profile. The second was the Meyers-Briggs Type Indicator test. I've been assigned many labels in life. Junior-high teachers labeled me poor at math, and because I was quiet in school, I was called conceited, arrogant, and antisocial. Out of school, I was derisively called computer nerd, geek, or jock. Most of the labels were superficial, only helping people around me feel better. The labels, assigned by those who didn't really know me, never helped explain my personality. The Meyers-Briggs test explained everything. It also gave me a new label—INTJ: Introverted, iNtuitive, Thinking, Judging.

A summary INTJ profile by Marina Margaret Heiss from February, 2005 describes me well:

> To outsiders, INTJs may appear to project an aura of "definiteness," of self-confidence. This self-confidence, sometimes mistaken for simple arrogance by the less decisive, is actually of a very specific rather than a general nature; its source

lies in the specialized knowledge systems that most INTJs start building at an early age. When it comes to their own areas of expertise—and INTJs can have several—they will be able to tell you almost immediately whether or not they can help you, and if so, how. INTJs know what they know, and perhaps still more importantly, they know what they don't know.

INTJs are perfectionists, with a seemingly endless capacity for improving upon anything that takes their interest. What prevents them from becoming chronically bogged down in this pursuit of perfection is the pragmatism so characteristic of the type: INTJs apply (often ruthlessly) the criterion "Does it work?" to everything from their own research efforts to the prevailing social norms. This in turn produces an unusual independence of mind, freeing the INTJ from the constraints of authority, convention, or sentiment for its own sake.

INTJs are known as the "Systems Builders" of the types, perhaps in part because they possess the unusual trait combination of imagination and reliability. Whatever system an INTJ happens to be working on is for them the equivalent of a moral cause to an INFJ; both perfectionism and disregard for authority may come into play, as INTJs can be unsparing of both themselves and the others on the project. Anyone considered to be "slacking," including superiors, will lose their respect—and will generally be made aware of this; INTJs have also been known to take it upon themselves to implement critical decisions without consulting their supervisors or co-workers. On the other hand, they do tend to be scrupulous and even-handed about recognizing the individual contributions that have gone into a project, and have a gift for seizing opportunities which others might not even notice.

In the broadest terms, what INTJs "do" tends to be what they "know." Typical INTJ career choices are in the sciences and engineering, but they can be found wherever a combination of intellect and incisiveness are required (e.g., law, some areas of academia). INTJs can rise to management positions when they are willing to invest time in marketing their abilities as well as enhancing them, and (whether for the sake of ambition or the desire for privacy) many also find it useful to learn to simulate some degree of surface conformism in order to mask their inherent unconventionality.

Personal relationships, particularly romantic ones, can be the INTJ's Achilles heel. While they are capable of caring deeply for others (usually a select few), and are willing to spend a great deal of time and effort on a relationship, the knowledge and self-confidence that make them so successful in other areas can suddenly abandon or mislead them in interpersonal situations.

This happens in part because many INTJs do not readily grasp the social rituals; for instance, they tend to have little patience and less understanding of such things as small talk and flirtation (which most types consider half the fun of a relationship). To complicate matters, INTJs are usually extremely private people, and can often be naturally impassive as well, which makes them easy to misread and misunderstand. Perhaps the most fundamental problem, however, is that INTJs really want people to make sense. This sometimes results in a peculiar naïveté, paralleling that of many Fs—only instead of expecting inexhaustible affection and empathy from a romantic relationship, the INTJ will expect inexhaustible reasonability and directness.

Probably the strongest INTJ assets in the interpersonal area are their intuitive abilities and their willingness to "work at" a relationship. Although as Ts they do not always have the kind of natural empathy that many Fs do, the Intuitive function can often act as a good substitute by synthesizing the probable meanings behind such things as tone of voice, turn of phrase, and facial expression. This ability can then be honed and directed by consistent, repeated efforts to understand and support those they care about, and those relationships which ultimately do become established with an INTJ tend to be characterized by their robustness, stability, and good communications.

I already knew I was different from most people but didn't understand how many standard deviations out toward the lunatic fringe of the bell curve I resided. I wasn't a physical freak on the football field, but in the general male population less than two percent of men have the classification INTJ. A female INTJ is even rarer at less than one percent. After receiving my surprising new label, I asked a trusted friend to review the test results and share her opinion. Surely I couldn't be that weird, antisocial, or different, but I'd asked the right person for feedback. Like always, she was candid but kind and strong enough to tell me the obvious truth: "Yes, Dan, this is exactly you." The results of the MBTI test and her feedback helped me understand many puzzling episodes from my past.

The INTJ label put my escape from the chaos of a second-grade classroom fully into context. As an adult, I've had similar panic attacks.

Only three years ago I ate the full cost of a plane ticket the day before Thanksgiving, the busiest travel day of the year. Already worn down from work, dealing with regulators, attorneys, staff—and, worse, commuters sharing the road—when I arrived at the airport terminal, a crescendo of harried force began an assault on my senses. After standing in a crowded check-in line of impatient, pushy travelers, I knew other punishments were waiting for me. First, I'd have to wade through the robotic bureaucracy of the TSA. After that I'd be forced to stand in the claustrophobic jetway before being herded into a stuffy, cramped aircraft full of screaming kids on their first flight. I couldn't do it. Like the second-grade boy in full panic mode, I escaped into the cool night air of San Francisco before calling my father telling him I wouldn't be making the trip. I assured him I'd be home in five weeks for Christmas but there was absolutely no way I could board the suffocating tube of aluminum.

The test shed a light on how I could lead conversations in the office, engaging everyone at multiple layers of abstraction, but with the same people three hours later in a neighborhood pub silently sip on a beer for hours. If I'm the host of a party or event, I can work a room like a debutante's mother, approaching complete strangers, introducing myself with a warm smile—but I'm an actor with a job to do. The test certainly helped me understand my relationships with women. An enigma to women and often to myself, I might as well have been raised in a different culture, speaking a foreign language. The test results explained why most women had to work so hard to get past my formidable defense layers. I've always had deep emotions, but to express them, I had to trust someone completely. It's a challenge that continues, even more so today.

When often asked, "Why don't you smile more? Are you upset?" the silent speech bubble drawn above my head would scream, "Pay attention! Can't you see my eyes are dancing? I'm observing. Listening. Absorbing. Everything around me." It helped me recognize that when people were trying to fix me by bringing me out of my shell, their solution was usually to talk more, not less. I've never been rude enough to say it, but I've often thought, '*If you want to bring me out of my shell, why don't you talk less? How about using sentences where every other word out of your mouth isn't I, me, or my?*' The test results helped me understand that when I go to a party, I'm often relieved the hosts have a dog I can befriend. It explained how I've come to depend on noise-canceling earbuds protecting me from the roar of a coffee shop or crowded airplane. It explained my continued reluctance to accept rides to a party because I have no easy way to make an "Irish exit" calling it an early evening.

When I'm at a party that lasts too long, it feels like my nerves are exposed to the air. Eventually, when my bones start to ache like I have the flu, I have to leave. My sensitivity to chaotic energy is perfectly illustrated in a photograph from an important game against a heated high-school rival. I had sat shoulder to shoulder with my teammates in a silent, tension-filled pregame locker room but three minutes before kickoff, when team members excitedly gather together to jump up and down screaming encouragement at each other, I stood alone outside the frenetic bubble of excitement. Only five feet away from my teammates I might as well have been on the other side of the planet. As the captain I should have been in the center of the mass of humans screaming at the top of my lungs. I wasn't afraid of the violence of the game to come, but I couldn't get in the huddle.

As layer after layer of my inner personality was pulled back by the test I felt like an infant, learning how to breathe on my own for the first time. I finally had a more accurate description for my social awkwardness other than weird, conceited or shy. Although my parents were exceedingly social, with close friends at the house for cards, cocktails and dinner every weekend, they never tried to force me to be more outgoing. While I've often felt different and uncomfortable, I've never had a single moment feeling shame or guilt about my reserved personality. Always extremely private and self-reflective I became aware for the first time that I certainly wasn't alone. Joining me were millions who needed significant amounts of downtime completely away from people to recharge.

Understanding the INTJ label certainly helped me understand my career. It helped me understand why working at a floor-to-ceiling white-board, living in a dense network of ideas and strategic planning, seemed so natural. Intuitively I could see the patterns and interfaces before synthesizing fluid concepts into solid plans of action—not only of technical systems and people but also difficult-to-verbalize abstract concepts and approaches. Using analogy, metaphor, and a flow of images, I could develop strategies with elaborate contingencies, sharing the intuitive logic with staff, helping them grasp the long-range concepts. The whiteboard was a two-dimensional window into my multidimensional mind.

Work was easy. Unlike many of my co-workers, it wasn't natural for me to worry about getting a project done without hurting anyone's feelings or making them the slightest bit uncomfortable. Throughout my career I'd watch co-workers paralyzed at the beginning of a project. A large part of their emotional process was to make sure everyone was comfortable and no one's feelings got hurt. Once that was accomplished they could get to the real job of completing the project. The problem was that at the beginning of almost every project, everyone is naturally anxious because the project is new, with many unknowns. Everyone *should* be nervous at that point, so I never worried about it. I couldn't imagine going to my boss when a project was late and explaining we had to get everyone's input and make sure no one was upset before proceeding.

With a new label and huge perspective shift in personal awareness, I wasn't shy, I started interviewing and quickly found a challenging position: managing a large technology staff at a huge national bank. My new position, while interesting, also reminded me of my most difficult problems at, or outside of work: people.

The first problem was hiring staff. Although I could teach technology, banking and process, it was practically impossible to teach curiosity, courage, or character. Like height on a basketball court or speed on a football field, candidates either had those attributes or not. I was looking for experts in learning as opposed to experts in a particular technology. A new candidate would have to learn our business, technologies and processes, quickly. Trying to explain this concept to some of the more bureaucratic, check-the-box HR staff was often futile and frustrating. During the screening process unless a resume listed one-hundred percent of every technology we used, HR would often pass on exceptional candidates. When I asked them why a candidate bubbling with curiosity, interested in learning new things and growing as an individual would come to the bank if they already met one-hundred percent of our criteria, I was often met with blank stares.

I was forced to explain that curious, motivated people with resiliency and resourcefulness weren't simply looking for a job, they wanted to grow. When I told HR that I only wanted three position titles, Junior Problem Solver, Senior Problem Solver and Complex Problem Solver, with corresponding compensation packages, their heads exploded. I didn't need software engineers. I needed problems to be solved. Even as an INTJ, I realized hiring staff was often more of an art than a science. My intuition rarely failing me, I usually knew within the first fifty-one seconds of an interview if the person in front of me was going to receive an offer.

For the first six to ten weeks at a new company I've always attended as many meetings as possible to observe the communication styles and my new staff's decision-making processes. The difference in those early weeks was I rarely spoke. I listened and absorbed, constantly taking notes. After becoming comfortable with the daily dynamics, I eventually asserted my presence and unique way of viewing the world. I've been in hundreds if not thousands of meetings, but the most important have been where I wasn't invited.

Purposefully entering my new staff's meetings twenty minutes after they began I'd often discover the meetings' content was nothing but a random series of pointless observations. Although I knew exactly how the meetings were going—they were little more than cocktail-party social exchanges with a few three-letter acronyms thrown in for good measure—I was often forced to politely ask, "How's the meeting going?"

"Great!"

"Can you share the meeting agenda with me?"

"Oh, we don't do that here."

"You don't do what?"

"We've never used agendas. We just get together and talk. You know. Well, we…collaborate."

"OK. Then what's the purpose of the meeting?"

"Project priorities. We have hundreds of projects we're working on."

"How do you decide where to begin prioritizing? How will you know if your meeting is a success? How do you differentiate between a discussion loaded with assumptions and implications or specific decisions with concrete, measurable objectives?"

"Well, we just sort of…you know…wing it. Well, we do a lot of brainstorming. We get together and discuss things. It's kind of like a consensus team-building meeting."

When I asked for specifics, I received obvious, transparent, and dull generalizations hidden in politically-correct euphemisms. The meeting attendees were completely confused. There was no tangible structure that could be measured or managed. No project plans. No structured architecture. Socratic, critical thinking was nowhere to be seen. They were having an after-work social hour in the office—with the same sense of urgency. There was nothing in the room but empty thought bubbles floating in the air.

Slowly looking around the table, meeting the eyes of each person, I shared, "It seems that the business teams, in particular their managers with decision-making responsibilities, weren't invited."

"Well, they just sort of tell us what they want. We've always done it that way."

"Are their project requests written down, or does the request just informally happen in the office hallways?"

"They're too busy to be bothered with documentation."

"OK. So when you've loosely guessed at the relative importance of their vague project requests when do you meet with them to share your prioritization so they'll know when to expect the software and begin training their staffs?

As I received the expected looks of terror I had to carefully explain that they were accepting all the risk by unilaterally prioritizing competing projects for the various business units without any understanding of metrics or relative value to the business. Unperturbed and unsurprised, I was forced to take over the meeting and introduce them to a new concept—prioritization based on math and measurement, not emotions.

"Is the business happy with IT now?"

"Well, no, not really. They derisively call us 'the black hole where projects go to die.'"

"Have you shared a list of completed projects for the year?"

"We don't have time for that. And if we did, it would seem like bragging."

"Then how does anyone objectively measure how IT is performing?"

As another group of embarrassed staff members kept their eyes glued to the table, I began helping by putting projects into initial categories of *critical*, *important*, and *next in queue*. As we discussed a minor project that had been on the list for over three years. I also introduced a surprising new acronym: IYD.

"What's IYD?"

"'In Your Dreams.' It looks like there are at least two hundred projects with more measurable value than this one."

"We can't do that. We need to get this done. It's embarrassing. It's been on the list for over three years. The business expects it as soon as possible, and if it doesn't get it, management will be upset."

"Sounds like they've been unhappy for a long time, but they're smart. Can you define the metrics of 'ASAP'? What're the criteria for deciding? Where are their ROI numbers and business justification other than an emotional 'We want it!' Do we have a yes/no I.T. Embarrassment flag on your spreadsheet? If the project's priority is low and if a nonexistent ROI allowed it to sit on the list for this long, my suggestion is to remove it. Completely."

"Can we work on the project while we do the other projects?"

"Absolutely not. If the critical projects with the highest ROI are late, how can we possibly explain that we squeezed this project in just because we were embarrassed? After the meeting I'll share the priorities with the business units asking for their input. I'll also tell them we're removing that project for good."

"What if someone from the business asks me to work on a project not on the critical list?"

"You're an adult professional working on higher-priority projects. Tell them no, or ask them to come speak with me."

"They'll be upset."

"Well then you have a problem. And a choice. If you say yes, doing the project under the covers, you'll be teaching me you're a child and I can't trust you. Then I'll be upset. Who would you rather upset? To help you, I'll ask the business managers to tell their staff not to informally insist on squeezing in their low priority projects."

After introducing and integrating the black-and-white concepts of emotionless prioritization, I began to enjoy working for the bank but was eventually lured away by a tough, direct, and no-nonsense Chinese woman at a huge securities-trading company. During the interview I knew within minutes I wanted to work for her. More importantly, I wanted to work side by side with her. I could feel her focus and discipline. I respected her and wanted to be around her penetrating, contagious energy.

After accepting the job offer, I managed the staff and activities of the bank's international back-office trading applications. Working with this powerful woman was easy: she knew exactly what she wanted. Tough but consistent, she never engaged me in a moment-by-moment Easter-egg hunt forcing me to discover and rediscover which way her emotional compass was pointing. Over lunch one day I joked with her that she was such a logical, direct thinker that I considered her a guy, in drag. Unfortunately, other companies saw her talent. Only ten weeks after my arrival, when she and I had hit our stride together, she was offered an executive position at a Bay Area dot.com. Her departure created a corporate reorganization forcing me to report to a gentleman out of our New York City office.

I tried giving my new boss the benefit of the doubt, but after the first few conference calls I realized he wasn't as black and white as my former boss. I had to work extremely hard to understand exactly what he wanted. I had to work even harder to hold him to a decision, however vague. Although he was using all the right words and acronyms, he wasn't committed to their deeper, strategic meanings. I was back on the Nebraska practice field again. My new boss was just like the graduate assistant coach: another actor playing a role. Without substance, the dull words from my new boss's well-practiced script were just as empty and passionless.

Arriving in San Francisco a month later to meet his new staff, he was wearing the expected suit and correct color of tie, but his empty handshake matched the intensity of his words on conference calls. It was a physical act with no depth or commitment. The day after his departure, I began looking outside the bank for a company led by someone to whom the value of a handshake meant everything.

CHAPTER TWENTY-SEVEN

Flipping my graduation tassel, at 12,500 feet

Come to the edge.
We can't, we're afraid.
Come to the edge.
We can't, we'll fall.
Come to the edge.
And they came.
And he pushed them.
And they flew.
—Guillaume Apollinaire

Almost a year ago today, an hour before leaving the office for another ski weekend, I asked a key staff member to calculate the ROI on her worry and guilt. Less than eight hours after that unusual meeting I had my emotional breakdown on the Cliff, the catharsis setting a year's worth of activity in motion. The next day the release of physical rage on the Wave guided me back to the simple pleasure of personal growth: competing against myself by setting challenging if not impossible goals. I've spent the last fifty-one weeks diligently preparing for this weekend. Day by day, using process and discipline, I've methodically executed my plan to challenge my nemesis, "Daddy."

After a short Friday-morning flight from San Francisco, I arrived at Perris Valley Skydiving an hour east of Los Angeles. From the moment I strolled into the main compound area I was sure I'd made the correct choice. Although Perris is a huge, world-class facility, I felt welcome, walking through grassy rigging areas watching hundreds of skydivers skillfully pack parachutes while discussing free-fall formations in a dozen different languages. Everyone was friendly, typically giving a respectful nod of recognition even to strangers like me. Soaking in the atmosphere of another nomadic tribe of adventurers, I spent the day taking video, watching the jumps, and getting a feel for the rhythm of skydiving. As the day slipped by I was also trying to wrap my head around the fact that in less than twenty-four hours I'd be doing the same thing: jumping from an airplane. I'd been planning this weekend for an entire year and expected to be nervous but I certainly wasn't prepared for the series of surprises tomorrow would bring.

I slept well and after making the short Saturday-morning drive to the drop zone I met Andy, my instructor and tandem partner for the day. For forty-five minutes, with almost military precision, Andy carefully explained what we would do in the plane, falling at terminal velocity, floating under the canopy, and finally how we would land.

As I pulled on a jumpsuit everything seemed to be going as expected until I received the first of the day's surprises. For the last six months I've watched hundreds of online videos. I specifically targeted videos of skydivers jumping from one of Perris's main aircraft, a Twin Otter with the large exit door on the left side of the plane. Then I'd stand on my living room couch, my left foot hanging over the cushioned edge imagining I was stepping off twelve thousand feet to the carpeted floor.

Unfortunately, this was the weekend of a large skydiving event. Competition jumpers from around the world had come to Southern California to perform intricate, hundred-person formations as they fell to the earth. Their jump planes, the entire fleet of the Twin Otters, would fly to eighteen thousand feet providing the altitude necessary to complete the choreographed flight dances. Because all the Twin Otters were busy Andy casually mentioned we'd be using the last plane available: A Skyvan. Appropriately nicknamed the "Flying Pig," the aircraft is little more than a short, fat, rectangular aluminum box fitted with wings. My surprise jumping from a different type of aircraft was compounded when I was told the exit door of the Pig opens at the back, similar to a military C-130 cargo plane. If I wanted the Navy Seal HALO skydiving experience, this was the closest way to do it.

Andy and I climbed into the plane with a dozen excited skydivers. Because we were the only tandem pair on the flight we would jump last. Moving as far forward as we could, we squeezed onto uncomfortable metal seats before clicking on our seatbelts. Trying to absorb the activities around me, I watched the hydraulic rear cargo door close, trapping me inside, before the Pig's powerful engine began coughing and snorting, building up the necessary torque and horsepower to propel us down the long runway. Matching the excited rhythm of my heartbeat, the Pig bounced down the concrete and gently lifted off the ground beginning the slow, circular ascent to our jump altitude.

My third surprise of the day arrived less than five minutes before we jumped. Over the din of roaring engines, Andy yelled at me to stand up and move my back closer to him so he could attach our harnesses. After the last reassuring click of metal joining us together, Andy adjusted the rig, cinching and tightening each thick nylon strap. When he was done strapping us together, he casually yelled into my ear his plan to exit the cargo door with a backflip! I was incredulous. I'm not a gymnast or a high-wire trapeze artist. I was trapped inside of a plane. I was also strapped and trapped onto Andy. Now I'm going to be performing a backflip out of a plane. Really? I definitely hadn't prepared for this possibility and yelled at him to repeat his plan.

As the roar of the engines backed off, signaling our arrival at the jump altitude, the jumpmaster calmly walked to the rear and pushed the button for the cargo door. Inch by inch the hydraulic door crept open, exposing an endless blue horizon. Within seconds the jumps began. One by one, almost nonchalant in mannerism and demeanor, each skydiver took a single step and dropped from sight.

I've spent an entire year moving up my ski hill metaphor, working on my ability to relax under the pressure of pure fear. I've been preparing for this moment using every physical and mental technique in my toolbox, but with each passing second it's becoming difficult to think and practically impossible to stay calm. I tried relaxing, breathing as slowly and deeply as possible, but the realization of what I was doing really began to sink in. My heart-rate is accelerating and my mouth is as dry as a desert. I can't swallow, and my tongue is made of cotton balls stealing every drop of moisture. As soon as the last jumper dropped out of sight, Andy and I stood up.

The videographer I hired to record the moment was at the exit door, waiting for Andy and I to make our jump. My legs just inside of his, Andy and I began an awkward waddle to the exit door. As we inched closer and closer to the rear of the plane, my job was to simply look up at the ceiling—probably to prevent a last-second panic attack creating a dangerous situation.

I hadn't prepared for a backflip 12,500 feet out of the back of a Pig…but the exit was easy. I didn't have the sensation of falling where my stomach is in my throat; nor did I feel we were tumbling out of control. Within a few seconds we regained a stable free-fall position.

As the earth rushed up at us, I was surprisingly comfortable, like I was back in the dry heat of the iFly wind tunnel. I didn't have a single thought about dying or any type of emergency such as the chute not opening. The videographer skillfully flew up to us smiling the entire time while he took video of us performing horizontal spins. I'd read about the abstract concept of time compression during a first skydive and although we fell for only fifty seconds, it felt compressed into about ten. My sense of time distorted, everything was happening so fast I forgot I was wearing an altimeter, a crucial safety device for a skydiver.

As we plummeted to our deployment altitude of five thousand feet Andy pointed at his altimeter before motioning for me to pull the pilot chute out into the airflow. I had practiced checking my altimeter before pulling an imaginary pilot chute dozens of times at iFly, but it took a moment before I realized what he was asking me to do. Trying to coordinate a glance at the altimeter on my left hand while reaching back with my right hand for the pilot chute, I was fumbling and grasping, trying to find the plastic handle. Again and again I missed it. With green-and-gold agricultural fields getting bigger every second Andy couldn't wait any longer and pulled the pilot chute out into the wind releasing the main canopy.

While it's the part of the skydive with the slowest speed and definitely the lowest decibel levels the parachute opening began the most unexpected, frightening part of the day. The first problem was I didn't know how the opening of the canopy would feel. From 125 miles per hour to just under 20, the deceleration was so swift I felt like a rag doll being jerked out of control. But after the canopy fully inflated I had a much larger problem.

Just like on the climbing wall, I was suspended in a nylon harness. The huge difference now was that I had a nylon parachute above me and the ground four thousand feet below. I'd spent practically all of my skydiving visualization time focusing on the decisive moment I'd exit from the plane followed by sixty seconds of high-speed freefall. I'd also diligently prepared for the technical aspects of the landing approach. The problem was that I hadn't invested much, if any, time imagining my sneakered feet dangling four thousand feet above the ground. It had been an afterthought.

Dependent on a few pounds of nylon, moment by moment my fear escalated until Andy snapped me back to the task at hand, telling me to grab the steering toggles and turn the canopy to the right. Seconds before I'd been out of control, my mind shifting into an overdrive of panic. Now I had something to do. The problem was I had no idea how the canopy would perform. Never having been under a parachute, I didn't know how hard to pull on the toggles to perform a turn. I was tentative, concerned that if I made a mistake and pulled too hard, I'd put us in an unrecoverable spin, causing us to cut away and deploy the reserve.

As Andy watched me meekly pulling down on the toggle, he reached up, aggressively pulling it down, putting the parachute into an aggressive, full banking right turn. Surprised by the stability of the canopy, I relaxed into the situation. I stopped thinking and began to *feel*. Once I realized I was under an aerodynamic wing, just like another windsurfing sail, I calmly said, "*OK, I get it. This is how it feels when a stable parachute turns.*" After descending gently to the setup zone we finally had to get ready for the landing.

Because a canopy is nothing more than a wing, the landing pattern on a parachute jump is broken down into three sections similar to, but much shorter than, commercial aircraft approaches. The landing pattern under a parachute is the downwind leg, the base leg, and the final approach back into the wind. As we descended from our downwind leg to our base leg, we were at an altitude of about five hundred feet. At this height, falling will kill you, but I was beginning to get a real understanding how the canopy was performing. When we made our final turn at 250 feet, I was able to sense our ground speed and understood fairly accurately where we were going to land. Closer and closer we descended until we were speeding fifteen feet above the ground, ready to flare the parachute for a gentle landing.

I had done it! I'd jumped out of an airplane! For someone who purposely hasn't walked across the Golden Gate Bridge and is too afraid to hike up Half Dome at Yosemite, leaping from a plane was more than the achievement of another personal goal. It became another validation. All I need to be happy is to set a huge, almost impossible goal before executing a detailed plan. The process is simple, but not easy. The black ski run of my process completed, tomorrow is the final step: the double black. I'll be jumping without the safety of an expert strapped to my back.

CHAPTER TWENTY-EIGHT

It's only a handshake

Thoughts are things; they have tremendous power. Thoughts of doubt and fear are pathways to failure. When you conquer negative attitudes of doubt and fear you conquer failure. Thoughts crystallize into habit and habit solidifies into circumstances.

—Bryan Adams

The final interview, the last step before a job offer was made, had been scheduled for only an hour: from 1:00 until 2:00 p.m. At 6:00 p.m. I was still at the conference room white-board sharing ideas and approaches with the Chairman of the Bank. Our personal chemistry and thought processes fully in sync, we discussed how technology and business could merge creating better solutions. At the end of the one-hour meeting turned five he made a job offer. Flattered and surprised, I shook his hand before asking for a week to give him an answer. I was in the final stages with a competing company and needed time to finish those interviews.

The next Thursday, the day before my commitment to the Chairman was due, the owner of the second company called, postponing my interviews again because of scheduling conflicts. After sharing I had shaken his competitor's hand a week before agreeing to give an answer the next day, I was given a critical piece of information when he responded, "What's the big deal? You didn't sign a legal contract. It's only a handshake. It doesn't mean anything." With this simple statement of his values, he was telling me exactly how he would treat me if I worked for him. His word would mean nothing. I wanted to work for and with a man where the value of a handshake meant everything. That evening I made an important phone call accepting a job offer, beginning a tremendously satisfying thirteen-year relationship that continues to this day.

Although it was never a specific goal, within a couple of years I reached the pinnacle of a technology career: Chief Information Officer, CIO. I had the corner office, the title, salary, and was on the Board of Directors. I was responsible for the worldwide technology of a private bank with millions of dollars in budget and a huge staff. As in the athletic world, each time I moved up a level everything became exponentially more difficult. Being the CIO didn't mean my life was easier or that I was able to simply command people what to do. It was exactly the opposite of having power. I had responsibility.

Most fascinating was that I'd been here before. Yes, the time was different, and so was the geography. Even the problems to solve were different. But my feelings were exactly the same. I was the captain of the football team again. The people sitting next to me, whether in a locker room or in a large conference room depended on me and I didn't want to let them down. Comfortable with the huge responsibilities of leadership, I enjoyed solving difficult problems with intellectual, motivated people. It was rewarding leading others, especially in a crisis. When complicated, high-pressure situations required an immediate decision, often with little information, my reassuring presence helped everyone remain calm.

Ironically, my strength in the office is a skill not typically attributed to introverts: communication. Much of my time was spent as a glorified translator, explaining to the business how technologies' constantly changing black box of three-letter acronyms would benefit their operations. When I wasn't translating technology on a white-board, I was explaining balance sheets, mortgage amortizations and present-value cash flow modeling to software engineers. Although timelines, costs, and priorities were often points of contentious discussion, people rarely left meetings with me confused or frustrated. They usually felt more knowledgeable and confident. Quickly getting to the core issue of a problem, I used pictures, analogy, and metaphor to simplify difficult concepts into a language people could understand. Not only was I a translator, I was a trusted teacher.

Surprisingly, the best part of being a CIO with an INTJ personality were the social aspects. As a group we were solving tangible problems and polite conversation, although necessary for group dynamics and cohesion, was a minor component. The biggest relief being in charge was that I wasn't constantly being interrupted. Cocktail parties often feel like competitions where I'm forced to raise my voice just to be heard. In meetings with staff or peers I could take my time, carefully deliberating what to say and even speaking more softly than normal, forcing staff to lean in and pay more attention.

Although my title provided the initial respect and authority, without saying a word the intensity of my INTJ stare under stress usually did the rest. The penetrating intensity of my had multiple layers of meaning. The first was, "Get to the point." The next was, "If you can't simplify the concepts verbally, at least draw us a picture." Finally, my unblinking eyes never leaving the gaze of the other meant, "If you can't draw a simple, structured picture, you don't understand the problem or solution well enough, so quit wasting everyone's time."

I love the mental stimulation and physical grind of work. I've had a great professional career that has challenged me with interesting technical, banking, and staff problems. Unfortunately, the more successful I became in my career the worse it became in my personal life. Casual and intimate relationships were still my Achilles' heel, even at home.

After not seeing them since Christmas, I'd flown back to Nebraska in May to visit my parents. On top of the astronomical odds of a couple staying together for fifty-two years since high school, their communication styles are completely different. When I play golf with my father we can spend five hours in the cart saying little more than "Nice swing tempo" or "Great speed on that putt." We might even have short tee-box to fairway discussions about sports, work or extended family. With minor variations in subject and intent, it's the same conversation we had when he taught me to play chess: ninety-nine percent focused silence dedicated to the task at hand, one-percent talk.

My mother is completely different. Not only does she want to talk, she's compelled to share every minute of every day since last seeing me. While I have a hard time remembering what I ate for breakfast she can describe in exacting detail what she had for lunch twenty-one years ago to the day, what the weather was like, and what stories were shared among her many friends. Within an hour of my arrival I had been trying to listen to her excitedly tell me about her best friend's, second cousin's, next-door neighbor's bad experience at a new restaurant with a rude waiter in a distant state. Lost and unable to follow the meandering twists and turns of her multilayered story about complete strangers, I couldn't hide my disinterest or confused facial expressions. I couldn't follow the conversation and was frustrated knowing I'd forget everything in less than an hour. She might as well have been speaking Spanish. As my jet-lagged eyes glanced over to the TV a few too many times, with an exasperated sigh, she said, "You're not listening to me."

"I'm trying to follow the story, but I don't know who these people are."

"I just told you who they were!"

As the tension escalated I knew I couldn't give her my INTJ death stare or ask her to draw a simplifying flowchart on a white-board so I asked, "Maybe if you tell me the end of the story, I can follow along to where it's going."

"My story doesn't have an end. I haven't seen you for months—I'm just telling you about my life!"

"No. You're sharing whatever vague thought that randomly pops into your head. This particular story is about a stranger, five degrees removed, whom you've never even met. More importantly, I'll never meet her either. I don't care about these people or their inconsequential problem with a rude waiter. I care about what *you're* doing."

A microsecond later, I was filled with regret. I'd really never snapped at her. Ever. Until seeing the hurt and disappointment in her eyes I'd never realized she wasn't sharing information I could use in the future. She was just happy to see her son, sharing her excitement in an unbroken stream of semi-unconnected thoughts and words. That was the moment when fifty-two years of social bewilderment washed away. With that insight I began to consider that perhaps social interactions, especially at parties, were similar. Although they usually weren't talking about anything substantive, people were sharing their energy—lots of it. It was exactly the opposite for me. I've always protected every ounce of energy, saving it for the intensity of work, the pleasure of reading, investigating ideas, a few close friends and my long list of personal goals.

On my next visit to Lincoln I arrived with a new approach to interactions with my mother. I'd recreate the golf-cart quietness my father and I shared by taking her to matinee movies. That way we could be together but being the considerate woman she is, she couldn't talk my leg off disturbing the people seated around us. It worked great. We'd see the movie, spending time together, and have a late lunch afterward to discuss the movie and its specific message and structure. On the flight back to San Francisco after a particularly pleasant trip to Lincoln, I wondered if my new revelation about communication and energy sharing could help me with personal relationships.

With a couple of marriages and a half dozen serious relationships it was obvious I'd never been afraid of commitment, so I decided to try again, likely for the last time. I'd never been reluctant to approach women I found attractive but problems with the initial encounters usually rested with me. I certainly didn't need attention or validation from just any woman. While nice for a moment or two, it didn't boost my ego if strange woman flirted with me. They didn't know *me*. They were merely engaging with their projected image of who they wanted me to be, a huge difference many, if not all, men miss.

The problem with the initial contacts was that I was impatient, struggling to let the music of the relationship dance begin. Averse to wasting time on small talk, within the first five minutes, I wanted a woman naked with her clothes on. *Who is she? What are her dreams and goals? What does she believe in? How does she live her life? Could she add to my life, offering deep emotions and insights I can't find in myself? After introducing me to new emotions, can she help me learn to express them? Fully. Can our demons play well with each other?* Unless I knew those things up front, it often felt like I was wasting time.

I was smart enough to avoid dating women in the office but after too many awkward attempts at the gym, grocery store, and gas pump, I decided on an approach the opposite of the romanticized "love at first sight" chance encounter. Falling in love was easy. Having sex was even easier. Finding someone to engage my soul seemed impossible. As unspontaneous as it sounded I joined a popular online dating site providing access to the profiles of thousands of women. Only an e-mail away, attractive photos were the initial filter, but the words in the profile were the key to eliminating incompatible women where a relationship, especially with me, would never work. It was the next best thing to formal interviews for a date.

Of course I also had to create a profile, a reciprocating window into my wants and desires. Being in a relationship was important to me but what did I really need? Instead of posting a fuzzy picture of myself in a baseball cap and sunglasses with a lackluster tagline, "Hey, what's up? Let's get together for a drink," I spent weeks carefully thinking about what I wanted. I read women's profiles and even those of other men. I also spent a lot of time painstakingly revisiting old relationships.

A couple of former girlfriends expected me to overlook the minimal effort of microwaved Tater-Tots and hot dogs, but I've savored made-from-scratch meals prepared by others that would make a gourmet chef nod in appreciation. I've endured girls pretending to be women who thought foreplay consisted of little more than timidly grabbing my crotch, the signal that as the 'man' I was expected to take charge, but have been brought to within an inch of my life, a woman's erotic power unleashed in a meticulous execution masquerading as seduction. I've heard a dispassionate "I love you" from women who had no idea who I was, but I've watched love pour from a woman's eyes without a syllable. I've dated women (for a very short time) whose intellectual world revolved solely around fashions of the day, yet have had conversations with others whose fervent insights and deep logic made me discard long-held beliefs quicker than taking out the trash.

As I wrote and rewrote the profile, it was becoming exceedingly clear about what I didn't need. Although physical attraction was important, a statuesque model who turned the heads of friends or strangers wasn't necessary. I didn't need to be in a relationship to satisfy my physical needs. I could handle the release of physical tension myself, pun intended. I'd never fantasized about what type of tuxedo to wear at the formal events of awkward small talk—weddings and receptions. Validating my emotional commitment to a woman with a financial contract called marriage seemed like a contradiction. I think I'd be a great father, but the thought "I'd like to raise children" has never entered my mind. I certainly didn't want to be in a relationship just because everyone else was doing it. The furthest thing from my mind was to be in a relationship with a 'companion', just so I wouldn't be alone. Most of the time I liked being alone.

Eliminating what I didn't need helped me understand my relationship needs were intellectual compatibility, deep emotional intimacy, and finally, physical chemistry. Ironically, this was exactly the opposite of what I'd done in the past. Fueled by barely contained hormones, too many relationships began with lustful eyes and ended at the insistent desire between my legs. If the relationship continued long enough to build on more than physical desire, the focus might slowly shift up to the center of emotion in my chest. Rarely would a relationship's trajectory make its way to the grayish three-pound organ between my ears asserting its need for constant stimulation. I knew she would be difficult to find, but if a woman couldn't stimulate me intellectually or capture my emotions, no matter how good looking she was or how talented she was in bed, it would never be enough. After at least a hundred iterations and dozens of crushed paper balls frustratingly thrown in the trash, I finally settled on:

> If you often feel like an ocean of emotion that keeps running into puddles and if against your better judgment you still enjoy the company of men, please keep reading.
>
> If you're seeking magic, where conversation with a man while dining in public transcends into an intimate, almost spiritual connection, perhaps we have much in common. Many say the woman I want to share my life with does not exist. I prefer to believe she exists in all her feminine wonder. Perhaps that is you, nature's mythical unicorn.
>
> If you're a vixen from the femme fatale clan, drown me in your mystery. If you're provocative and cerebral, astonish me with your character while I patiently pull back each protective layer of your soul. Strong enough to surrender to your strength, I ache for a sultry muse who inspires me to share my successes and failures in the calm harbor of her heart.
>
> I relish the company of introspective, discerning women. Being somewhat competitive (sic), I find it mildly amusing I don't mind losing a well thought out argument to a woman I respect. I didn't say I liked it, I just don't mind it. I prefer women not easily influenced by those around them. If you feel safer following the crowd or are constantly worrying what your girlfriends are thinking, we are definitely not a good fit. In short, I enjoy the company of independent women who make conscious decisions about what they want to experience and believe in life. If we are to become friends, partners and lovers, I will eventually expect you to stand with me in the center of the fire of life.
>
> I am both a cliché and anomaly. Working in the technology and financial arena as a senior executive, I'm driven, ambitious and disciplined. Living and working abroad extensively, 日本語を話せますか?、I'm well educated and continue to actively increase my knowledge of myself and the world. To strangers or casual acquaintances, I can be reserved, distant and cold: MBTI-INTJ. Once I build a necessary level of trust and respect, I warm up quickly. Long past the party and bar stage of my life I find

small talk mind-numbing and exhausting. My preferred social outlets are intimate dinners with stimulating discussions or long afternoons hiding together on the floor of a bookstore aisle. My work requires me to be assertive and extroverted, yet I regain my strength from significant downtime alone. I tenaciously guard my energy for those closest to me, with whom I spend it happily and freely.

Privately I am expressive, gentle and vulnerable. Though at times I can be overly burdened by my gender, I am a passable cook, give great massages and am conversant in subjects other than cars, fishing and sports. I consider loyalty and character far more than convenient words or hollow outdated ideas. As much as I love the intensity and adrenaline rush of high-risk sports (windsurfing, motorcycles, martial arts) I also enjoy live theater, quiet evenings over a chessboard and brushing my lover's hair while unwinding from the day's events.

I love the differences between men and women, the subtlety of flirty banter and intellectual women with a touch of bad girl, sort of the bespectacled librarian in a pencil skirt. The lack of emotional intimacy and courage in most relationships leaves me empty and unfulfilled and thus, I'm no longer interested in the white picket fence and all it implies. I need a woman who has the strength to wrap me around one of her delicate manicured fingers and the confidence to carry it off with a delightful, irresistible style. After the extended foreplay of psychology, passion and endurance have turned me into your prized possession, I want to feel the private, unspoken power of your upraised eyebrow from across a crowded room.

So, if you can use your mind like a feather, a scalpel, or a sledgehammer, if you're fluent in the languages of the body, and can pull down the walls of my masculine pride with little more than a whisper, I would love to speak with you.

PS. If your current strategy is pretending to be the needle coyly hiding in the haystack, at least make a little noise in there, I've been saving a seat for you.

The long hours working on the profile were frustrating but it seemed to work. It was flattering to come home to an inbox of e-mails, but I was only trying to pique the curiosity of a single woman. Some women were gracious enough to write that while we weren't a match, they wanted to compliment the writing and wish me luck in my search. Other women "winked" at me, the website's version of an inviting but passive smile in a bar. Foreshadowing their level of relationship commitment—they were interested, but not more than the effort of a single click of a mouse. A real man, whatever that is, was supposed to be the pursuer of a woman. Reciprocating their level of effort, I ignored every wink. I even received e-mails from women who loathed what I wrote and weren't shy to castigate my unrealistic need for the Nietzschean *Überfrau*. Anything worthwhile I've done in my life has been challenging, if not impossible, so why settle for just any woman with a pulse?

A month after joining, I opened a long e-mail from the woman who would become my third wife. An attractive corporate professional, she enjoyed many of the same interests, outlooks, and activities. She was frighteningly smart but combined it with deep, compassionate emotions. Her extroversion balancing my introversion, our first dinner was a perfect harmony of chemistry, humor, and intelligence. She was a dream come true. After a two-year courtship followed by a wedding on an isolated beach on Maui, our early years were filled with romance, snow-ski holidays, trips to Maui, and carefree evenings watching movies while sharing a bottle of wine. I was married to a fantastic woman, living with her in one of the great cities of the world.

It still wasn't enough.

She was a healthy human being, but I was plagued with the same problems. Every intimate relationship has been a delicate balancing act. From my first experience with love in high school to my third wife, I've been trapped in an inflexible, triangular prison. On one side are my deep needs for raw emotional intimacy and absolute, uncompromising trust. On the next are my huge demands for privacy, independence, and solitude. The last side, the culminating closure of my emotional prison, is my complete disdain for stagnation and complacency. I've never been able to find the key to escape my self-made trap.

After a long day of necessary but forced extroversion at work communicating on the phone, in person, or through e-mail, the last thing I wanted was to rehash it all when asked, "Tell me about your day sweetie." The stamina of her social reservoir far exceeding mine, I knew she was trying to support the relationship, but I didn't have the energy to think or talk. She was curious enough to listen and smart enough to understand, but I had zero interest in explaining projects and especially didn't want to delve into recurring problems with staff or peers. As long as she was squeezed shoulder to shoulder with me in our loveseat, I was happy to nurse a glass of wine for hours, decompressing without a single word.

If asked something as innocuous as, "What do you want to do for dinner?" it only took a microsecond for a spiral of internal questions a thousand layers deep to emerge. *How does she seem to feel tonight? What are her favorite foods? Did we have that recently?* When I didn't have the energy to consider dozens of mental options and simply blurted out exactly how I felt— "I don't care"—it sounded like I didn't love her. I loved her exactly the same as the day we were married, but "I don't care" was a plea for help: *I've made a thousand decisions today. Please help me turn off my mind by telling me exactly what to do. Don't burden me with the responsibility of another decision.* I didn't need a leather-clad dominatrix barking orders at me, but sometimes it would have been easier just to be told what we were doing, when and with whom, without my input.

If I'd arrive home to a surprise of strange cars in the driveway, graciously communicating with her girlfriends was practically impossible. It was worse at weekend social events. Sometimes hugging my mother and father felt awkward, so the Marin County expectation of meeting strangers with a pretentious pseudo-European hug instead of a handshake was overwhelming. I hated it. An unexpected relationship problem was that the more I loved and respected my wife, the more protective I became of her.

I started life exceedingly naïve, believing most people were honest and good. Unfortunately, the longer I lived and the more cruelty I witnessed the more I felt like a police officer, forced to develop thick emotional calluses just to survive. If one of her girlfriends treated my wife poorly, which was sadly all too common, she could forgive and forget moving on for the sake of their relationship. I could do neither. Embarrassing my wife and making it difficult to socialize as a couple, I could be harsh, cold, and unforgiving. I expected an apology—not in contrite words, but in action, a change in behavior toward my wife. It also never surprised me that if I disliked one of her girlfriends, it was practically assured I didn't like anything about the husband.

Eventually, although neither of us wanted it to happen, we began drifting apart. After a perfect first dinner and a few years of bliss, years four and five were difficult and by the time year six arrived the relationship had run its course. After nature's biological reproductive chemistry of dopamine, serotonin, and oxytocin had evaporated, we'd been reduced to roommates. The irony is that in the beginning, I simply wanted to be next to her—grocery shopping, doing laundry, and life's other mundane activities.

But familiarity didn't breed contempt. It replaced mystery, intrigue, and excitement. The irony is that for each vulnerability and weakness I exposed, the newness and mystery of my personality was diminished. I didn't, and still don't, know how to be open and mysterious at the same time. I couldn't find the balance of being a stable husband and exciting lover. If such a balance even exists.

It certainly hadn't been a function of disinterest or neglect, from either of us. She could fill parts of her relationship needs with girlfriends, but most of my social needs came from work or solely from her. I probably overthought every detail from every angle. It was probably too much. I struggled, wondering how to be the mysterious guy she had first met and at the same time be the dependable partner. It also wasn't enough just to be in a relationship. I had to know where we were going, together.

I needed our relationship to have a purpose, almost like an important work project or personal goal. There were three parties: husband, wife, and the relationship itself. How did each of the parties get what they needed without losing themselves? How could I continue to grow as a man without growing distant from a woman or the relationship? Does each party have to grow at the same pace? What if both people are growing, just not in the same direction? Simply being in love and together wasn't enough. At least for me.

As we went through the legal process of ending a marriage existing only on paper I began long evenings staring at a wine glass wondering what had happened. The strange thing is I could accept the pain because it was a reflection of how much the relationship had meant to me. I couldn't just walk away with an indifferent shrug, ready for a rebound relationship. Devastated at losing someone I'd finally thought was my soul mate, my experiences falling in and out of love with women have always caused me the greatest amount of pain. It's been sheer torture in every conceivable way. Because of that I began to consider that probably the best thing for me was to remain a bachelor, get a dog, or develop a 'Dan User's Manual' I could hand to a woman before entering long-distance relationships that came with two-year, renewable terms.

CHAPTER TWENTY-NINE

Revelations

A mind that is stretched by new experience,
can never go back to its old dimensions.
—Oliver Wendell Holmes

Last night was spent relaxing on the hotel bed, savoring yesterday's success before meticulously reviewing a stack of well-used skydiving books. Mentally rehearsing a perfect performance free-falling at terminal velocity I eventually drifted asleep, immersed in rolling waves of anticipation.

I'm here. Today, *I complete my goal.* Out of bed before sunup, a steaming cup of black coffee elevated my already intense focus. Driving to the jump site reflecting on the previous fifty-one weeks, warm rays of opportunity greeted me from the eastern horizon. Exactly a year ago today on the drive home from the emotionally charged weekend of the Cliff, I had the unequivocal realization it had become exhausting avoiding fear, in all its forms. After that I decided to spend a year in the arena of my weaknesses explicitly challenging Daddy with increasingly difficult situations.

Using my body as a wing I've learned how to fly in a wind tunnel. I've soared in a glider over Lake Tahoe, survived four Gs in a military dogfight, and embraced the confidence-building stability of a helicopter roaring over the peaks of snow-capped backcountry mountains. I've learned moving towards fear, hanging off the side of a motorcycle at a hundred miles per hour draws my mind into the quiet space of a chess match. I've driven Formula Three cars up to the razor's edge of my ability and entered a submerged cage, expecting to see great white sharks. I've skied Portillo, Chile, and windsurfed Punta San Carlos and Maui's north shore. Yesterday I jumped from a plane with an instructor strapped to my back.

I've done the work: research on the physiology of fear, homework on skydiving techniques, structured incremental improvements, and hours of intense visualization. I've grown to recognize Daddy's subtle but relentless dialogue of fear and doubt. It's been a fantastic fifty-two weeks overflowing with deep insights and personal growth. The year, and my project, ends today with the most dangerous double-black-diamond ski run of my life: my first solo skydive.

After arriving at Perris, getting registered, and signing the last set of liability waivers for the year, I was pleasantly surprised to discover I'd be the only student in today's class. My instructor would be Patrick, a world-champion skydiver. Classroom instruction began promptly at 9:00 a.m. and would continue until 3:00 p.m., when I was scheduled for my first jump.

Patrick began by laying out the structure of the day and how we would progress together. It was a lot of information, but fortunately he was patient, communicating with ease the necessary information to keep me safe. For the first hour of instruction, the material was little more than a refresher of what I'd been studying. Absorbed in the moment, I found that the second hour progressed smoothly. My problems began in the third hour with a verbal pop quiz. Technically, I knew the information but when Patrick challenged me, asking random questions about sequence or timing, I froze up, struggling to give the correct answer. My hesitation in answering triggered a cycle of doubt. In the short span it had taken to answer a few simple questions, much of my preparation and confidence was slipping through my fingers.

As each second of the classroom's digital clock passed by, well-known feelings of dread reemerged from the shadows. I was back in another calculus exam, unprepared to perform. The possibility of getting hurt or worse was remote, but I began fighting an overwhelming sense that I was spiraling out of control. During the glider and Air Combat flights, and certainly at yesterday's tandem jump, I had had an insurance policy: a highly skilled person ready to take over if I made a mistake. In less than four hours I'd be alone, completely dependent upon my ability to perform under extreme pressure.

During short classroom breaks, I strolled the grounds, desperately trying to relax. With a series of breaths deep into my abdomen, I felt my confidence returning until the droning of an aircraft engine overhead brought my attention to skydivers making their morning jumps. On one hand it was beautiful. The plane was sowing the air with seeds. One by one, the tiny specks fell until they exploded into colorful flowers, creating a floating garden in the sky. On the other, I struggled. Trying to hold the awkward position of looking straight up, the tension in my neck—and my mind—was increasing exponentially; I knew I'd soon be up there as well.

I knew the information and had a detailed plan. I'd diligently prepared, breaking the jump into three manageable pieces: the critical leap from the plane, the sixty-second freefall, and finally, the quiet canopy-ride to the landing zone. Most, if not all, of my focus was on leaping from the plane. I had spent hours, at home, driving in the car, and even taking morning showers imagining a confident step from the door of a plane into thin air. If I couldn't step into empty space, the free-fall skills I'd developed in the wind tunnel would be pointless. Then I visualized skillfully free-falling toward the earth for hours, my breathing as controlled as a Buddhist monk deep in meditation. My visualization turned to physical confidence when I learned to fly in a wind tunnel.

I've spent an entire year focused on my internal game, but as the canopies gently floated to the landing area I knew I'd made a critical mistake. I couldn't get yesterday's terror under the canopy out of my mind. Other than pictures in a textbook, I also didn't know much of anything about how the equipment I was trusting to save my life would perform. A parachute canopy uses the same aerodynamic physics, the Bernoulli principle, as a windsurfing sail, but until yesterday I didn't know how it would feel flying through the air. I've also only had one repetition pulling on the risers to make a turn. Yesterday's tandem jump. Today was only the third time I'd ever touched a parachute rig. I'd never watched anyone pack a canopy and had no idea how it would deploy from the container. Compounding my equipment ignorance, thoughts of yesterday's fumbled attempts to find the handle of the pilot chute swirled in my mind. Everything was accelerating out of control.

I've lived a life in a protective bubble of confidence built on grinding preparation. On a racetrack I could develop my skills starting out at much slower speeds staying within my comfort zone. It was the same incremental progression in windsurfing, snow skiing, or practicing the martial arts. The problem is I couldn't find a way to execute the necessary repetitions under a canopy at seventy-five percent of my abilities. Magnifying the sensory overload from yesterday's tandem jump was a deep feeling I'd panic, unable to manage my emotions in case of an emergency malfunction. I had to perform perfectly the first time out or suffer the consequences.

I'm grateful for a lifetime gauntlet of challenges but today's activity, my self-imposed confrontation with fear, has turned into severe pain. I'm suffocating from the inside out. This fear is a thousand times worse than the Cliff, neighborhood trees, or a concrete diving platform. In an agonizing release of pressure, every molecule of preparation, discipline and work instantly evaporated. Completely broken and defeated, it was over.

Thirty minutes before strapping on a parachute I told Patrick I couldn't do it. I didn't think I should jump unless I had absolute confidence in my ability to perform under tremendous pressure. Telling him wasn't difficult. I've had to do many things much harder. I've had to fire employees whom I considered close friends. I've had to look into the helpless, searching eyes of a woman and tell her I was no longer in love with her. I've survived the full impact of despair while sitting on a hospital bed helplessly holding my sister's hand, knowing there was nothing I could do to prevent her death. In comparison, although I didn't enjoy it, telling Patrick was easy. And surprising.

Patrick's unexpected response was gracious acceptance. He didn't try to make me feel guilty or weak, pressuring me to jump. He quietly mentioned my logic was sound and inquired when—not if—I would like to try it again in the future. It was a nice way of saying this was nothing more than a minor setback on the way to a long-term goal. In a moment of candid vulnerability, he shared that even as a world-champion skydiver he was still terrified of heights. He'd made over fifteen thousand jumps, but he quivers with fear when looking over the side of a tall building.

I left Perris smothering under a heavy, wet blanket of defeat. During the drive to the hotel disbelief forcefully invaded my brain. Worse was the painful feelings of disappointment flooding every cell of my body. I've had the instantaneous surge of adrenaline in high school and college after stupidly becoming involved in alcohol-induced fistfights. During those moments of physical invincibility, adrenaline had dulled any pain but the aftermath was awful. The shame and embarrassment from an ego-driven loss of control was bad enough, but the adrenaline pumping through me with no physical outlet caused me to shake painfully for hours.

This pain was similar.

Disoriented and exhausted, I laid in bed all evening staring at the hotel ceiling endlessly replaying every second of the day. Hour after hour the deafening silence of the hotel room crushed me with the indifferent, oppressive weight of failure. I know these feelings well, but after adding one more to my long list this failure was leading me through an early-morning mist where answers to questions nagging me my entire life began swirling. *Why do I engage in such intense activities? Why is it vital to keep pushing so hard? How and when did the relentless desire for personal growth turn into such an addiction?*

Peering back at me through the fog of failure, the look in Patrick's eyes as we shook hands opened a hidden door to understanding. Piece by piece, memory by memory, the intricate jigsaw puzzle of my life was becoming clear. It took fifty-two years completely avoiding my fear of heights to arrive at my implosion at the Cliff. After that it only took a fifty-two-week project challenging fear to reach my first revelation.

For an extreme introvert, content to be alone for days at a time, the irony and overwhelming paradox of my life is that *everything* has been about relationships with a small number of people I can count on two hands. I don't need, or want, any more than that.

From ten years old until I graduated from college the impossible challenge of being a running back in the NFL consumed me. I never yearned for money or seeing my face on the cover of Sports Illustrated. My dreams weren't about scoring touchdowns, reading my name in the newspapers or being interviewed on sports television. As an introvert I couldn't imagine anything worse than being famous, unable to quietly enjoy a dinner without constant interruptions from my 'fans'. All of it would have been nice for a moment, a nice validation my work had paid off, but eventually all the clippings, awards, and trophies would be packed away in cardboard boxes, little more than distant memories.

Until today I'd never understood exactly how relationships and my NFL dream were intertwined. The answer was incredibly simple, easily captured in two, five-second blocks of time. Those tiny segments of time could have happened within a ten-minute span on August 5, 1981—5:00 p.m. to 5:10 p.m.—at Saint Vincent College in Latrobe, Pennsylvania, the home of the Pittsburgh Steelers' summer training camp.

The first five seconds could have happened after a long, hot practice. Slowly walking off the practice field, my shoulder pads hanging from the helmet in my hand, I'd have heard familiar voices calling out to me. "Cass. Danny Cass. Over here." Turning to the voices, a few high-school and college teammates were leaning on the chain-link fence separating fans from the practice field. They had flown in to watch practice before joining me for dinner and a few beers later that evening. Standing at the fence while silently shaking their hands, I understood without a word why the countless hours of training were worth it. I had their respect—not because I'd signed an NFL contract, but because I'd followed my dream: I never gave up and had overcome the impossible odds.

1974: My first tribe leading the way

The next five-second segment could have happened moments after leaving my friends at the fence for a post-practice lifting session. After entering the practice-complex weight room, the team's center, a bearded giant of a man looks at me with a nod of respect before telling the others, "OK, he's here now. We can get started." The men that would be blocking for me were waiting: For me.

My first tribe, forty-four years later

Challenging fear became the ante into my internal game helping me remember the currency of exchange I value the most. All I've ever wanted was a firm handshake, an almost imperceptible nod, and a penetrating look of respect in someone's eyes. I love the intense, respectful bow from one martial artist to another before and after sparring, but more than anything I wanted the single nod of respect from one man—a teammate in a weight room—his silent acknowledgment that I belonged with him in the NFL.

Patrick's handshake was the hidden answer to why the "What do you want for your birthday?" question has always been so frustratingly elusive. Especially after becoming an adult, I've never wanted presents, either for my birthday, Christmas or Valentine's Day. I usually told people, "Don't get me anything. I already have enough things." More specifically, Patrick opened my eyes to the more important "What do I want" in life question.

The words, "I just want to be happy", have never passed over my lips. I don't measure my success with integers in a bank account, a title on a business card, or what type of car I drive. Being liked, popular or famous has never been on my long list of goals. How many strangers click a mouse indicating they're my 'friends' means practically nothing to me. A good day of life isn't a function of avoiding stress or fear.

I'm not a complex Renaissance man. I simply want to be understood. To do that someone has to be curious and patient enough to unwrap me, layer by layer. If they're not curious about me as a man, it's an indication of their curiosity about life and I want them to leave me alone. I've known the feelings of being liked and loved. What's exceedingly rare is being understood. Patrick understood me, practically without a word. The realization was unbelievable. Stunned by the irony of my first revelation, yesterday's fifty-two seconds in freefall brought me to the denouement of the next.

I am *not* afraid of heights.

How could I be? I jumped out of an airplane. On purpose. I certainly wasn't afraid while falling. As soon as we stabilized into freefall, I relaxed, completely confident of maneuvering exactly as I'd done dozens of times in the wind tunnel. Everything changed the instant the canopy snapped open, leaving me dangling in the harness. It was the opposite of my experience on the climbing wall. In one moment I was frozen on the wall, terrified I'd fall. In the next I sat back into the security of the harness completely relaxed at exactly the same height. How can these two experiences in the harness be so completely different?

It's because I'm terrified of being out of control.

I've often woken up from dreams where the physical emotions were more vivid than memories from actual events in my past, but I've never had a single dream falling to my death. I've had a recurring nightmare standing helplessly on the ground watching a hot air balloon swaying uncontrollably thousands of feet in the air. As the winds increase I watch one passenger after another tumble out of the basket plummeting to their deaths. The horrifying nightmare—and my sleep—always ends with the frustrating realization that although I want to help, there is nothing I can do. All of my dreams are about control.

I've also had countless dreams showing up for exams completely unprepared. After quickly scanning the test questions I realize I have no idea of the subject matter. None. I've also had nightmares watching teammates rush out of a locker room to play a football game while I frantically search my duffle bag for a misplaced mouthpiece or helmet. My worst nightmares are when I'm being held off the ground by a screaming, faceless mob of humanity. Passing me from one group of hands to the next, they ignore my frantic pleas to be let go.

Experience, the brutal but painfully efficient teacher is where I've always grown the most. It was only during the six months of torture watching my sister wither away from cancer that I began to grasp that control is an illusion. Getting laid off and the pain of being fired forced me to jump-start my career, bluntly saying exactly what I thought, control and consequences be damned. It took thirty years of social awkwardness to arrive at a personality test confirming my intuition. Instead of being shy, I was actually trying to protect and control my energy, particularly my emotions. It took me years to understand why trust in an intimate relationship was paramount for me—a literal On-Off switch with no settings in between.

Am I really afraid of heights? Either the vertigo-inducing feelings looking over the railing of a tall building or the sudden deceleration trauma hitting the ground after a long fall? The simple answer? No. A walking enigma carrying a massive backpack of paradox, contradiction and irony, my fear isn't heights, it's being out of control. Especially with my emotions. Caution and preparation my insurance policy, I overthink and over plan because I'm afraid I won't be able to handle terrifying levels of love and compassion, anger and rage, just below the surface. The irony is I know those levels exist. I've felt them and so have people close to me. To continue discovering what I'm capable of as a man, and as a human being, I've got to explore everything, living on the razor's edge of control.

Epilogue

Through fear, I'm becoming more as a man

What I'm talkin' about is a game...
a game that can't be won. Only played.
—Will Smith
The Legend of Bagger Vance

When a 1st-degree black belt is earned in the martial arts it's commonly understood the student is nowhere close to being an expert. With a minimal set of fundamental skills, not only is it not the end, it's only the first step of a long, arduous journey into self-awareness. The first training session as a first-degree begins by tying the crisp new black belt into a perfect knot before stepping onto the dojo floor. Each subsequent session begins and ends with the tying and untying ritual until after years of training, the fraying threads of the belt turn white, symbolizing the purity of the beginner's mind and the beginning of the next journey.

Did I earn another black belt in life's dojo? When the pair of blue eyes stared back from the hotel's bathroom mirror this morning did I see a failure? Did I notice twinges of regret after an entire year of effort ended in crushing defeat?

No. I've been here before.

I've circled back to another beginning, exactly where I started 365 days ago, swimming in familiar feelings of failure and satisfaction, insight and growth. A year ago fear became the essential ingredient reigniting the motivation of a man in a relentless pursuit of growth. The opposite of threatening, competition, adversity and failure have always been where my truths have been found. From a ten-year-old boy's impossible NFL goal to the inspired idea in a ski hill parking lot to leap from a plane, it's been critical to nourish and stubbornly protect every dream fueling the engine of my life.

I've returned from the wilderness of my fear but I'm certainly not the victorious conqueror returning to throngs of cheering citizens. Instead of marching into a roaring stadium triumphantly displaying my bloody trophy—Daddy's severed head on a stake—I've returned with him at my side. When I unknowingly accepted the fear of heights as a boy I didn't understand its primary purpose was to help me expand. Every time I begged fear to leave me alone it was patiently waiting for me at the next crossroad. It's all part of the process. Inextricable parts of life, struggle, challenge, and problems are the preconditions for growth. Fear's purpose wasn't to hold me back or keep me safe. Fear was my hidden grain of sand in the oyster shell, the tiny irritant designed to create the beauty of the pearl.

When lying down to sleep, I often wonder: *If I don't wake up tomorrow morning, what would I regret?* I'm not perfect, but more importantly, I don't want to be perfect. How interesting would life be if it were perfect? Failure tastes different than success. It's more tangible. Subtle. Interesting. That's why I've always grown far more from my many mistakes, failures, and defeats.

I don't regret any of my personal failures, but I continue to carry the heavy burden of my relationship difficulties. I don't know what's worse—not knowing what I want in a relationship or knowing exactly what I want but not being able to find it. I certainly regret how I broke up with girlfriends in high school, college, or soon after. I should have been honest, bluntly telling them that although I wanted my feelings to be different I couldn't force it. Thinking it was cruel to hurt them I compounded the problem letting the passionless relationship drag on, callously letting them figure it out on their own. The truth was that I was uncomfortable with the relationship-ending confrontations and conflict.

It took me years to learn the incredibly frustrating lesson that I could only love someone as much as they loved themselves. When someone was smart enough to tell me exactly what I wanted to hear, I instead of believing the consistent patterns of their actions, I naïvely believed the nuanced sophistry hidden within the words. I also didn't realize that not only were they lying to me, worse is they were often lying to themselves. It's only recently that I've been learning how to forgive myself for being so incredibly stupid. It took me far too long to recognize that people without self-control usually found it easier to manipulate and control other people. It's also incredibly painful to look back at how I forced my way through life, trying to get to the next achievement as quickly as possible. I regret not understanding the simple fact that the world, and people, are always changing. Nothing is static. Ever. My worst mistakes have always occurred when I looked externally for success and happiness. It's always been inside of me, but I've often needed reminders.

I've always used the space most people call a garage as a miniature sporting goods store. But the gear isn't just toys for boys. Like the brushes of an artist or a musician's instruments, all of the sports equipment are tools of expression and escape—for a man. Since arriving in San Francisco, hanging next to golf clubs, windsurfing wetsuits, and snow-ski gear was my crisply ironed, white Tae Kwon Do gi, its red belt loosely draped over the middle of the hanger. One early morning while racing to leave the house for another ski trip I took a moment to pull the sweat-stained belt off the hanger before nostalgically tying it around my waist. As the soft cotton completed the intricate, twisting journey to a perfectly formed knot, the sounds, smells, and intensity of the dojo flooded my senses.

In the mid-eighties, I trained extremely hard, quickly moving up the ranks. Hour after hour, belt by colorful belt, in only eighteen months I earned my red belt. Only a few months and one test away from earning a first-degree black belt, being laid off in Omaha forced my move to Wichita. I tried training on my own, planning to go back to Omaha to test, but it wasn't the same. Missing the physicality of sparring and the camaraderie of the locker room I slowly drifted away from the satisfaction and discipline of my martial-arts training.

The soft cotton belt awakening long-forgotten memories, before I knew it I was moving through the garage slowly performing punches, blocks, and kicks at imaginary adversaries. At the end of a sequence designed for defense and counterattack I was stunned when my invisible opponent viciously hit me back, his unexpected blow an answer to a feeling plaguing me for years. Every time I left the house to ski, windsurf, or golf, the garage door closing in the rearview mirror, I felt off balance, wondering what critical piece of equipment I'd left behind. I hadn't forgotten anything: each visit to the garage was a subconscious reminder as painful as a punch to the face. My feelings were the bitter, acrid taste of an unfinished project: I'd missed the opportunity to earn my black belt.

For a moment I tried to rationalize it was pointless and silly: a single individual on a planet of seven billion earning a black belt wouldn't change or improve anything. After that I tried the convenient excuse my goal was unrealistic—I should act my age distracting myself with television, the Internet or vicariously wrap my happiness in the weekly win-loss records of a local sports team.

To avoid weekly reminders driving away from home I could have sold my gi in a garage sale or donated it to Goodwill. I could have chosen denial, hiding the gi, and my desires, in a box in the basement. Every option ending with an overt exclamation point of regret, I chose a different path and joined a school in San Francisco with a phenomenal world-champion instructor. Although it was difficult getting my forty-nine-year-old-body back into the physical demands of Tae Kwon Do, within a year I earned my black belt. Externally the belt meant nothing to the world. Internally it meant everything: it was a tangible symbol I was growing again.

Although I don't have a parachute rig hanging in my garage as a reminder (yet), I expect yesterday's AFF failure will silently torture me with similar feelings of incompleteness: the dull ache of another unfinished project and missed opportunity. New doors of opportunity and insight opened when I decided to confront fear and the high probability of failure. The irony is that even if I'd successfully completed the AFF jumps, played in the NFL, or achieved any other goal, I'd always be faced with the eventual, ironic question, "OK, now what?"

All this would lead to even more profound questions: what would I do with my life if, or when, I get exactly what I want? If I could create it, what would my perfect day on this planet look like?

These new questions were both depressing and exhilarating. It would never end: the eternal recurrence, incarnate. Every time I slay Daddy his offspring evolves, coming back stronger, *for* me. No matter how much I grow as a man, the universe patiently responds with a simple but knowing smile. "You've grown again Dan, but you can't stay here, and you can't go back. The only way is forward. Life doesn't have a finish line. A new challenge, uniquely designed for you, is waiting just around the corner."

Explicitly challenging Daddy began the chemical reaction, the alchemy necessary to expand the fascia of my soul. When the boiling fluids of life softened the metal, slowly molding and expanding the limitless capacity of my cup, I could finally see the answer isn't 'out there'. *I'm not on an external quest, trying to acquire an object called the Holy Grail. The Holy Grail is inside of me.* It has always been there.

I've only begun to scratch the surface of what I'm capable of as a man. There will always be something to learn. Somewhere to grow and expand. Something difficult, and thus interesting, to do. Physically I'm fifty-three, but my soul, masquerading behind the playful innocence of the ten-year-old boy continues to search for neighborhood trees to climb. I'm curious what I'm capable of mentally, physically, and emotionally into my sixties and even later.

The tentacles of my mind are holding on to everything. I'm living a life, but I'm also creating one as well. It hasn't even been twenty-four-hours but I'm already building a new plan to become a competent skydiver. The glider and Air Combat adventures stirred an interest in learning to fly. I still haven't broken eighty on a golf course or become fluent in Japanese. I haven't looped or pulled a perfect bottom turn windsurfing at Ho'okipa. I've yet to see the Aurora Borealis in person. There are more than a hundred books I want to read. I haven't skillfully driven a GT3 Cup car around the Nürburgring.

Maybe I'll begin working toward a second-degree black belt. Perhaps I'll even write another book, the ending highlighted by an AFF skydiving certificate. My monumental challenges with personal relationships, control, and trusting my emotions, patiently wait for me. Somewhere in the future, I have an upcoming date with death. I'm curious what will happen. In some bizarre way, everything seems perfectly laid out.

The only thing I can do now is look in the mirror, accepting the universe's next challenging gift. Often satisfied but never content, the only time I've ever been happy is during the journey into personal growth. Even though failure and struggle, success and satisfaction in every form are waiting for me, I'm at peace now.

Acknowledgments

So many people have been involved, directly or indirectly, with this project and my life. These are the people, living or in the next life, to whom I owe so much.

I owe my parents, Paul and Linda, a debt I could never repay. I've never had a single moment in my life when I doubted they loved me. Ever. I received unending, unconditional love and support from the moment of my birth, which can be summed up by the fact they never missed a sporting event I participated in my entire athletic career. Not only did they never miss a game, my father rarely missed attending a football practice. I just assumed all parents were the same until I saw the deep pain in a friends' eyes when they told me their parents never attended any of their games, recitals, or performances.

To my coaches from junior-high school through college, thank you for imposing discipline and consequences on a bunch of young men who needed boundaries and shared adversity. These coaches took lumps of impressionable clay and molded us into men, using character, integrity, and commitment. Like my parents, I have no idea how I could ever repay them.

I owe each classroom teacher thanks not only for imparting subject knowledge to me, but most importantly, for caring enough to challenge me every day. I used to resent that whatever I did wasn't good enough for many of my instructors—in particular, the late Mr. Nagle. A high-school algebra teacher, he cared enough and knew exactly how to press my competitive buttons. On the top of a barely passing exam, he wrote in red ink, "Dan, would you be proud of this performance in front of fifteen thousand people at Seacrest Field on Friday night?"

I'd be remiss if I didn't acknowledge my handful of close friends who put up with my complete focus on sports at the expense of relaxing with them on the weekends. I'd often show up at a party and have a few beers before quietly leaving to get home to bed. I never felt more accepted than when they simply shrugged their shoulders in resignation, knowing they couldn't pressure me to change and respected me enough not to try.

Every athlete I've competed against has been critical to my development as a man. Most were complete strangers, but they provided the opposition necessary for me to grow. They fueled my desire to train and prepare. I thought I was competing against them, but I was wrong. I've always been competing against myself. Without their external challenge, I wouldn't have learned to compete internally.

Finally, I'd like to thank every artist, whether a musician, actor, director, or writer, whose work inspired me to grow, striving to reach my potential as a human being. Sometimes a short scene in a movie or paragraph in a book became a match, setting my mind ablaze with new possibilities.

About the Author

Athlete, adventurer, author, and introvert, Dan has lived and worked around the world: Bermuda, Lisbon, Toronto, Vancouver, San Francisco, Shanghai, Bangalore, Maui, and Japan. To fund his lifestyle, Dan has worked in the banking, finance and technology industry since 1986 in various roles from software engineer to consultant to Chief Information Officer. Born and raised in Nebraska, Dan played collegiate football at the University of Nebraska and at the University of Nebraska at Kearney. Divorced with no children, he lives in Northern California. When not challenging himself with adventure sports, the martial arts, and work, Dan spends much of his time refining his golf swing and studying the Japanese language.

www.ingramcontent.com/pod-product-compliance
Lightning Source LLC
Chambersburg PA
CBHW061425040426
42450CB00007B/909
* 9 7 8 0 9 9 9 2 7 5 7 0 2 *